THE SPIRIT AND THE CHURCH: ANTIQUITY

Stanley M. Burgess

Hendrickson Publishers, Inc.
Peabody, Massachusetts

ISBN 0-913573-10-8

To Ruth, with gratitude

CONTENTS

SECTION TWO: FROM NICEA TO AUGUSTINE

ACKNOWLEDGEMENTS

We are grateful to the following for granting us permission to reprint copyrighted materials:

Abingdon Press, Nashville, Tennessee, for an excerpt from Elaine Pagels, *"Gnosticism," The Interpreter's Dictionary of the Bible, Supplementary Volume,* © 1976.

Ave Maria Press, Notre Dame, Indiana, for excerpts from Edward D. O'Connor, *Pope Paul and the Spirit,* © 1976.

Cambridge University Press, New York, for excerpts from Burton Scott Easton, translator, *The Apostolic Tradition of Hippolytus,* © 1934.

Catholic University of America Press, Washington D.C., for excerpts from Sister Thomas Aquinas Goggin, translator, *St. John Chrysostom: Commentary on St. John the Apostle and Evangelist,* Vols. 33 and 41 in *The Fathers of the Church,* © 1957, 1960; for excerpts from Virginia Woods Callahan, translator, *St. Gregory of Nyssa: Ascetical Works,* Vol. 58 in *The Fathers of the Church,* © 1967; for an excerpt from *Early Christian Biographies,* © 1952.

Concordia Publishing House, St. Louis, for an excerpt from E. R. Kalin, "Inspired Community: a glance at canon history," *Concordia Theological Monthly* 43, © 1971 Concordia Publishing House.

Epworth Press, London, for excerpts from C. R. B. Shapland, translator, *The Letters of St. Athanasius Concerning the Holy Spirit,* © 1951.

Eerdmans Publishing Company, Grand Rapids, Michigan, for excerpts from Michael Ramsey, *Holy Spirit,* © 1977. Used by permission.

Evangelical Theological Society, for excerpts from Harold Hunter, "Tongues-Speech: A Patristic Analysis," *Journal of the Evangelical Theological Society* 23, © 1980.

Harper and Row, New York, for an excerpt from Paul Tillich, *A History of Christian Thought,* © 1968; for an excerpt from Jeffrey B. Russell, *A History of Medieval Christianity: Prophecy and Order,* © 1968; for excerpts from James M. Robinson, general editor, *The Nag Hammadi Library,* © 1981.

Oxford University Press, Oxford, for excerpts from Werner Foerster, editor, *Gnosis: A Selection of Gnostic Texts,* © 1972, 1974.

Paulist Press, Ramsey, New Jersey, for excerpts from Joseph F. Christopher, translator, *Augustine: The First Catechetical Instruction,* Vol. 2 in *Ancient Christian Writers,* © 1946; for excerpts from Louis A. Arand, translator, *Augustine: Faith, Hope and Charity,* Vol. 3 in *Ancient Christian Writers,* © 1947; for excerpts from James A. Kleist, translator, *The Didache,* Vol. 6 in *Ancient Christian Writers,* © 1948; for an excerpt from William

P. LeSaint, translator, *Tertullian: Treatises on Marriage and Remarriage*, Vol. 13 in *Ancient Christian Writers,* © 1951; for an excerpt from Robert T. Meyer, translator, *Palladius: The Lausiac History*, Vol. 34 in *Ancient Christian Writers,* © 1965.

Pontifical Institute of Medieval Studies, Toronto, for an excerpt from Paul J. Fedwick, *The Church and the Charisma of Leadership in Basil of Caesarea,* © 1979. By permission of the publisher.

Charles Scribners' Sons, New York, for excerpts from Jean Danielou, *From Glory to Glory*, translated by Herbert Musurillo, © 1961.

Society for Promoting Christian Knowledge, London, for excerpts from W. K. L. Clarke, translator, *The Ascetic Works of St. Basil,* © 1925.

Stanford University Press, Stanford, California, for an excerpt from Hans von Campenhausen, *Ecclesiastical Authority and Spiritual Power in the Church of the First Three Centuries,* © 1969.

Theological Studies, for excerpts from James L. Ash, Jr., "The Decline of Ecstatic Prophecy in the Early Church" (June 1976).

Viking Penguin Incorporated, New York, for an excerpt from Jean Doresse, *The Secret Books of the Egyptian Gnostics*. With an English translation and critical evaluation of *The Gospel According to Thomas*. Translation by Philip Mairet. Originally titled *Les livres secrets des gnostiques d'Egypte,* © 1960 by Hollis and Carter, Ltd., London. Reprinted by permission of Viking Penguin Inc.

Westminster Press, Philadelphia, for an excerpt from John Burnaby, translator, *Augustine: Homilies on I John*, Vol. 8 in *The Library of Christian Classics,* © 1955; for an excerpt from William Telfer, translator, *Cyril of Jerusalem and Nemesius of Emesa*, Vol. 4 in *The Library of Christian Classics,* © 1955.

INTRODUCTION

"We have not so much as heard whether there be a Holy Ghost."
(Acts 19:2)

So certain Ephesian Christians answered Paul's inquiry, "Have ye received the Holy Ghost since ye believed?" Sadly, a similar response could have been anticipated had the same question been posed to individual believers at virtually any other time in the Christian Era. While most Christians have used His name in their religious practices, they have been woefully deficient in their knowledge of the Holy Spirit. The Spirit has always been the "dark side of the moon" in Christian theology. His Person has been long ignored and His work largely unrecognized. The result has been that part of the very heart of God—His plan and His resources for the Church as experienced through the ministry of the Paraclete—has been obscured over past centuries. Msgr. Maurice Laudrieux correctly referred to the Spirit as "The Forgotten Paraclete."[1] In 1897 Pope Leo XIII deplored the fact that the Spirit is so little known and that His divine mission is so little appreciated by us:

> These sublime truths, which so clearly show forth the infinite
> goodness of the Holy Ghost towards us, certainly demand that we
> should direct towards Him the highest homage of our love and
> devotion. Christians may do this most effectually if they will daily
> strive to know Him, to love Him, and to implore Him more earnestly;
> for which reason may our exhortation, flowing spontaneously from a
> paternal heart, reach their ears. . . . All preachers and those having
> care of souls should remember that it is their duty to instruct their
> people more diligently and more fully about the Holy Ghost . . . so
> that errors and ignorance concerning matters of such moment may be
> entirely dispelled, as unworthy of "the children of light."[2]

No facile explanation will suffice to account for this significant omission in the thought and writings of Christian theologians over a span of nearly two thousand years. However, several factors appear to have contributed. Perhaps the most likely reason for such

1

disregard has been the difficulty of understanding and of defining the essence of God and, therefore, of His work within the Church through His Spirit. Hilary of Poitiers succinctly expressed the problem in these words, "I cannot describe Him whose pleas for me I cannot describe."[3] To a certain extent the doctrine of the Spirit has been avoided because it involves the most complex question of all Christian theology, the problem of the Trinity. We are told in Scripture that the Spirit reveals to us the Son, through whom we are enabled to know the Father.[4] But who is to reveal the Spirit? Admittedly, the inner life of God remains ineffable.[5] It does not admit to formulation and cannot be readily communicated from one soul to another. It only can be understood through concrete action with the Persons and only by participating in the Person of the Spirit, incorporating us into the Son, in whom we are led to the Father as His children. Yet the action of the Holy Spirit in our souls is so quiet and so continuous that it is barely perceived. He who breaks into our lives, unbounded by natural restraints, is a Person gentle. Yet He is God active within us. While we have constant reminders of God the Father, and our calendars bring to mind the advent, death and Resurrection of the Son, we neglect the Spirit—God in action in the world of men.

A certain vagueness surrounds the very conception of Spirit. Clearly there are linguistic inadequacies in our English terms "ghost" and "spirit," which have come to be used in ways very foreign to that of the breath connotation of the Hebrew *nesamah*, or the meaning of wind-breath of the Hebrew word *ruah*, or the Greek word *pneuma*. Ghost now connotes the bizarre, while spirit implies something without substance. But the problem is not limited to language. Our imaginations readily can conceive of the Father as Ancient of Days and the Son in the form of man, but we have problems conceptualizing the Holy Spirit as a Person. More often than not, the third Person in the Godhead is portrayed as a stream, a fire, or a dove. Rarely is the Spirit anthropomorphized, however.

The doctrine of the Trinity, including that of the Holy Spirit, is so comprehensive, so intertwined with other doctrines, that its proper treatment has demanded a broad sweep, a command of knowledge, theological and otherwise, which few in the history of the Church have possessed. The tendency has been for doctrine to develop from intermittent reactions against perceived heresy, which in fact has resulted in emphasis being placed on particular points of view. In turn, these intermittent reactions have come to be mistaken for the infallible voice of the whole Church giving the whole truth. The ancient Church tended to absorb pneumatology into Christology. From Augustine onward through the Middle Ages the major theological thrust in the West was soteriological, with accompanying major intellectual struggles over the definition or the description of the saving work of Christ. The tendency to view the work of the Spirit as that of applying the salvation accomplished by Christ to mankind continued with the reformers of the sixteenth century and the Protestant and Catholic pietists of the Early Modern period, with the result that the doctrine of the Holy Spirit did not develop alongside the other major tenets of the Christian faith. Even in the twentieth century, Pentecostals and Charismatics, whom one might expect to have a keen interest in the doctrine of the Spirit, have been less anxious to define the divine power of the Spirit than to possess it. With their theology of experience, they have shown more concern for the gifts than for the Giver.

To a certain extent it would seem that the doctrine of the Spirit has been shunned by those concerned with theological development because it has been seen as the sphere belonging to extremists or enthusiasts. There is clear evidence through Christian history that theologians of the mainstream Church (hereafter referred to as the "major tradition") have discounted charismatic experiences and even the subject of the Spirit due to their impression, whether justified or not, that the enthusiasts (hereafter referred to as the "minor tradition") were engaged in an effort to domesticate the divine.[6] Time and again people of the Spirit have been accused of emphasizing experience (gifts of the Spirit) over character (fruits of the Spirit).[7] Ultimately, reaction against the minor tradition has resulted from perception by the major tradition of the dangerous threat which the enthusiasts pose to order in the Church.[8]

The Christian centuries have witnessed a tension—sometimes waxing, sometimes waning, but always present—between the major and minor traditions in the Church. Jeffrey R. Russell sees this tension between what he describes as the spirit of order and the spirit of prophecy as inevitable:

> The Church was necessarily a failure in that its organizational structure muffled the immediacy of the religious experience. Its search for *order* frustrated *prophecy*. Yet this search was also completely necessary. Christianity can get along neither within the Church nor without it. The demise of Gnosticism, which had no lasting ecclesiastical organization, is evidence that without a structure and a system of authority, no body of doctrines can long endure: either it will undergo such strange metamorphoses as to make it unrecognizably different from its origins, or else it will simply perish. It was the necessary work of the Church, and a work in which it was quite successful, both to keep the doctrines of Christ alive and to keep its development of his teachings within the boundaries of a recognizable tradition.[9]

It was equally inevitable that prophetic elements either became sectarian or existed in the mainline Church only at the cost of severe internal tension and institutional disapproval. In ancient Hebrew society tension developed between priests and kings on the one hand, and prophetic types on the other. The very term "prophet" in Hebrew (*nabi*) can mean "madman." Jesus Himself was a prophet, misunderstood by the established order, and even by His own. During the entire Christian Era, those who have represented themselves as the "true Church," as part of an invisible and spiritual body of believers, also have contrasted themselves to the institutional Church, which they have correlated with a political and social order. Of course, the Holy Spirit has been claimed by both sides in this tension between prophecy and order. By the prophetic, He has been seen to move in a wind-like manner, difficult for most to discern, impossible for anyone to control or to limit. Prophets have viewed themselves as instruments of the Spirit as He breaks into this world, superseding natural laws or processes, allowing man to experience God's revelation and grace in forms foreign to the institutional Church. By those defending the established order, the true operation of the Spirit is always orderly—He is present in figures of authority, acknowledged in creeds, liturgies, hymns, and doxologies, having already led man into all truth.

Modern representatives of the minor tradition have continued to emphasize prophetic qualities (religious experience, the direct leading of the Holy Spirit, and Spirit gifts—especially tongues) to the exclusion of any real treatment of the broader Spirit question—an understanding of the third Person in the Godhead as the Agent who brings to man that grace and truth which is the character of God and the ultimate provision for man from the inner life of God. The Spirit's coming is seen as a great, new event in the series of divine saving acts. A few within this tradition even have deemphasized the intimate connection of the Spirit with Christ in favor of viewing the third Person as an independent reality and a center of new actions. Many Pentecostals have pictured a quasi-Deistic Spirit—present for a First Cause of the Spirit ("the early rain"), a dramatic creative act in the Spirit-created, Spirit-led first century Church, and largely dormant until the coming of a Last Cause of the Spirit ("the latter rain"), a twentieth-century outpouring among Pentecostals and Charismatics.[10] This approach does not consider the intimate involvement of the Spirit in the full panorama of the redemptive act of God—creation, inspiration, Incarnation, and life-giving Resurrection—nor does it recognize the continuous involvement of the Spirit in the life of the Church.

Fortunately, both Pentecostal and Charismatic historians have begun to recognize that the Spirit has given charismata in every epoch of Christian history.[11] Unfortunately, the emphasis still is limited to gifts, not upon the full range of the Spirit's activity in the life of the Church.

Understandably, the major theological tradition in the West has more adequately recorded the growth of Spirit doctrine in the institutional Church.[12] However, it also has tended to stress the role of the Spirit in terms of the Person and work of Jesus Christ. While the Spirit is recognized to have a unique role in the redemptive act of God, that role is limited to being merely instrumental, applying the salvation accomplished by Christ to mankind. The Third Person thereby is subordinated to the Second. This tradition also tends to discount any legitimate role for the prophetic type after the establishment of canon. The Spirit works within order. His action is restricted to ecclesiastical structures. Charismatics of Church history are pictured as enthusiasts, drawing the faithful away from established truth toward dangerous aberrations, dividing the Body of Christ with dreams of continued prophetic inspiration. The major tradition by and large still fails to acknowledge that present vitality of the Spirit, which Michael Ramsey, Archbishop of Canterbury, insists is the essence of the living Church:

> But while indeed the Church's sacramental and apostolic order witnesses to the historical givenness of gospel and Church, there is need to remember the continuing lively action of the Spirit whereby alone the believers are Christ's body. The many charismata shared among the Church's members are not personal qualities or possessions so much as constant actions of the Spirit in which the liveliness of God touches human lives.[13]

To a certain extent the sharp distinction between major and minor traditions has faded in the brilliant light of Church renewal experienced in our century. In his forward to *The Holy Spirit in the Ancient Church* (1911), Henry Barclay Swete wrote, "In our own time the doctrine of the Holy Spirit has aroused an interest which seems likely to grow and extend as attention is increasingly fixed on the spiritual side of human nature."[14] Interest in fact has grown, but far beyond what Swete could have anticipated and for reasons other than he foresaw. Pneumatology has assumed a new prominence in our time, both in theological study and in Christian life.[15] The Church as a whole has experienced renewal, and, in turn, there has been an increased awareness that renewal is the work of the Spirit. Most apparent, of course, has been the so-called Charismatic Renewal, which began shortly before 1960 and subsequently has embraced churches representing the major tradition with a new emphasis on life in the Spirit. The theology of this movement is distinguished by its center, the Holy Spirit, and by its emphasis on experience. The result has been an expansion of Spirit consciousness and a new level of expectation of Spirit activity.

This new Spirit emphasis has prompted theologians from various mainline Christian groups to reevaluate the place of the Third Person in, and the relationship of the renewal to, their long-established traditions.[16] The major tradition has come to recognize the new movement as "The Third Force in Christendom,"[17] "The Third Ecclesiology,"[18] and "The New Reformation."[19] Pope John XXIII on December 8, 1962, at the conclusion of the first session of Vatican II, declared the movement for renewal to be a "New Pentecost . . . a new advance of the Kingdom of Christ in the world."[20] Several years later his successor, Paul VI, who has come to be known as the Pope of the Holy Spirit, declared:

> We must point out something new in contemporary spirituality, not just within our own fold, but also among those who are near to us, and sometimes even among those who are far off. It is esteem for the charismatic elements of religion over the so-called institutional ones. It is the seeking after spiritual facts into which there enters from without a certain indefinable energy which, to some extent, persuades the one who experiences it that he is in communication with God, or more generically with the Divine, with the Spirit in an indeterminate sense.

> The breath-giving influence of the Spirit has come to awaken latent forces within the Church, to stir up forgotten charisms and to infuse that sense of vitality and joy which in every epoch of history marks the Church itself as youthful and up-to-date, ready and happy again to proclaim its eternal message to the modern age.

> How wonderful it would be if the Lord would again pour out the charisms in increased abundance, in order to make the Church fruitful, beautiful and marvelous, and to enable it to win the attention and astonishment of the profane and secularized world.[21]

The Eastern Christian world, long known for a more prominent pneumatology, also has experienced a renewal which gives the Spirit an even greater place than before. The Metropolitan Ignatius of Latakia, in addressing the 1968 Assembly of the World Council of Churches at Uppsala, declared:

> Without the Holy Spirit God is far away.
> Christ stays in the past,
> the Gospel is simply an organization,
> authority a matter of propaganda,
> the liturgy is no more than an evolution,
> Christian loving a slave morality.

> But in the Holy Spirit,
> the cosmos is resurrected and grows
> with the birth pangs of the Kingdom,

the Risen Christ is there,
the Gospel is the power of life,
the Church shows forth the life of the Trinity,
authority is a liberating science,
mission is a Pentecost,
the liturgy is both renewal and anticipation,
human action is deified.[22]

While pneumatology now plays a much more prominent place in the Church, Christians have only begun to recognize the wealth of Spirit theology and activity within their own tradition, let alone to understand and appreciate the pneumatology and Spirit dynamics of the competing tradition. The present work is a study of the order/prophecy tension—a struggle between major and minor traditions. As such it recognizes theological insight and Spirit activity in both traditions. Acknowledging that in every epoch the Holy Spirit is invading *ruah* as well as indwelling *pneuma,* it attempts to examine both the development of Spirit theology and the life of the Spirit in the Church together as an interrelated whole. There is reason to assume that the most fruitful times of the Spirit have been those occasions when representatives of prophecy and order have cross-fertilized each other. Each tradition has much to learn from the other. To this end, it shall be my purpose to recover for the reader a deeper and wider vision of the Person and the workings of the Spirit by tracing the Church's understanding of the third Person as God at once beyond and within. This volume is devoted to the ancient Church, from the end of the first century to the end of the fifth century A.D., a time of great growth in theological understanding of the Spirit, and a period which witnessed early conflicts between prophecy and order in the Christian world and the Church's first efforts to institutionalize the Spirit's activities. The method pursued will be descriptive and historical, rather than exegetical. For the purpose of providing the reader with a better grasp of the depth of insight and intensity of conviction apparent in the early Christian writers, selected passages in translation have been incorporated into the narrative.

Notes to Introduction

[1]Quoted in Deborah Pease Armstrong, "And in the Holy Ghost," *The Life of the Spirit* 7 (May 1953): 497.

[2]John J. Wynne, trans., *The Great Encyclical Letters of Pope Leo XIII* (New York and Cincinnati: Benziger Brothers, 1903), 435-436.

[3]Hilary of Poitiers, *On the Trinity* xii 56, *Nicene and Post-Nicene Fathers* Second Series (Grand Rapids: Eerdmans, 1979), IX, 233 (henceforth NPF).

⁴John i:18; xiv:9,17; xv:26; xvi:13-14.

⁵E.g., see Hilary of Poitiers, op. cit., ii.6-7, NPF 2nd Series IX, 53-54.

⁶Representative of this viewpoint is R. A. Knox, *Enthusiasm: A Chapter in the History of Religion* (Oxford: Clarendon Press, 1962).

⁷See the discussion of Montanism on pp. 55-56. cf. p. 132.

⁸It must be recognized that our evidence for much of the Christian Era is badly slanted by the fact that such peoples of the Spirit in the minor tradition did not leave significant historic record, or that such evidence has been destroyed by those fearful of its implications. An example of such a writing is Tertullian's, *On Ecstasy* in six books, which might have given us valuable evidence into the development of his theology of the Spirit, as well as provide primary evidence from the Montanist camp, had it not disappeared. Tertullian, whom the Spirit possessed, and, at the same time quickened with an understanding of the nature and work of the Third Person of the Trinity, is a rare example of an individual who combined experience with explanation. He stands as a representative, albeit during different periods of his life, of both major and minor traditions. See Jerome, *Lives of Illustrious Men* xxiv, NPF 2nd Series 3: 369, for evidence of Tertullian's *On Ecstasy.*

⁹Jeffrey Burton Russell, *A History of Medieval Christianity: Prophecy and Order* (New York: Crowell, 1968), 5. Russell has identified the tension between prophecy and order as one of the fundamental conflicts in medieval Christianity. I am suggesting that this tension was not born in the Middle Ages and that it certainly did not cease with the coming of modernity.

¹⁰According to David duPlessis, "Golden Jubilees," *International Review of Missions* 47 (April 1958): 193-194, "The Holy Spirit continued in control until the close of the first century, when He was largely rejected and His position as leader usurped by man. The results are written in history. The missionary movement halted. The dark ages ensued." A similar view is expressed by Frank Stagg, E. Glenn Hinson, and Wayne E. Oates, *Glossolalia: Tongue Speaking in Biblical, Historical, and Psychological Perspective* (Nashville and New York: Abingdon, 1967), 67, who call the centuries between the apostolic and modern Spirit outpourings "the long drought."

¹¹Beginning with Robert Chandler Dalton, *Tongues like as of Fire* (Springfield, MO: Gospel Publishing House, 1945); Klaude Kendrick, *The Promise Fulfilled* (Springfield, MO: Gospel Publishing House, 1959); and Bernard L. Bresson, *Studies in*

Ecstasy (New York: Vantage Press, 1966), numerous authors have examined the history of the charismata in the Church. They include but are not limited to the following: Wade H. Horton, ed., *The Glossolalia Phenomenon* (Cleveland, TN: Pathway Press, 1966); George H. Williams and Edith Waldvogel, "A History of Speaking in Tongues and Related Gifts," in Michael P. Hamilton, ed., *The Charismatic Movement* (Grand Rapids, MI, 1975), 61-113; Stanley M. Burgess, "Medieval Examples of Charismatic Piety in the Roman Catholic Church," in Russell P. Spittler, ed., *Perspectives on the New Pentecostalism* (Grand Rapids, MI: Baker, 1976), 15-26; Eusebius A. Stephanou, "The Charismata in the Early Church Fathers," *The Greek Orthodox Theological Review* 21 (Summer 1976): 125-146; and Harold Hunter, "Tongues-speech: A Patristic Analysis," *Journal of the Evangelical Theological Society* 23, no. 2 (June 1980): 125-137. In each of these the emphasis has been on gifts, not on the full range of the Spirit's activity in the life of the Church.

[12]Of special importance are Henry Barclay Swete, *The Holy Spirit in the Ancient Church* (London: Macmillan, 1912); Howard Watkin-Jones, *The Holy Spirit in the Mediaeval Church* (London: Epworth, 1922); and Howard Watkin-Jones, *The Holy Spirit from Arminius to Wesley* (London: Epworth, 1929). R. A. Knox, *Enthusiasm,* (note 6 above) is a classic evaluation of the history of the minor tradition by a champion of the major. Another such work is George B. Cutten, *Speaking in Tongues* (New Haven, CT: Yale University Press, 1927), who treats the charismata exercised in the medieval and early modern Church from a strongly negative perspective. Other useful works include Geoffrey F. Nuttall, *The Holy Spirit in Puritan Faith and Experience* (Oxford: Basil Blackwell, 1946) and Eugene Egert, *The Holy Spirit in German Literature until the End of the Twelfth Century* (The Hague and Paris: Mouton, 1973).

[13]Michael Ramsey, *Holy Spirit* (Grand Rapids, MI: Eerdmans, 1977), 127-128.

[14]Swete, op. cit., 7.

[15]See George S. Hendry, *The Holy Spirit in Christian Theology* (Philadelphia: Westminster, 1956), 20ff.

[16]Paul D. Opsahl, ed., *The Holy Spirit in the Life of the Church from Biblical Times to the Present* (Minneapolis: Augsburg, 1978), addresses the dilemma faced by the Lutheran Council in the United States in rethinking the place and importance of the Holy Spirit in Lutheran theology.

[17]Henry Pitt Van Dusen, "The Third Force in Christendom," *Life* 44 (9 June 1958): 13.

[18]Leslie Newbigin, *The Household of God: Lectures on the Nature of the Church* (New York: Friendship Press, 1954), 82-83.

[19]Henry Pitt Van Dusen, "Caribbean Holiday," *Christian Century* 72 (17 August 1955): 946-947.

[20]Floyd Anderson, ed., *Council Daybook: Vatican II, Sessions 1 and 2* (Washington, D.C.: National Catholic Welfare Conference, 1965), 150.

[21]Quoted in Edward D. O'Connor, *Pope Paul and the Spirit* (Notre Dame, IN: Ave Maria Press, 1978), 42, 188, 201.

[22]Quoted in Michael Ramsey, op. cit., 126-127.

SECTION ONE: BEFORE NICEA

INTRODUCTION

During the first three centuries of the Christian Era, the Church was in constant peril from a hostile Roman state, which periodically persecuted the faithful. But the Church also faced danger from competing religions which rivaled the still young faith for the affections of the people, from philosophies which challenged the reasonableness of its doctrines, and from heresies which grew up within its ranks. The earliest non-canonical writers in the Church, the Apostolic Fathers, chose to address immediate concerns of local churches. From the mid-second century onward, however, the greater challenges to the Church were answered by two new groups of Christian writers: the Apologists, who tried to convince Roman leaders that the Christians had done nothing to deserve the persecution being inflicted on them, and the polemicists, who tried to counter the influence of heretical movements.

With the writings of the Apologists and the polemicists the pace of doctrinal formulation accelerated. Their basic emphasis, however, was on Jesus Christ, the Logos, at the expense of the other basic teachings of the Church. Among those doctrines which remained largely undeveloped in the pre-Nicene period was that of the Holy Spirit. In part this was due to the fact that deliberate formulation of such doctrine could not be attempted until the Church had fully settled the previous question about the divinity of Christ. To be sure, the Holy Spirit appeared alongside the Father and the Son in early creeds and doxologies, and such writers as Tertullian and Origen vindicated His place in the Trinity. But the Holy Spirit was not yet a topic of great theological discussion; consequently, the treatment of the Spirit in this period suffered from imperfect formulae and a lack of precise terminology.

There is strong evidence of the Pauline view of the ministry of the Holy Spirit in the Church throughout the pre-Nicene era. The place of the prophet remained prominent into the second century, although prophetic ministry appears to have declined somewhat in

12

the third century. Modern scholars do not agree about the extent of that decline nor its reason. Adolph von Harnack, who represents the traditional Protestant emphasis on *sola scriptura,* suggests that prophecy ceased with the establishment of the canon. ''The New Testament, though not all at once, put an end to the situation where it was possible for any Christian under the inspiration of the Spirit to give authoritative disclosures and instructions.''[1] On the other hand, James L. Ash, Jr. denies that the sources signal the end of a charisma of prophecy and argues for a distinction between the inspiration of canon by the Spirit and the Pauline charismata, which continued to be experienced, indeed, espoused by orthodoxy, throughout the pre-Nicene period. Furthermore, he suggests that the decline in the prophetic ministry resulted from the inability of bishops and prophets to find common goals for the Church.

> Instead of declaring theological war on ecstatic prophecy, they [the bishops] simply captured it and used it for their own ends, a process which was at the same time less traumatic and far more effective. The charisma of prophecy, then, became the special province of the bishop, and the relics of the dying gift were to remain ever beneath the episcopal mitre.[2]

This trend begins in the *Didache,* Ignatius, Polycarp, Irenaeus, and Hippolytus and culminates in the writings of Cyprian, the respected Bishop of Carthage, who claimed to be able to do virtually everything that the prophetic Montanists did.

While Ash contends that Pauline charismata continued after the establishment of the canon, Everett R. Kalin demonstrates that the early church fathers also understood inspiration to extend beyond the close of the canon.[3] Kalin points out that, while the leaders of the early Church called the Scriptures inspired, they did not suggest that non-Scripture was not inspired. The canon was unique, but not because it alone was inspired. Inspiration was attributed also ''to bishops, monks, martyrs, councils, interpreters of Scripture, various prophetic gifts, and to many other aspects of the church's life.''[4] Eusebius attributes one of Constantine's sermons to divine inspiration, as does Gregory of Nyssa in referring to one of the commentaries written by his brother Basil. Clement of Rome and Origen even claim that their own writings are inspired. The only use of the term ''noninspired'' by ancient Christian writers was with reference to heretical documents. Kalin concludes that the early Church did not distinguish the apostolic age from all subsequent ages as the only time in which the Holy Spirit was experienced in full measure. The early Christian Church

> saw itself to be living under the ongoing inspiration of the Holy Spirit who was poured out at Pentecost. It took seriously the promise given in the 16th chapter of the Gospel of John: ''When the Spirit of truth comes, He will guide you into all the truth.'' That community did not

believe that the canonization of the Scriptures had cancelled that promise. Early Christians had no trouble believing that the New Testament documents were given by inspiration of God. After all, they knew that such documents emerged from their own life of Spirit-directed confession to Jesus Christ, and knew themselves to be an inspired community.[5]

The issue of Scripture versus Spirit, seen in Harnack's argument that prophecy could not coexist with an established canon, and in Blackman and Grant's insistence that inspiration necessarily ended with the setting of canon,[6] is but a modern extension of that tension between order and prophecy which was apparent before A.D. 325. Similarly, the very fear of all mystics and ecstatics which many modern Protestants share with Harnack, Blackman, and Grant also is expressed in the writings of second and third century polemicists who argue against the ecstatic excesses of the Montanists. Eusebius distrusts "unnatural ecstasy" and the way in which Montanus raved "and began to chatter and talk nonsense, prophesying in a way that conflicted with the practice of the Church."[7] Hippolytus attacks leaders of the "New Prophecy" for not judging their prophecies "according to reason."[8] Epiphanius claims that true prophets prophesied while retaining their reason.[9] It is important to note, however, that these early Christian writers react only against those excesses which they considered unnatural. They do not disavow the continuation of Christian prophecy. Before John Chrysostom (A.D. 347-407) in the East and Augustine of Hippo (A.D. 354-430) in the West, no church father suggested that any or all of the charismata were intended only for the first century Church.

This section will deal with the struggle between prophecy and order in the broader context of the Church's growing awareness of the Spirit's Person and offices from the end of the first century A.D. to the calling of the first great council at Nicea in 325. After briefly examining the writings of the Apostolic Fathers, who offered but little to development in Spirit theology, we will concentrate on those heretics and Christian aberrants who challenged the early Church toward greater self-understanding, and on the doctrinal formulations concerning matters of the Spirit by the Apologists and the polemicists who responded to such challenges.

Notes to Introduction

[1]Adolph von Harnack, *History of Dogma* (New York: Russell and Russell, 1958), 2:53.

[2]James L. Ash, Jr., "The Decline of Ecstatic Prophecy in the

Early Church," *Theological Studies* 36, no. 2 (June 1976): 250. Cf. Karl Holl, *Enthusiasmus und Bussgewalt beim griechischen Mönchtum: eine Studie zu Simeon dem Neuen Theologen* (Leipzig: J.C. Hinrichs, 1898), and *Gessammelte Aufsätze zur Kirchengeschichte II, der Osten* (Tübingen, verlag von J.C.B. Mohr (P. Siebeck), 1928), 44-67, who argues that charismatic authority played an enduring role in the history of the Church. He states that this was especially true in Eastern Christianity where charismatic authority maintained its legitimacy in the monastic tradition.

³E.R. Kalin, "Inspired Community: A Glance at Canon History," *Concordia Theological Monthly* 43 (September 1971): 541-549.

⁴Ibid., 547.

⁵Ibid.

⁶E.C. Blackman, *Marcion and His Influence* (London: SPCK, 1948), 33ff., and Robert Grant, *The Letter and the Spirit* (New York: Macmillan, 1957), 75. Both writers are mentioned by Kalin, p. 543. H. Paulsen, "Die Bedeutung des Montanismus für die herausbildung des kanons," *Vigiliae Christianae* 32, no. 1 (1978): 19-52, reverses Blackman and Grant's argument by insisting that the canon was not at issue in the controversy between Montanism and the mainline Church. Rather, the Montanists provoked the larger Church to an exclusive limitation of the scriptural tradition and to fix a normative interpretation of it.

⁷Eusebius, *Church History* v. 16, *Nicene and Post-Nicene Fathers* Second series (Grand Rapids: Eerdmans, 1975), 1:219 (henceforth NPF).

⁸Hippolytus, *Philosophumena* viii.19, trans. by F. Legge (London: SPCK, 1921), 2:114.

⁹Epiphanius, *Panarion* xlviii.2, in Pierre de Labroille, ed., *Les sources de l'histoire du montanisme* (Fribourg: Librairie de l'Universite (O. Gschwend), 1913), 117.

CHAPTER ONE

THE APOSTOLIC FATHERS

The earliest church fathers, usually designated Apostolic Fathers, were individuals who are known, or may reasonably be presumed, to have associated with and derived their teachings directly from one of the apostles. Their writings are contemporary with the latest canonical books and, therefore, do not represent a chronological break in the continuity of early Christian teaching. However, these successors of the spiritual giants of the New Testament were men of lower stature and poorer capacity, whose works lack the originality and freshness of canonical writings. The writings of the Apostolic Fathers are derivative in that they tend to replicate the ideas and language already familiar in the Gospels and the Epistles. Invariably, the Apostolic Fathers produced occasional pieces of a pastoral orientation, evoked by local contemporary needs, rather than works of systematic theology. As such they did not provide as much important material on early Christian thought and practice as one might hope. Indeed, the scholar is made to wonder whether these scattered writings really indicate the true level of vitality in the early Church.

The Apostolic Fathers are concerned with the Trinity, of course, but there is no marked development in trinitarian theology over levels reached in New Testament writings. They have inherited from the young Christian tradition a series of doxologies, baptismal and trinitarian formulae which express the general orientation of the faith. When referring to these traditional declarations, the Apostolic Fathers confirm their belief in the Spirit's personhood and divinity and ascribe to Him the divine tasks of inspiration of Scripture and of giving His gifts to believers.

On occasion the terms "Spirit" or "Holy Spirit" are used imprecisely. For example, the *Shepherd of Hermas* appears to identify the Son or Word of God with the Holy Spirit, representing the latter as the divine principle of the incarnate Christ. At one point Hermas speaks of the Holy Spirit as the Son of God.[1] Such statements are not surprising, however, because the Spirit is still "a primary fact of Christian experience, rather than a subject for investigation and exact definition."[2]

1. CLEMENT OF ROME

In the last decade of the first century A.D. a feud over leadership broke out in the church at Corinth. Presbyters who had been appointed by the apostles or their successors had been deposed by insubordinate younger members. The church at Rome addressed a letter to the church at Corinth rebuking such practices. Although this document is known as 1 Clement, we are not certain of its authorship because the best manuscripts of the documents do not identify the author as Clement of Rome. Dionysius of Corinth (ca. A.D. 170) is the first to ascribe it to Clement.

The letter makes only ten references to the Holy Spirit, and more than half of these refer to the role of the Spirit in inspiring the Old Testament Scriptures. Here are two samples: "Look closely into the Scriptures, which are the true utterances of the Holy Ghost."[3] "Let us act according to that which is written (for the Holy Spirit saith . . .)."[4] In the Old Testament Clement also finds evidence of the Holy Spirit revealing Jesus. For example, in his discussion of Isaiah 53, Clement asserts, "The Holy Spirit had declared regarding Him."[5] Clement also uses Old Testament passages to give evidence of the working of the Spirit in his own day. While discussing Psalm 34:11ff., he declares that Christ himself calls His people by the Holy Spirit.[6]

The Holy Spirit's role of inspiration operates in the everyday life of the New Testament Church. The apostles share the inspiration of the Prophets and go forth with "full assurance of the Holy Ghost."[7] They test or prove the bishops and deacons whom they appoint by the Spirit.[8] St. Paul writes to the Corinthians under the influence of the Holy Spirit.[9]

Clement also believes that he is inspired by the Holy Spirit in writing his Epistle to the Corinthians.[10] However, he does not give the same prominence as Paul to the Spirit's place in the normal Christian life, nor does he suggest that the Corinthian church of his day was experiencing a life in the Spirit as described by the Apostle in 1 Corinthians 12 through 14. Somewhat wistfully he reminds his readers in Corinth of those earlier times in which all were blessed with "a profound and abundant peace . . . and . . . had an insatiable desire for doing good, while a full outpouring of the Holy Spirit was upon you all."[11] He admonishes his readers, "Let your whole body, then, be preserved in Christ Jesus; and let every one be subject to his neighbor, according to the special gift (charisma) bestowed upon him."[12]

While it is not uncommon for early Christian writers to be inexact in their expressions about the relationship of the Trinity, as judged by later standards, Clement of Rome on several occasions speaks of the Father, the Son, and the Holy Spirit together, with a clear understanding of the separateness and the divine status of the Spirit.

> Having therefore received their orders, and being fully assured by the resurrection of our Lord Jesus Christ, and established in the word of God, with full assurance of the Holy Ghost, they went forth proclaiming that the kingdom of God was at hand.[13]

> Why are there strifes, and tumults, and divisions, and schisms, and wars among you? Have we not all one God and one Christ? Is there not one Spirit of grace poured out upon us? And have we not one calling in Christ?[14]

Clement also coordinates the Father, the Son, and the Holy Spirit in an oath, "As God lives, and the Lord Jesus Christ lives, and the Holy Spirit, who are at once the faith and the hope of the elect."[15]

The Bishop's letter reveals that nothing has been added to the New Testament doctrine of the Spirit. In fact, there is strong evidence of a decline in the Church's apprehension of the meaning of the dispensation of the Spirit from the time of the Pauline letters to the last decade of the first century A.D.

2. PSEUDO-CLEMENT

The *Second Epistle of Clement* or Pseudo-Clement, an anonymous homily probably of Corinthian origin, appears to have been written between A.D. 120 and 140. While its tone is highly moral and it is strong in faith, the work is difficult to follow, for the thought is inconsistent and the metaphors are mixed. It has but one reference to the Holy Spirit:

> Now the Church, being spiritual, was manifested in the flesh of Christ, thereby showing us that, if any of us guard her in the flesh, and defile her not, he shall receive her again in the Holy Spirit; for this flesh is the counterpart and copy of the spirit. No man therefore, when he hath defiled the copy, shall receive the original for his portion. This therefore is what He meaneth, brethren; Guard ye the flesh, that ye may partake of the spirit. But if we say that the flesh is the Church and the spirit is Christ, then he that hath dealt wantonly with the flesh hath dealt wantonly with the Church. Such an one therefore shall not partake of the spirit, which is Christ. So excellent is the life and immortality which this flesh can receive as its portion, if the Holy Spirit be joined to it. No men can declare or tell those things which the Lord hath prepared for His elect.[16]

This passage illustrates the error into which certain early Christian writers fell, namely, failing to distinguish between the Son and the Holy Spirit. Like the *Shepherd of Hermas*, the author of this letter views the preexistent Son as Spirit. In addition, he believes that man's flesh is a copy of the Spirit. No one who has corrupted the flesh (the copy) may keep the Spirit (the original).

As with most of the Apostolic Fathers, the style of Pseudo-Clement is loose, there is an absence of arrangement in the topics and no system in its teaching. But of greatest importance for our study is the author's lack of understanding of the Person and the work of the Holy Spirit who played such a prominent role in the New Testament Church at Corinth.

3. IGNATIUS OF ANTIOCH

The letters of Ignatius, bishop of Antioch, written about two decades after 1 Clement, reveal a leader full of spiritual power, with a genuine awareness of the work of the Holy Spirit in the Church. Surprisingly, the number of direct references to the Holy Spirit are not many. Perhaps the work of the Spirit was regarded as so much a part of the normal life of the Church that frequent mention seemed unnecessary. We know that the Apostle Paul addressed the issue of the Spirit most frequently when a specific problem or question arose, rather than as a subject to be dealt with in each of his letters.

In the letter to the Philadelphians Ignatius states his conviction that he is moved upon by the Holy Spirit and speaks as the Spirit gives him utterance:

> For though some would have deceived me according to the flesh, yet my spirit is not deceived; for I have received it from God. [Shorter version: "yet the Spirit, as being from God, is not deceived."] For it knows both whence it comes and whither it goes, and detects the secrets of the heart. For when I was among you, I cried, I spoke with a loud voice—the word is not mine but God's—Give heed to the bishop, and to the presbytery and deacons. But if you suspect that I spake thus, as having learned beforehand the division caused by some among you, He is my witness, for whose sake I am in bonds, that I learned nothing of it from the mouth of any man. But the Spirit made an announcement to men, saying as follows: Do nothing without the bishop; keep your bodies as temples of God.[17]

Ignatius's comments are reminiscent of John 3:8, "The wind bloweth where it listeth, and thou hearest the sound thereof, but canst not tell whence it cometh, and whither it goeth: so is every one that is born of the Spirit." His writings are more characteristically Pauline than Johannine, however. The remainder of the passage given above is reminiscent of Paul's declaration to the elders at Ephesus that they had been made overseers of the church by the Holy Ghost (Acts 20:28). The tradition of prophets continues from the New Testament but is inseparably joined in Ignatius's mind, as it is in such later writers as Cyprian, with the ordered hierarchy of bishops, presbyters, and deacons. The tension that later would develop between prophecy and order has not yet become apparent, however.

Ignatius also is conscious of the daily work of the Holy Spirit in the lives of believers. He likens them to

> chosen stones, well fitted for the divine edifice of the Father, and who are raised up on high by Christ, who was crucified for you, making use of the Holy Spirit as a rope, and being borne up by faith, while exalted by love from earth to heaven.[18]

Not only does the Spirit serve as a rope lifting man from earth to heaven, He also lifts the Christian to the place prepared for him in the Church. "Why," asks Ignatius, "through a careless neglect of acknowledging the gift (charisma) which we have received, do we foolishly perish?"[19] In his letter to Polycarp, Ignatius entreats his contemporary to pray that the invisible realities might be revealed in him in order that he "be deficient in nothing, and mayest abound in all gifts."[20] Addressing believers at Smyrna, Ignatius calls the church there one "that has mercifully obtained every kind of gift (charisma) and is deficient in no gift."[21]

Ignatius speaks of the Trinity together in two passages,[22] one of which has the order of Son, Father, and Spirit. He also recognizes that Jesus Christ "was conceived in the womb of Mary, according to the appointment of God, of the seed of David, and by the Holy Ghost."[23]

4. POLYCARP OF SMYRNA

Near the end of the first century A.D., one of the disciples of the apostle John, Polycarp, Bishop of Smyrna, wrote to the church at Philippi. His letter contains only one reference to the Spirit, and scholars do not agree whether Polycarp intends to refer to the Holy Spirit or to the spirit of man. "It is, indeed, a noble thing to cut oneself off from the lusts that are rampant in the world. Lust of any kind makes war upon the Spirit."[24]

Polycarp was martyred several decades later (A.D. 155 or 156). His last words are preserved by a writer from Smyrna who makes two references to the Spirit. One contains the phrase, "the immortality of the Holy Spirit."[25] The other has become well-known. In his last moments with his eyes lifted upward and his spirit soaring, Polycarp utters words which serve as the earliest known doxology in which the Holy Spirit is exalted together with the Father and the Son:

> I glorify Thee through the eternal and heavenly High Priest, Jesus Christ, Thy beloved Son, through whom be glory to Thee together

with Him and the Holy Spirit, both now and for the ages to come. Amen.[26]

5. THE DIDACHE

An early second century document, the *Didache* (or the *Teaching of the Twelve Apostles*), is the first writing of the Apostolic Fathers in which an account of charismatic ministry is given. According to the author, the Church was still experiencing the ministry of itinerant teachers, prophets, and apostles, who apparently had equal importance to the ordained, resident ministry.[27] The author seems to accept itinerant and resident ministries as equally normative in the Church. This is consistent with his contention that the Father wishes that a share of His own charismata be given to all.[28] Readers are exhorted to receive itinerant prophets as the Lord.[29] They apparently speak in a similar kind of vocal ecstasy that characterized Paul's time. They teach, lead in giving thanks, and exercise their gifts during religious services.[30] They can celebrate the Eucharist in their own words at the length they please, or order an agape feast at their discretion, although they cannot eat of it.[31] They can collect money for the needy brethren without giving an account of how they dispose of the gifts.[32] They may clothe their teaching in symbolic terms which are not open to criticism.[33]

The author does not recommend an unqualified trust in all self-proclaimed prophets, however. Believers are exhorted to be concerned about false prophets, "If anyone says in ecstasy, 'Give me money,' or something else, you must not listen to him. However, should he tell you to give something for others who are in need, let no one condemn him."[34] Not everyone that speaks in the Spirit is a prophet, "except he has the ways of the Lord about him."[35] Among other considerations, this means that, under ordinary circumstances, no true prophet would spend more than two days in any given local church.[36]

The author warns his readers not to despise an authentic prophet, lest they commit the unpardonable sin of blasphemy against the Holy Spirit.[37] Rather, they are to judge whether the prophet has the "ways of the Lord" or not. Obviously, this author differs from St. Paul on how one should discern the teachings of prophets. Paul insists on spiritual discernment, while the writer of the *Didache* condemns any such spiritual judgments. The gift of "discernment of spirits" appears to have passed from the churches to which this work is addressed. The only test remaining is that of personal character.

6. THE EPISTLE OF BARNABAS

The writer of the *Epistle of Barnabas* (or *Pseudo-Barnabas*) is unknown. Internal evidence suggests that the document was written between A.D. 70 and 132, and that the author may not have been connected with the apostles in any way.

The author recognizes that the Spirit has the dual function of inspiration and prophecy. As the teacher of Old Testament heroes, the Spirit speaks to the heart of Moses,[38] who, in turn, speaks in the Spirit.[39] Abraham in the Spirit looks forward to Jesus,[40] and Jacob by the Spirit sees a type of the Christian Church.[41]

Under the New Covenant the work of the Holy Spirit continues. According to this writing the gift of prophecy and the indwelling of the Spirit are connected. "He personally prophesies in us and personally dwells in us."[42] Both prophecy and Spirit presence are considered normative for those who share in the divine provision. The writer exclaims with gratitude, "And so I am exceedingly, in fact beyond all measure, cheered as I think of your happy and glorious endowments. So deeply implanted is the gift of the Spirit that has been graciously vouchsafed to you."[43] "I really witness in your community an outpouring upon you of the Spirit from the wealth of the Lord's fountainhead."[44]

The writer also declares that Christ comes to those who have been prepared by the Spirit.[45] The body of the baptized, as in Christ himself, is to be considered as the vessel, or the dwelling place of the Spirit.[46]

7. THE SHEPHERD OF HERMAS

The Shepherd or *The Shepherd of Hermas* was circulated generally in both the Eastern and Western Churches soon after the middle of the second century A.D. The Shepherd, the divine teacher, communicates to the narrator, Hermas, by precept or allegory, lessons which are to be disseminated for the edification of the Church.

The picture of the Holy Spirit as portrayed in *The Shepherd* is more mystically framed than in the other Apostolic Fathers. Hermas is carried away by the Spirit when he sees his visions. In an attempt to describe the true form of prophecy, Hermas includes accounts of his visions, as well as revelations and transportations in the Spirit. One of his primary concerns is to advise Christians of the importance of proving by their conduct those who claim to have gifts of the Holy Spirit.

The false prophet has no power from the divine Spirit in him and answers Christians according to their questions, giving them the words they want to hear. "For being empty, he gives empty answers to empty inquirers."[47] However, no spirit given by God needs to be questioned. It speaks all things of itself because it is from the Holy Spirit. The pretender exalts himself and attempts to take the prominent role in the assembly. He takes on airs, is unblushing and talkative, surrounds himself with luxuries and many other deceits, and takes money for prophesying, or if he cannot get it, does not prophesy. The false prophet who has an earthly spirit avoids assemblies of righteous men, choosing rather to associate with doubters and the vain. Whenever he comes into a group where the Holy Spirit is present, he becomes fearful and unable to speak.

On the other hand, the true prophet who has the heavenly Spirit is quiet and humble and abstains from wickedness, vanity, and the desires of the present world. He prophesies only when God chooses for him to speak. Whenever he comes into the assembly of righteous men, the Angel of the Spirit of prophecy fills him and he speaks as the Lord wishes.

While it is clear from Hermas's writings that the Holy Spirit alone accredits the true prophet, he strongly admonishes Christians to try the prophet by his deeds and his life. They are instructed to trust the Spirit that comes from God and has power, but to place no trust in the earthly, empty spirit, which has no power and comes from the Devil.[48]

Equally significant to the life of the Church is the role of the Holy Spirit as teacher and sanctifier of believers. The writer recognizes that the first teachers of the faith "walked in righteousness and truth, even as they received the Holy Spirit. Such persons, therefore, shall enter in with the angels."[49]

It is possible to grieve the Spirit through unrighteous behavior. Both doubt and anger sadden the Spirit of God:

> Wherefore remove grief from you, and crush not the Holy Spirit which dwells in you, lest He entreat God against you, and He withdraw from you. . . . Wherefore put on cheerfulness, which always is agreeable and acceptable to God.[50]

A similar warning occurs in Commandment Five:

> If you be patient, the Holy Spirit that dwells in you will be pure . . . . But if any outburst of anger takes place, forthwith the Holy Spirit, who is tender, is straitened, not having a pure place, and He seeks to depart. . . . For the Lord dwells in long-suffering, but the Devil in anger. The two spirits, then when dwelling in the same habitation, are at discord with each other, and are troublesome to that man in whom they dwell.[51]

This strange passage suggests that both the Holy Spirit and an evil spirit can possess man at the same time. This is the only known reference in ancient Christian writings before the development of hagiographic literature (lives of the Saints) to the possibility that a

Christian might be demon possessed.

Hermas's description of the relationship between the Son and the Holy Spirit is confused. The following passage will illustrate how difficult it is to determine his exact views:

> The holy, preexistent Spirit, that created every creature, God made to dwell in flesh, which he chose. This flesh, accordingly, in which the Holy Spirit dwelt, was nobly subject to that Spirit, walking religiously and chastely, in no respect defiling the Spirit; and, accordingly, after living excellently and purely, and after labouring and co-operating with the Spirit, and having in everything acted vigorously and courageously along with the Holy Spirit, He assumed it as a partner with it. For this conduct of the flesh pleased Him, because it was not defiled on the earth while having the Holy Spirit. He took, therefore, as fellow-councillors His Son and the glorious angels, in order that this flesh, which had been subject to the body without a fault, might have some place of tabernacle, and that it might not appear that the reward of its servitude had been lost, for the flesh that has been found without spot or defilement, in which the Holy Spirit dwelt, will receive a reward.[52]

Hermas herein fails to distinguish between the Son and the Spirit, a confusion that exists in numerous other second and third-century writers. At one point he states explicitly, "That Spirit is the Son of God."[53]

In other passages Hermas appears to be confusing the Holy Spirit with the human spirit. An example is found in Commandment Three:

> Love the truth, and let nothing but truth proceed from your mouth, that the spirit which God has placed in your flesh may be found truthful before all men; and the Lord, who dwelleth in you, will be glorified, because the Lord is truthful in every word, and in Him is no falsehood. They therefore who lie deny the Lord, and rob Him not giving back to Him the deposit which they have received. For they received from Him a spirit free from falsehood. If they give him back this spirit untruthful, they pollute the commandment of the Lord, and become robbers.[54]

Hermas's confusion on the nature of the Holy Spirit and on the relationship of the Spirit to the Trinity is a confusion that will reappear in the controversies of the fourth century and will occupy the Church for several subsequent centuries as it struggles to more adequately define the Godhead.

Notes to Chapter 1

[1]*Shepherd of Hermas*, Similitude Ninth i, *Ante-Nicene Fathers* (Grand Rapids: Eerdmans, 1976), 2:43 (henceforth ANF).

[2]Henry Barclay Swete, *The Holy Spirit in the Ancient Church* (London: Macmillan, 1912), 16.

[3]Clement of Rome, *First Epistle to the Corinthians* xlv, ANF 1:17.

[4]Ibid., xiii, ANF 1:8.
[5]Ibid., xvi, ANF 1:9.
[6]Ibid., xxii, ANF 1:11.
[7]Ibid., xlii, ANF 1:16.
[8]Ibid.
[9]Ibid., xlvii, ANF 1:18.
[10]Clement of Rome, *First Epistle to the Corinthians* lviii, in J.B. Lightfoot, ed., *The Apostolic Fathers* (Grand Rapids, MI: Baker Book House, 1980), 40.
[11]Ibid., ii, ANF 1:5. Eusebius A. Stephanou, "The Charismata in the Early Church Fathers," *The Greek Orthodox Theological Review* 21 (1976): 128-129, argues that silence on the charismata does not suggest their absence any more than the silence of certain New Testament books. "We cannot logically expect a teacher or pastor to include the totality of belief and practice each time he took up the pen to write."
[12]Clement of Rome, op. cit., xxxviii, ANF 1:15.
[13]Ibid., xlii, ANF 1:16
[14]Ibid., xlvi, ANF 1:17.
[15]Ibid., lviii, Lightfoot, 38.
[16]*Second Epistle of Clement* xiv, Lightfoot, 49-50.
[17]Ignatius, *Letter to the Philadelphians* vii, ANF 1:83.
[18]Ignatius, *Letter to the Ephesians* ix, ANF 1:53.
[19]Ibid., xvii, ANF 1:56.
[20]Ignatius, *Letter to Polycarp* ii, ANF 1:99.
[21]Ignatius, *Letter to the Smyrnaeans*, superscription, ANF 1:86.
[22]Ignatius, *Letter to the Magnesians* xiii, ANF 1: 64-65; and *Letter to the Ephesians* ix, ANF 1:53.
[23]*Letter to the Ephesians* xviii, ANF 1:57.
[24]Polycarp, *Epistle to the Philippians* v. 3, *Ancient Christian Writers* (New York: Newman Press, 1975), 13:78 (henceforth ACW).
[25]Ibid., xiv. 2, ACW 6:97.
[26]*The Martyrdom of Polycarp* xiv.3. ACW, op. cit.
[27]*Didache* xv.1-2, ACW 6:24.
[28]Ibid., i.5, ACW 6:15.
[29]Ibid., xi.1, ACW 6:22.
[30]Ibid., x.7, xi.1-2, xiii.1-2, ACW 6:21, 22, 23.
[31]Ibid., xi.9, ACW 6:22.
[32]Ibid., xi.12, ACW 6:22-23.
[33]Ibid., xi.11, ACW 6:22.
[34]Ibid., xi.6, 12, ACW 6:22-23.
[35]Ibid., xi.7-8, ACW 6:22.
[36]Ibid., xi.5, ACW, op. cit.

³⁷Ibid., xi.7, ACW, op. cit.
³⁸*Epistle of Barnabas* xii.2, ACW 6:54.
³⁹Ibid., x.2, ACW 6:51.
⁴⁰Ibid., ix,7, ACW 6:50.
⁴¹Ibid., xiii.5, ACW 6:56-57.
⁴²Ibid., xvi.9, ACW 6:61.
⁴³Ibid., i.2, ACW 6:37.
⁴⁴Ibid., i.3, ACW, op. cit.
⁴⁵Ibid., ix.2, 7, ACW 6:49, 50.
⁴⁶Ibid., vii.3, xi.8-9, ACW 6:47, 53-54. Cf. this with Ignatius's use of the simile "stones."
⁴⁷*Shepherd of Hermas*, Commandment Eleventh, ANF 2:27.
⁴⁸Ibid., ANF 2:27-28.
⁴⁹*Shepherd of Hermas*, Similitude Ninth xxv, ANF 2:52.
⁵⁰Commandment Tenth ii, ANF 2:26-27. Swete, 26-27, points out that Hermas's teaching that the Holy Spirit is defiled and Hermas's suggestion that the Spirit pleads against the sinner are not compatible with teachings in the New Testament.
⁵¹*Shepherd of Hermas*, Commandment Fifth i, ANF 2:23-24.
⁵²*Shepherd of Hermas*, Similitude Sixth vi, ANF 2:35-36.
⁵³*Shepherd of Hermas*, Similitude Ninth i, ANF 2:43.
⁵⁴*Shepherd of Hermas*, Commandment Third, ANF 2:21.

CHAPTER TWO
THE RESPONSE OF THE
EARLY APOLOGISTS

Whereas the occasional writings of the Apostolic Fathers mirrored the biblical proclamation, the Apologists made the first hesitant attempt to conceptualize and interpret Christian theology with the aid of the dominant philosophy of the period. As the first systematic theologians, they ushered in a period of intensified doctrinal formulation. Their common objective was to defend the Church against objections raised by intelligent contemporaries in the Graeco-Roman world, especially against the charge that Christians were "atheists" and, therefore, subversives. They also pointed out defects in the ideas of paganism. In addition, they attempted to demonstrate that Christianity fulfills a longing in the minds of pagan people.

The Apologists sought to defend their fundamental beliefs in terms most acceptable to the non-Christian inquirer. In so doing, they depended strongly on their philosophic training for both arguments and language. The truth that is common to both Christians and pagans must be emphasized. Their starting point was the claim that Christ is the truth to which both the Scriptures and the wisdom of the philosophers directly lead. The divine Logos spoke to the prophets and His truth was revealed though the great pagan thinkers.

The doctrine of the Logos so dominated the attention of the Apologists that it overshadowed, even cramped, the articulation of pneumatology. The Holy Spirit played a relatively indistinct role in their theology. In fact, the doctrinal language used at this time was still immature. The Apologists at times used the word "spirit" in an unclear manner to indicate the preexistent nature of Christ and the third Person in the Godhead. Furthermore, the word "Spirit" was used for all three Persons of God.

It is not difficult to recognize theological difficulties in the Apologists' treatment of the Holy Spirit. Such difficulties probably were inevitable, given the task and the degree of experimentation that were demanded of these writers. On the other hand, much of this experimentation resulted in long-range gains in the articulation of what became orthodox teaching. For example, the Apologist Athenagoras anticipated with remarkable accuracy certain conclusions to which experience and reflection brought the best Christian thinkers of the next several centuries.[2]

1. JUSTIN MARTYR

Justin Martyr (ca. 100-165 A.D.), the most important of the Apologists, refers to the Holy Spirit on numerous occasions. He is the first Christian writer to attempt to define the relationship between members of the Trinity—an attempt that was not fully satisfactory, at least as viewed by later trinitarians. On two occasions he coordinates the Father, Son, and Holy Spirit:

> For, in the name of God, the Father and Lord of the universe, and of our Saviour Jesus Christ, and of the Holy Spirit, they then receive the washing of water.[1]

> There is then brought to the president of the brethren bread and a cup of wine mixed with water; and he taking them, gives praise and glory to the Father of the universe, through the name of the Son and of the Holy Ghost, and offers thanks at considerable length for our being counted worthy to receive these things at His hands.[2]

Justin appears to subordinate the Son to the Father, and the Holy Spirit to the Son in the following passage: "We reasonably worship Him [Christ], having learned that He is the Son of the true God Himself, and holding Him in the second place, and the prophetic Spirit in the third."[3]

Here Justin is attempting to represent Christian teaching on the Trinity as in accord with best Greek philosophy which frequently presented levels of deity, resulting from the Neoplatonic belief in emanation. The subordination of the second and the third Persons appears to be one of rank and function only. There is little evidence to suggest that Justin is a true forerunner of Arius, Macedonius, or Eunomius, who make distinctions within the Trinity on matters of essence and nature.

Justin's difficulty is in part his inability to differentiate between the functions of Son and Spirit. This certainly is true in his description of the role of the Holy Spirit in the Incarnation:

> It is wrong, therefore, to understand the Spirit and the power of God as anything else than the Word, which is also the firstborn of God, as the foresaid prophet Moses declared; and it was this [Spirit] which, when it came upon the Virgin and overshadowed her, caused her to conceive, not by intercourse, but by power.[4]

Justin attempts to answer the claim that no prophet had risen from among the followers of Christ. He explains that the Spirit had rested and ceased His gifts with the coming of Christ, and then returned, giving them to the followers of Christ. The gifts which the Old Testament community formerly enjoyed now have been transferred to the Christian believers.

> It is accordingly said, "He ascended on high, He led captivity captive, He gave gifts unto the sons of men." And again, in another prophecy it is said: "And it shall come to pass after this, I will pour out My Spirit on all flesh, and on My Servants, and on My handmaids, and they shall prophesy." Now, it is possible to see amongst us women and men who possess gifts of the Spirit of God.[5]

Again he reminds fellow Christians:

> Daily some [of you] are becoming disciples in the name of Christ, and are quitting the path of error, who are also receiving gifts each as he is worthy, illumined through the name of this Christ. For one receives the spirit of understanding, another of counsel, another of strength, another healing, another of foreknowledge, another of teaching, another of the fear of God.[6]

Apparently, these gifts were being exercised throughout the Christian world as well as certain of those charisms listed in 2 Corinthians 12:

> For numberless demoniacs throughout the whole world and in your city, many of our Christian men, exorcising them in the name of Jesus Christ, who was crucified under Pontius Pilate, have healed and do heal, rendering helpless and driving the possessing devils out of the men, though they could not be cured by all the other exorcists, and those who used incantations and drugs.[7]

According to Justin, the Holy Spirit also is responsible for the inspiration of the prophets, "There were, then, among the Jews certain men who were prophets of God, through whom the prophetic Spirit published beforehand things that were to pass, ere ever they happened."[8]

The Holy Spirit is intimately linked with the process of Redemption. This is apparent in Justin's writings on the Incarnation, as well as on baptism, in which the believer is regenerated in the name of the Father, the Son, and Holy Spirit.[9] Again, the Spirit is referred to as the power of God.[10] The work of the Spirit in the life of the believer is such that Justin declared, "Is there then such and so great power in our mind? Will the mind of man see God at any time it is uninstructed by the Holy Spirit?"[11] The very Church is holy because God dwells in it in the Person of the Holy Spirit.[12]

2. TATIAN

Justin Martyr's dependence on the thought of the philosophers, especially Plato, and his belief that the great truths of Christianity

had been taught before Christ's time were shared by most of the
Apologists. The most important exception is Tatian, a pupil of
Justin, who scorns all paganism including Platonism, and argues in
his *Admonition to the Greeks* that it is the Holy Spirit alone who
gives man immortality:

> The soul is not in itself immortal, O Greeks, but mortal . . . if it
> continues solitary (lives alone), it tends downward towards matter,
> and dies with the flesh; but, if it enters into union with the Divine
> Spirit, it is no longer helpless, but ascends to the regions whither the
> Spirit guides it.[13]

Because the soul must be united with the Spirit, Tatian suggests
that "It becomes us now to seek for what we once had, but have
lost, to unite the soul with the Holy Spirit, and to strive after union
with God."[14]

The Holy Spirit, according to Tatian, is God's representative
within the soul,[15] the wings of the soul,[16] but not within all souls,
not even within all believers. Rather, He is within some of the just.
"The Spirit of God is not with all, but, taking up its abode with
those who live justly, and intimately combining with the soul, by
prophecies it announces hidden things to other souls."[17]

The Spirit provides protection against evil spirits as well as
matter. "Being armed with the breastplate of the celestial Spirit, he
will be able to preserve all that is encompassed by it."[18] More
specifically, in countering evil spirits, Tatian declares, "Only by
those whom the Spirit of God dwells in and fortifies are the bodies
of the demons easily seen, not at all by others."[19] Not only is there
protection in the Spirit, there also is healing. "If any one is healed
by matter, through trusting to it, much more will be healed by
having recourse to the power of God."[20]

In the use of such expressions as God's ambassador or deputy,
and as minister of the incarnate Word, Tatian seems to imply
subordination, at least in function. However, he never directly
addresses this question. Nor does he concern himself with other
basic questions of the Holy Spirit's Person and work.

3. ATHENAGORAS

Athenagoras was a contemporary of Tatian, although his spirit is
very different from Justin's pupil. In fact, Athenagoras more
closely resembles Justin in that he finds positive value in the truth
found in pagan philosophy. In his elegantly written, *A Plea for the
Christians*, Athenagoras asserts that Plato knew the basic points of
the Christian doctrine of God.[21] Indeed, it was Platonism which led
Athenagoras to a clear-cut definition of the relationship of the
Holy Spirit to the rest of the Trinity:

> The Son of God is the Logos of the Father, in idea and in operation;

for after the pattern of Him and by Him were all things made, the Father and the Son being one. And, the Son being in the Father and the Father in the Son, in oneness and power of spirit, the understanding and reason of the Father is the Son of God. But if, in your surpassing intelligence it occurs to you to inquire what is meant by the Son I will state briefly that He is the first product of the Father, not as having been brought into existence (for from the beginning, God, who is the eternal mind, had the Logos in Himself, being from eternity instinct with Logos); but inasmuch as He came forth to be the idea and energizing power of all material things, which law like a nature without attributes, and an inactive earth, the grosser particles being statements. "The Lord," it says, "made me, the beginning of His ways to His works." The Holy Spirit Himself also, which operates in the prophets, we assert to be an effluence of God, flowing from Him, and returning back again like a beam of the sun. Who, then, would not be astonished to hear men who speak of God the Father, and of God the Son, and of the Holy Spirit, and who declare both their power in union and their distinction in order, called atheists?[22]

Athenagoras seems to be teaching, at least by implication, a doctrine of essential procession. In this he is much ahead of his time.

At another point in the *Plea*, Athenagoras presents a capsule version of his understanding of the relationship of the Trinity:

We acknowledge a God, and a Son his Logos, and a Holy Spirit, united in essence, the Father, the Son, the Spirit, because the Son is the Intelligence, Reason, Wisdom of the Father, and the Spirit an effluence, as light from fire.[23]

These statements stand as the first attempt by a Christian writer to give something like a philosophy of the trinitarian position—statements that are remarkably close to the Catholic dogma of the Trinity as it is ultimately defined.

Athenagoras deals in some detail with the role played by the Holy Spirit as the Inspirer of the writers of Scripture.

But we have for witnesses of the things we apprehend and believe, prophets, men who have pronounced concerning God and the things of God, guided by the Spirit of God. . . . it would be irrational for us to cease to believe in the Spirit from God, who moved the mouths of the prophets like musical instruments, and to give heed to mere human opinions.[24]

[You] cannot be ignorant of the writings either of Moses or of Isaiah and Jeremiah, and the other prophets, who, lifted in ecstasy above the natural operations of their minds by the impulses of the Divine Spirit, uttered the things with which they were inspired, the Spirit making use of them as a flute-player breathes into the flute.[25]

Athenagoras's analysis of the process of divine inspiration of the writers of Scripture reveals a keen awareness of the heights of human potential when aided by divine impetus and is in line with the Apologist's view that Christianity is a higher form of wisdom than Greek philosophy, which represents mere human wisdom.

4. THEOPHILUS OF ANTIOCH

Theophilus, bishop of Antioch, wrote his *Three Books of Autolycus* to a friend, with the purpose of persuading him of the truth of Christianity. He is the first Christian author to apply the word "trinity" to the Godhead.[26] The members of the Trinity are not named as Father, Son, and Holy Spirit, however; rather, they are God, His Word (*Logos*), and His Wisdom. Theophilus is not unique in calling the second person of the Trinity the *Logos*, for Justin Martyr, Tatian, and Athenagoras already had popularized the use of the word. The term "wisdom" is associated by Theophilus with the Spirit, the Spirit of Prophecy.[27] Both the Word and the Wisdom emitted from God before creation, and both were present with God at creation. (The text is somewhat confusing in that it can be read either that the Word and the Wisdom are separate identities or that they are one, "God, then, having His own Word internal within His own bowels, begat Him, emitting Him along with His own wisdom before all things.")

In creation the Holy Spirit moved on the face of the waters as a vital and vitalizing power:

> And by the Spirit which is borne above the waters he means that which God gave for animating the creation, as he gave life to man, mixing what is fine with what is fine. For the Spirit is fine, and the water is fine, that the Spirit may nourish the water, and the water penetrating everywhere along with the Spirit, may nourish creation. For the Spirit being one, and holding the place of light, was between the water and the heaven, in order that the darkness might not in any way communicate with the heaven, which was nearer God, before God said, "Let there be light."[28]

> So the whole creation is contained by the spirit of God, and the containing spirit is along with creation contained by the hand of God.[29]

Theophilus also recognizes the role of the Holy Spirit in prophecy, although he does not limit it to the Hebrews. The Greeks also had been selected for such gifts:

> But men of God carrying in them a bold spirit and becoming prophets, being inspired and made wise by God, became God-taught and holy, and righteous. Wherefore they were also deemed worthy of receiving this reward, that they should become instruments of God, and contain the wisdom that is from Him, through which wisdom they uttered both what regarded the creation of the world and all other things. For they predicted also pestilences, and famines, and wars. And there was not one or two, but many, at various times and seasons among the Hebrews; and also among the Greeks there was the Sibyl; and they all have spoken things consistent and harmonius [*sic*] with each other, both what happened before them and what happened in their own time, and what things are now being fulfilled in our own day.[30]

At the same time, I met with the sacred Scriptures of the holy prophets, who also by the Spirit of God foretold the things that had already happened, just as they came to pass, and the things now occurring as they are now happening, and things future in the order in which they shall be accomplished.[31]

Notes to Chapter 2

[1]Justin Martyr, *First Apology* lxi, ANF 1:183.
[2]Ibid., lxv, ANF 1:185.
[3]Ibid., xiii, ANF 1:166-167.
[4]Ibid., xxxiii, ANF 1:174.
[5]Justin Martyr, *Dialogue with Trypho* lxxxvii-lxxxviii, ANF 1:243.
[6]Ibid., xxxix, ANF 1:214. Harold Hunter, "Tongues-Speech: A Patristic Analysis," *Journal of the Evangelical Theological Society* 23 (June 1980): 127-128, argues that while Justin Martyr excludes mention of tongues-speech in both lists of gifts (Dialogue 39 and Dialogue 87), it must be remembered that Justin's lists are taken from Isaiah 11:2-3, not from 1 Corinthians 12. He gives the main ingredients of each passage in parallel columns as follows:

1 Cor. 12:8-10	Dialogue 39	Isa 11:1-3	Dialogue 87
wisdom		wisdom	wisdom
	understanding	understanding	understanding
	counsel	counsel	counsel
knowledge		knowledge	knowledge
faith			
healing	healing		
miracles			
		might	might
	foreknowledge		
prophecy			
discern spirits			
	teaching		
tongues			
interpretation of tongues			
	fear of God	fear of the Lord	fear of the Lord

Hunter argues that Justin's dependence on Isaiah 11:1-3 is consistent with the patristic reliance on Old Testament authority, that the object of the apology was a Jew, Trypho, and that the concept of a "Sevenfold Spirit," derived from the Isaiah passage, was commonplace among patristic writers. Later, Tertullian will argue for the unanimity in thought of the Isaiah and 1 Corinthian passages. (*Against Marcion* v. 8.9, ANF 3:446.) Hunter's argument that the lists of gifts given in Dialogues 39 and 87 are Christianized forms of the list in Isaiah seems reasonable. For one thing, Justin does not list prophecy as one of the gifts in either Dialogue, although he discusses this charism in numerous places in his writings.

[7]*Second Apology* vi, ANF 1:190.

[8]*First Apology* xxxi, ANF 1:173. Also note *First Apology* 42-44, ANF 1:176-177.

[9]Ibid., lxi, ANF 1:183.

[10]Ibid., xxxiii, ANF 1:174.

[11]*Dialogue with Trypho* iv, ANF 1:196.

[12]For a discussion on this point see J.N.D. Kelly, *Early Christian Creeds* (Third Edition; New York: Longmans, 1972), 159.

[13]Tatian, *Admonition to the Greeks* xiii, ANF 2:70-71.

[14]Ibid., xv, ANF 2:71.

[15]Ibid.

[16]Ibid., xx, ANF 2:73-74.

[17]Ibid., xiii, ANF 2:71.

[18]Ibid., xvi, ANF 2:72.

[19]Ibid., xv, ANF 2:71.

[20]Ibid., xviii, ANF 2:73.

[21]Athenagoras, *Plea for the Christians* xxiii, ANF 2:141.

[22]Ibid., x, ANF II, 133. Abraham J. Malherbe, "The Holy Spirit in Athenagoras," *Journal of Theological Studies*, n.s. 20 (October 1969): 538-542, concludes that Athenagoras conceives of the function of the Spirit in the act of creation along the lines of the Middle Platonic World Soul.

[23]Ibid., xxiv, ANF 2:141. Malherbe, 541, suggests that in Athenagoras "the Spirit corresponds to the Logos, with the exception that the Logos is the agent through which God created the world, while through the Spirit He maintains and controls it."

[24]Ibid., vii ANF 2:132.

[25]Ibid., ix, ANF 2:133.

[26]Theophilus, *To Autolycus* ii.15, ANF 2:101.

[27]Ibid., ii.10, ANF 2:98.

[28]Ibid., ii.13, ANF 2:99-100.

[29]Ibid., i.5, ANF 2:90.

[30]Ibid., ix, ANF 2:97.

[31]Ibid., i.14, ANF 2:93.

CHAPTER THREE
THE CHALLENGE OF THEOLOGICAL ERROR AND PROPHETIC EXCESS

The Apologists defended the Church against philosophers and emperors. However, threats to Christianity did not come only from the outside. A still greater danger came from the threat of heresies within Christianity. Chief among these was Gnosticism, which challenged the realm of authority in the Church, including that of Holy Scripture, by the intrusion of secret traditions which asserted quite different things from what the biblical writings said. Another was the heresy of Marcion, who separated law and gospel, the Old and New Testaments, the Creator and the God of love. A third was Monarchianism, which opted for a unipersonal rather than a trinitarian view of the divine nature in order to preserve the unity of God. Finally, there was Montanism, not a heresy but rather a reaction against developing ecclesiasticism, a reaction of the Spirit against order, which came at a time when the Church could not tolerate prophetic excesses and extreme rigor in morals and discipline.

1. GNOSTIC RELIGIONS

The general label of "Gnosticism" is used to describe a wide variety of religious systems and ideas that flourished from the first through the third centuries A.D., with some continuing well into the Middle Ages. Gnosticism was both highly syncretistic and contemplative: syncretistic in that it drew from whatever doctrines it found valuable and contemplative in the common belief that, although mankind exists in ignorance and illusion, one can, through gnosis, attain spiritual liberation by which one achieves his own identity with the divine. Gnostic groups differed widely in ethical practice, in ritual, and in theology. Irenaeus, who writes against the Gnostics, relates that they "do not agree in treating the same points, but alike, in things and names, set forth opinions mutually discordant."[1] Their commonalities are described by Elaine Pagels:

> 1. There is an irreconcilable contradiction between the cosmic system of this world and the absolutely transcendent God. That God is often described negatively: the indescribable, unknowable, or nonexistent One; alternatively, the Abyss, Source, or Primal Beginning of all things.
>
> 2. The "I" of the Gnostic, the "spirit," or "inner man" is unalterably divine, and belongs to that divine being which transcends all creation.
>
> 3. The "spiritual" element, however, has become mingled with two distinct lower elements, and bound into the lower order of creation with them: first, with the body, dominated by sensual passions: second, with the soul, the center of psychic functions. The Spirit, hidden within soul and body like marrow within two layers of bone and flesh, has been entrapped within these lower elements. The person in whom it is hidden remains unaware of its presence.
>
> 4. Only an emissary from the divine world above—a savior, a redeemer, or a "call"—can release these bonds of confinement. Through gnosis the spiritual spark that lies dormant within the Gnostic is ignited, and the inner spirit is liberated so that one becomes aware of one's own true nature.[2]

Gnosticism was not restricted to any institutionalized religion. Most scholars now agree that it had non-Christian origins and amalgamated both Jewish and Christian elements with pagan ideas.[3] Often Gnosticism completely reversed the values of the systems that it incorporated. For example, since the world is material and evil, Yahweh, the creator God of the Jewish and Christian faiths, is depicted by numerous Gnostic writers as an evil demiurge (a subordinate god). In Christian Gnosticism the agent Wisdom is often identified with Christ. But because Christ delivers man from the enslavement of flesh, he can have no flesh. He only appears to have flesh. His body is a phantom that only seems to exist. From this docetic perspective the Incarnation and the Crucifixion, so basic to orthodox Christian belief, pale into illusion. Jesus becomes a spiritual being who adapts himself to human perception. In the *Second Treatise of the Great Seth*, for example, Jesus reveals to His believers that

> it was another . . . who drank the gall and the vinegar; it was not I. They struck me with the reed; it was another, Simon, who bore the cross on his shoulder. It was another upon whom they placed the crown of thorns. But I was rejoicing in the height over all the wealth of the archons and the offspring of their error, of their empty glory. And I was laughing at their ignorance.[4]

Gnostic religions, then, had a doctrine of salvation, but not in the traditional Christian sense. As the redeemed become aware of their true identity, that their inner self is unalterably divine and that they were generated from the true God, they are released from the dominion of the creator. Certain Gnostic groups initiated the recipient into union with the divine. All Gnostics, however, saw the redemption process as a movement toward full realization of the divine nature.

Although Christian Gnostics originally had much in common with early Christianity—a common estrangement from the contaminating world around them and an ideal which transcended life as we know it—they shared little with those second and third century Christians who had come to follow a more practical and conventional way of life and who considered the Gnostic vision to be a betrayal of the original position. Christian Gnostics came to be excluded from the larger church as heretics.

In Acts 8 we have a record of one of the earliest encounters between Christianity and Gnosticism. Simon Magus, who lived in Samaria, claimed that he or his companion Helena was the Holy Spirit. (Simon was not the founder of Gnosticism as Justin,[5] Irenaeus,[6] and others suggest.) When his early successes at Samaria ended with the arrival of Peter and John who possessed spiritual gifts, Simon sought to buy the gift of the Holy Spirit from the apostles.

Basilides of Alexandria, who claimed to be a disciple of the apostle Matthew, was a prominent Christian Gnostic in the period between A.D. 120 and 140. He asserted that a nonexistent deity made from nothing a nonexistent world. The Holy Spirit is not consubstantial with the sonship for it cannot rise to the highest spheres. After creation part of the sonship remains to be lifted up. The Spirit comes down from the elevated sonship upon the Son of Mary to accompany Him so that the sonship not yet elevated might pass upwards.[7]

This form of Gnosticism recognizes a connection between the Holy Spirit and sonship, which it lifts and illuminates. The anonymous author of the *Philosophumena*, writing about the teachings of Basilides, describes the Spirit-sonship relationship in these words:

> When one has put a delicate perfume into a vase, one may empty that vase with the greatest care, but the odour still remains after the perfume has been decanted . . . and the vase retains the odour even though it contains no more of the perfume. Thus it is with the Holy Spirit, separated from and deprived of the sonhood (from which it came forth): it keeps within itself, so to speak, the virtue of the perfume.[8]

The Spirit in Basilides's system is subordinate, not exercising divine

authority or power. In this belief, Basilides and his followers
anticipate the teachings of the Arians and the Macedonians of the
fourth century A.D.

According to Valentinus, another second-century Alexandrian
Christian Gnostic leader, one element of a Primal Dyad begets
within Silence other dyads: Father and Truth, Logos and Life,
Mankind and Ecclesia. From these emanate other aeons (eternal
beings that together form the fullness of the supreme being from
whom they emanate and between whom and the world they are
intermediaries), settling and strengthening the pleroma (the fullness
of being of the divine life). The least of the aeons is Wisdom, or
Sophia, who goes beyond the limits of her possibilities in
attempting to know the element of the Primal Dyad who is beyond
description. The result is disorder within the pleroma. The Primal
Dyad reestablishes order by producing two more aeons, Christ and
Holy Spirit. The product of Wisdom's passion, Achamoth,
therefore, has to be expelled from the pleroma. The aeons, wishing
to help Achamoth, produce a new aeon, Jesus, in whom their
fullness is to be found. Jesus frees Achamoth from passions, which
become matter. Finally, Jesus grants Achamoth knowledge from
on high. Christ descends on Jesus in his baptism, and leaves him
before his passion.[9] Meanwhile, Holy Spirit enters the aeons
invisibly, causing them to "bring forth the plants of truth."[10] *The
Apocryphon of John*, a tractate of the second century A.D.,
contains this revealing statement of a Valentinian understanding of
the function of Holy Spirit in the pleroma:

> And when the mother recognized that the cover of darkness was
> imperfect, then she knew that her consort had not agreed with her.
> She repented with much weeping. And the whole pleroma hears the
> prayer of her repentence and they praised on her behalf the invisible,
> virginal Spirit. And he consented; and when the invisible Spirit had
> consented, the holy Spirit poured over her from their whole fullness.
> For her consort had not come to her, but he came to her through the
> pleroma in order that he might correct her deficiency. And she was
> taken up not to her own aeon but above her son, that she might be in
> the ninth until she has corrected her deficiency.[11]

Despite the chaos of Gnostic theologies, apparent from the
passages above, the fervor of Christian devotion and spiritual life is
retained, even amplified, in Gnosticism. Those individuals who
recognize the presence of the Spirit within them are pneumatic, the
elect seed, as opposed to those identified with matter (hylics) or
with the soul (psychics).[12] With their dependence on the "higher
gift" of knowledge to comprehend the "secrets of the holy way"
and "the deep things of God," the Gnostics readily find a place for
the Holy Spirit. The Spirit is involved in the very act of
Redemption, the coming of gnosis. "When the wind of the world

blows, it makes the winter come. When the Holy Spirit blows, the summer comes."[13] However, the role of the Holy Spirit necessarily is limited to the realm of the intellect and excluded from the moral nature of man. Therefore, it is very difficult for the Gnostic to find a place for the Holy Spirit as presented in the Gospels. This can be seen in the following excerpts:

> This is the manner of those who possess (something) from above of the immeasurable greatness, as they stretch out after the one alone and the perfect one, the one who is there for them. And they do not go down to Hades nor have they envy nor groaning nor death within them, but they rest in him who is at rest, not striving nor being involved in the search for truth. But they themselves are the truth; and the Father is within them and they are in the Father, being perfect, being undivided in the truly good one, being in no way deficient in anything, but they are set at rest, refreshed in the Spirit.[14]

So will you not cease loving the flesh and being afraid of sufferings? Or do you not know that you have yet to be abused and to be accused unjustly; and have yet to be shut up in prison, and condemned unlawfully, and crucified [without] reason, and buried [shamefully], as (was) I myself, by the evil one: Do you dare to spare the flesh, you for whom the Spirit is an encircling wall?[15]

He who comes out of the world can no longer be detained, because he was in the world. It is evident that he is above desire . . . and fear. He is master over [nature]. He is superior to envy. If [any one else] comes, they seize him and throttle [him] . . . How will he be able to [hide from them? Often] some [come and say], "We are faithful," in order that [they may be able to escape the unclean spirits] and the demons. For if they had the Holy Spirit, no unclean spirit would cleave to them.[16]

And the Life of Heaven wishes to renew all, that he may cast out that which is weak and every black form, that everyone may shine forth with great brilliance in heavenly garments in order to make manifest the command of the Father, and that he may crown those wishing to contend well—Christ, being judge of the contest, he who crowned every one, teaching every one to contend. This one who contended first received the crown, gained dominion, and appeared giving light to everyone. And all were made new through the Holy Spirit and the Mind.[17]

Come, Holy Spirit and cleanse their inward parts and their heart, and seal them in the name of the Father and of the Son and of the Holy Spirit.[18]

Come, water from the living water, that which is from that which is, which also has been sent to us; rest which has been sent to us from the rest; power of salvation which comes from that power which conquers all things and is subject to its own will; come and dwell in these waters, so that the gracious gift of the Holy Spirit may perfectly be perfected in them.[19]

I invoke you, the one who is and preexisted, by the name [which is] exalted above every name, through Jesus Christ [the Lord] of Lords,

the king of the ages: give me your gifts which you do not regret
through the Son of man, the Spirit, the Paraclete of [truth].[20]

Because of their emphasis on special knowledge and their desire
to transcend the evil of the world around them, the Gnostics laid
considerable emphasis on the gifts of the Spirit. A tractate in the
Nag Hammadi Codices, *The Interpretation of Knowledge*, is given
over to the question of the gifts and the importance of their proper
exercise within the Church, "the Body of Christ." Apparently, the
author is writing to a community of Gnostic believers divided over
the issue of spiritual gifts. Some of those who exercised gifts
despised the "ignorant" who lacked gnosis. Others felt resentment
when their fellows refused to share their spiritual gifts, or envy
when the gifted took a prominent place in the congregation. The
author deals with these difficulties in the Body in the following
way:

> Moreover, it is fitting for [each] of us to [enjoy] the gift that he has
> received from [God, and] that we not be jealous, since we know that
> he who is jealous is an obstacle in his (own) [path], since he destroys
> only himself with the gift and he is ignorant of God. He ought to
> rejoice [and] be glad and partake of grace and bounty. Does someone
> have a prophetic gift? Share it without hesitation. Neither approach
> your brother jealously nor [. . .] chosen as they [. . .] empty as
> they [escape . . .] fallen from their [. . .] are ignorant of the fact
> that [. . .] in [this way they] have [. . .] them in [. . .] in order
> that they may [reflect] perforce upon the things that you want [them
> to think] about when they [think about] you. [For] your brother [also
> has] the grace [that is in you. Do not] belittle yourself, but [rejoice and
> give] thanks spiritually [and] pray for that [one in order that] you
> might share in the grace [that dwells] within him. Do not consider
> [him foreign] to you; rather, one who is yours, whom each [of] your
> fellow members received. [If] you [love] the Head who possesses
> them, you also possess the one from whom it is that these outpourings
> of gifts exist among your brethren.
>
> But is someone making progress in the Word? Do not be upset by this;
> do not say, "Why does he speak while I do not?" for what he says is
> (also) yours, and that which discerns the Word and that which speaks
> is the same power, The Word [. . . eye] or a [hand only, but they are]
> a [single] body. [Those who belong to] all [of us] serve [the Head
> together]. For each one of [the members reckons] it as a member.
>
> What now, do you think [of] as spirit? Or [why] do they persecute
> men of [this] sort to death? Aren't they satisfied to be with the soul
> and (so) seek it? For every place is [excluded] from them by [the] men
> of God so long as they exist in flesh. And when they cannot see them,
> since they (the men of God) live by the spirit, they tear apart what
> appears as if thus they can find them. But what is the profit for them?
> They are senselessly mad! They rend their surroundings![21]

This writer at times comes surprisingly close to Paul's position in
his treatment of the Church as the "Body of Christ" and of the
gifts listed in 1 Corinthians 12 and 14, and to the author of 1 John

2:20, "But ye have an unction from the Holy One, and ye know all things." However, *The Interpretation of Knowledge* is a distinctly Gnostic document. The author could not have stated with Paul in 1 Corinthians, "But we preach Christ crucified,"[22] or with the author of 1 John, "And every spirit that confesseth not that Jesus Christ is come in the flesh is not of God."[23] The jealous Gnostics are compared to the jealous and ignorant demiurge. The Gnostic cosmology is ever-present in such passages as "For the Father does not keep the Sabbath but does work on the Son, and through the Son he continued to provide himself with the Aeons."[24]

In several Gnostic texts appear glossolalia-like passages, although certain of these may have been Greek characters often repeated many times within the Coptic text expressing mysteries inexpressible. Some may simply be *nomina barbara*, barbarization of language. Selected passages follow:

> The second ogdoad-power, the Mother, the virginal Barbelon epititioch [. . .] the uninterpretable power, the ineffable Mother.

> And the throne of his [glory] was established [in it, this one] on which his unrevealable name [is inscribed], on the tablet [. . .] one is the word, the [Father of the light] of everything, he [who came] forth from the silence, while he rests in the silence, he whose name [is] in an invisible symbol. A hidden, [invisible] mystery came forth iiiiiiiiiiiiiiiiii [iii] eeeeeeeeeeeeeeeeeeee [ee o] ooooo oooooooooooooooo uu [uuu] uuuuuuuuuuuuuuuu eeee eeeeeeeeeeeeee aaaaaaa [aaaa] aaaaaaaaaaa oooooooooo[oo] oooooooooooo.

> ie ieus eo eu eo oua! Really truly. O Tesseus Mazareus Yessedekeus, O Living water, O child of the child, O glorious name, really truly, aion o on (or: O existing aeon), iiii eeee eeee oooo uuuu oooo aaaa [a], really truly, ei aaaa oooo, O existing one who sees the aeons! Really truly, aee eee iiii uuuuuu ooooooooo, who is eternally eternal, really truly, iea aio, in the heart, who exists, u aei eis aei, ei o ei, ei os ei (or: (Son) forever, Thou art what Thou art, Thou art who Thou art)![25]

Because of their desire to discredit the Gnostic leaders, polemicists were quick to point out any abuse of spiritual gifts. Irenaeus describes a follower of Valentinus, Marcus, as a charlatan who proclaimed himself to be a prophet capable of giving others the prophetic gift.

> But there is another among these heretics, Marcus by name, who boasts himself as having improved upon his master. He is a perfect adept in magical impostures, and by this means drawing away a great number of men, and not a few women, he has induced them to join themselves to him, as to one who is possessed of the greatest knowledge and perfection, and who has received the highest power from the invisible and ineffable regions above. Thus it appears as if he really were the precursor of Antichrist. . . . Pretending to consecrate cups mixed with wine, and protracting to great length the word of invocation, he contrives to give them a purple and reddish colour, so

that Charis, who is one of those that are superior to all things, should be thought to drop her own blood into that cup through means of his invocation, and that thus those who are present should be led to rejoice to taste of that cup, in order that, by so doing, the Charis, who is set forth by this magician, may also flow into them. Again, handing mixed cups to the women, he bids them consecrate these in his presence. When this has been done, he himself produces another cup of much larger size than that which the deluded woman has consecrated, and pouring from the smaller one consecrated by the woman into that which has been brought forward by himself, he at the same time pronounces these words: "May that Charis who is before all things, and who transcends all knowledge and speech, fill thine inner man, and multiply in thee her own knowledge, by sowing the grain of mustard seed in thee as in good soil.". . . It appears probable enough that this man possesses a demon as his familiar spirit, by means of whom he seems able to prophesy, and also enables as many as he counts worthy to be partakers of his Charis themselves to prophesy. He devotes himself especially to women, and those such as are well-bred, and elegantly attired, and of great wealth, whom he frequently seeks to draw after him, by addressing them in such seductive words as these: "I am eager to make thee a partaker of my Charis, since the Father of all doth continually behold thy angel before His face. Now the place of thy angel is among us: it behoves us to become one. Receive first from me and by me [the gift of] Charis. Adorn thyself as a bride who is expecting her bridegroom, that thou mayest be what I am, and I what thou art. Establish the germ of light in thy nuptial chamber. Receive from me a spouse, and become receptive of him, while thou art received by him. Behold Charis has descended upon thee; open thy mouth and prophesy." She then, vainly puffed up and elated by these words, and greatly excited in soul by the expectation that it is herself who is to prophesy. Her heart beating violently [from emotion], reaches the requisite pitch of audacity, and idly as well as impudently utters some nonsense as it happens to occur to her, such as might be expected from one heated by an empty spirit. . . . Henceforth she reckons herself a prophetess, and expresses her thanks to Marcus for having imparted to her of his own Charis. She then makes the effort to reward him, not only by the gift of her possessions . . . but also yielding up to him her person, desiring in every way to be united to him, that she may become altogether one with him.[26]

While most Christian Gnostic writers allow for the role of the Spirit in their cosmology, trinitarian doctrine as understood in the mainstream Church is not present, perhaps because of the emphasis placed on the incomprehensible nature of God and on the numerous emanations from God which place both the Son and the Holy Spirit in subordinate positions. It is true that the Father, Son, and Holy Spirit appear together in several Nag Hammadi writings, including the *Gospel of Philip*[27] and *The Acts of Thomas*.[28] However, numerous other triads exist, including the Father, Son, and Church in *The Tripartite Tractate*,[29] a "Triple-powered Spirit"—consisting of Existence, Life, and Mind—in *Allogenes*,[30] and the Father, Mother Barbelo (the name of a female aeon, usually in a high or even the highest place), and the Son in *The Gospel of the Egyptians* (*The Holy Book of the Great Invisible Spirit*).[31] Again in the *Trimorphic Protennoia*[32] we find a reference to "the Father, the Mother, the Son." There is a description in the *Apocryphon of John* of a mystical vision of the Trinity experienced by the beloved disciple. A voice announces to John, "I am the one who [is with you] always. I [am the Father]; I am the Mother; I am the Son."[33]

In several Christian Gnostic texts the divine Mother is described as the Holy Spirit. This may seem strange to those of us who use the Greek term for Spirit, *pneuma*, which is neuter. Perhaps the Gnostic writers have in mind the Hebrew term for Spirit, *ruah,* which is feminine. This certainly is true in the *Gospel of Philip* when the author argues that the virgin birth was the mysterious union between the heavenly Father and the Spirit who is both Mother and Virgin. He concludes that Christ was indeed born from a virgin—the Holy Spirit. The Spirit (*ruah*) is the mother of many. Against the orthodox version of the virgin birth, the author comments, "Some said, 'Mary conceived by the Holy Spirit.' These are in error. They do not know what they are saying. When did a woman ever conceive by a woman?"[34]

In the *Gospel of the Hebrews*, Jesus is said to speak of "my Mother, the Holy Spirit,"[35] while in *The Gospel of Thomas* Jesus contrasts His earthly mother and father, Mary and Joseph, with His divine Father and His divine Mother, the Holy Spirit. In the latter work the author declares that whoever becomes a Christian gains both a Father and a Mother, who is the Spirit.[36]

Christian Gnosis often has several sacraments, including baptism, Eucharist, unction, sealing, and bridal chamber. The *Trimorphic Protennoia* has a fivefold baptismal ritual called Five Seals.[37] Baptism and Eucharist have a completely different meaning from that expressed in the larger Church. Because Gnostic redemption is "the knowledge of the unspeakable Greatness," and "knowledge is the redemption of the inner man,"[38] baptism and the Eucharist are really superfluous. Yet, they do appear in several Gnostic writings, perhaps, as Foerster suggests, because the Gnostics broke away from movements which practiced sacraments, which they then transformed.[39]

Several Gnostic sacramental passages refer to the Holy Spirit. The first, from the *Gospel of Philip*, equates the Spirit with the blood of the sacrament:

> Because of this he [Jesus] said, "He who shall not eat my flesh and drink my blood has not life in him" (John 6:53). What is it? His flesh

> is the word, and his blood is the Holy Spirit. He who has received
> these has food and he has drink and clothing.
>
> The cup of prayer contains wine and water, since it is appointed as the
> type of the blood for which thanks is given. And it is full of the Holy
> Spirit, and it belongs to the wholly perfect man. When we drink this,
> we shall receive for ourselves the perfect man.[40]

In the same *Gospel of Philip* we have strong indication that the
unction of the Holy Spirit is of a higher order than the traditional
sacraments. In the first passage the author distinguishes between
baptism in water and baptism in the Holy Spirit:

> If one go down into the water and come up without having anything
> and says, "I am a Christian," he has borrowed the name at interest.
> But if he receive the Holy Spirit, he has the name as a gift. He who has
> received a gift does not have to give it back, but of him who has
> borrowed it at interest, payment is demanded.[41]

Similarly, anointing by the Holy Spirit is considered above that of
baptism.

> The chrism is superior to baptism, for it is from the word "chrism"
> that we have been called "Christians," certainly not because of the
> word "baptism." And it is because of the chrism that "the Christ"
> has his name. For the Father anointed us. He who has been anointed
> possesses everything. He possesses the resurrection, the light, the
> cross, the Holy Spirit. The Father gave him this in the bridal chamber,
> he merely accepted (the gift).[42]

It is always difficult to assess the long-term impact of fringe
groups, such as the Christian Gnostics, on the thought and practice
in the mainline Church. It is probable that the Gnostic's claim to be
set aside from other Christians by the possession of a gift of special
knowledge led to more than their estrangement from the larger
Church. One can assume that there also resulted an increased fear
of novelty and an atmosphere less accepting of those who claimed
to walk in the Spirit and to exercise His gifts.

2. MARCIONISM

Marcion, a wealthy shipowner from Sinope in Pontus, moved to
Rome shortly before A.D. 140. By 144 he was excommunicated by
the orthodox community and proceeded to organize his followers
into a movement rival to mainline Christianity, with churches
established in many parts of the empire. At one time, his church
had so many members that the final result of the conflict was
seriously in doubt.

Marcion's views were in some respects very much like the
Gnostics, although he arrived at them by a different approach.
Like the Gnostics, Marcion's system began with the problem of
evil. However, he did not share Gnostic ideas that salvation comes
by knowledge as opposed to faith, or that the work of the redeemer
reintegrates the human spirit with the divine element from which it

came. As Marcion saw it, the problem presents itself in terms of the Bible. The Old and New Testaments are in a state of contradiction. There are really two gods, one god of the Old Testament, the creator, who is in opposition to the God of love, the true God of the New Testament. For Marcion, the Incarnation was not only unnecessary, the very concept of a divine Redeemer participating in materiality was disgusting.

In a very real sense, Marcion's doctrine was an exaggerated Paulinism. He believed that Christianity was only to be understood in the light of the Apostle's message to the Gentiles, his distinction between law and grace, and his radical Christocentrism. However, Marcion's theory of two gods, his negative view of the Old Testament, and his Docetism clearly were not Pauline.

For our purposes it is significant to note that Marcion seemingly found no place for the Holy Spirit—a strange posture for someone so devoted to St. Paul. He apparently looked to no Spirit of God other than Christ himself, as the Giver of supernatural life. His opponent, Origen, insists that Marcion could not really have accepted Paul if he rejected the Paraclete and set aside the Gospel.

> For Marcion, rejecting the entire Gospel, yea rather, cutting himself off from the Gospel, boasts that he has a part in the [blessings of] the Gospel. Others, again (the Montanists), that they may set at nought the gift of the Spirit, which in the latter times has been, by the good pleasure of the Father, poured out upon the human race, do not admit that aspect [of the evangelical dispensation] presented by John's Gospel, in which the Lord promised that He would send the Paraclete; but set aside at once both the Gospel and the prophetic Spirit. Wretched men indeed! who wish to be pseudo-prophets, forsooth, but who set aside the gift of prophecy from the Church; acting like those (the Encratitae) who, on account of such as come in hypocrisy, hold themselves aloof from the communion of the brethren.[43]

Tertullian agrees with Origen that Marcion made the claim to prophetic ministry; however, we are told that Marcion denied ecstatic prophecy which his critics interpreted as a quenching of the Spirit.

> What "spirit" does he forbid us to "quench," and what "prophesyings" to "despise?" Not the Creator's spirit, nor the Creator's prophesyings, Marcion of course replies. For he has already quenched and despised the thing which he destroys, and is unable to forbid what he has despised. It is then incumbent on Marcion now to display in his church that spirit of his god which must not be quenched, and the prophesyings which must not be despised. And when he shall have failed to produce and give proof of any such criterion, we will then on our side bring out both the Spirit and the prophecies of the Creator, which utter predictions according to His will. Thus it will be clearly seen of what the apostle spoke, even of those things which were to happen in the church of his God; and as long as He endures, so long also does His Spirit work, and so long are His promises repeated.[44]

In another passage Tertullian again challenges Marcion to demonstrate the validity of his teachings by showing that charismata exist on Marcion's side, since they are "forthcoming from my side without any difficulty, and they agree, too, with the rules, and the dispensations, and the instructions of the Creator."[45]

Apparently, some of Marcion's followers held that the Paraclete was to be identified with the Apostle Paul, meaning probably that Jesus' promise of another comforter was chiefly fulfilled in the ministry and writings of St. Paul.[46]

Marcion's apparent rejection of the Holy Spirit resulted in the ablest defenders of the faith in the late second century—Tertullian, Irenaeus, and Origen—rising in support of the Church's belief in the third Person in the Godhead. And in so doing, they amplified and further developed the Church's doctrine of the Spirit.

One might speculate that, without the challenge of the Marcionists, it would have been less likely that these polemicists would have chosen to allude to the ongoing charismatization of the Church by the Spirit. In retrospect, it is clear that the Marcion challenge to the institutional church resulted in a clear witness to the continued functioning of the Spirit through His gifts in the late second and early third centuries.

3. DYNAMIC AND MODALISTIC MONARCHIANISM

Many Christian believers in the late second and the third centuries reacted against Logos theology. They were interested in having only one ruler (one God), not three, as they believed were present in Logos Christology. They stressed the "one man rule" or "monarchy" of the Father, rather than that of the Logos, whom they saw as a second God, or of a third, the Holy Spirit. Trinitarian teaching, such as found in Origen, they considered to be a tritheistic danger.

The dynamic Monarchians (or adoptionists) taught that Jesus was merely a man on whom the divine Spirit descended in baptism, giving him power for his messianic mission. The man Jesus was adopted, then filled by the Logos or the Spirit. But he was not God. Hippolytus describes one of the adoptionists, Theodotus of Byzantium, as teaching that

"... Jesus was a (mere) man, born of a virgin, according to the counsel of the Father, and that after he had lived promiscuously with all men, and had become pre-eminently religious, he subsequently at his baptism in Jordan received Christ, who came from above and descended (upon him) in form of a dove. And this was the reason, (according to Theodotus,) why (miraculous) powers did not operate within him prior to the manifestation in him of that *Spirit* which descended, (and) which proclaims him to be the Christ.[47]

Such individuals as denied Logos Christology also rejected the Fourth Gospel, in which the Logos idea appears. They stressed the literal interpretation of the rest of Scripture, rather than the allegorizing which they perceived to be present in Johannine writings.

While Theodotus of Byzantium was the leading dynamic Monarchian in the West, Paul of Samosata, a bishop of Antioch, was the leading figure in the East. He taught that the Logos and Spirit were qualities of God, not persons in a Godhead. These were names of powers or potentialities in God, but not persons in the sense of independent beings. Jesus was a man who was inhabited by the Logos. He developed in his being as he received more of the Spirit. Finally, he achieved eternal union with God, and ultimately, he received the status of God. The Spirit served to drive Jesus while on earth and, finally, to elevate him into the divine sphere.

Of Paul of Samosata, Malchion, who held the presidency of the Sophists' school at Antioch, writes:

> He does not wish to acknowledge that the Son of God came down from heaven. And this is a statement which shall not be made to depend on simple assertion; for it is proved abundantly by those memoranda which we sent you, and not least by that passage in which he says that Jesus Christ is from below.[48]

Malchion is not content simply to convey the heresy of Paul of Samosata. He proceeds to attack his character.

> Nor shall I say anything of the quackery which he practises in the ecclesiastical assemblies, in the way of courting popularity and making a great parade, and astounding by such arts the minds of the less sophisticated; nor of his setting up for himself a lofty tribunal and throne, so unlike a disciple of Christ; nor of his having a secretum and calling it by that name, after the manner of the rulers of this world; nor of his striking his thigh with his hand and beating the tribunal with his feet; nor of his censuring and insulting those who did not applaud him nor shake their handkerchiefs, as is done in the theatres . . . nor of putting a stop to the psalms sung in honour of himself in the midst of the Church, in the great day of the Paschal festival, which choristers one might shudder to hear.[49]

The modalistic Monarchians taught that God appears in different modes, in different ways. The first known leader was Noetus of Smyrna, probably a bishop of that city, who was condemned by a synod about A.D. 190. The anti-Monarchian, Hippolytus, tells us that

> Noetus, being by birth a native of Smyrna, and a fellow addicted to reckless babbling, as well as crafty withal, introduced (among us) this heresy which originated from one Epigonus. It reached Rome, and was adopted by Cleomenes, and so has continued to this day among his successors. Noetus asserts that there is one Father and God of the universe, and that He made all things, and was imperceptible to those that exist when He might so desire. Noetus maintained that the Father then appeared when He wished; and He is invisible when He is not seen, but visible when He is seen. And this heretic also alleges that the Father is unbegotten when He is not generated, but begotten when He is born of a virgin; as also that He is not subject to suffering, and is

immortal when He does not suffer or die. When, however, His passion came upon Him, Noetus allows that the Father suffers and dies. And the Noetians suppose that this Father Himself is called Son, (and vice versa).[50]

Praxeas, against whom Tertullian fought, also taught that God the Father was born through the Virgin Mary, and that He, the only God, suffered and died. Praxeas's teaching was particularly appealing to Christians who wanted to have God present on earth, participating among His creatures, Whom we experience when we see and hear Jesus.

Tertullian counters with the following:

> We, however, as we indeed always have done (and more especially since we have been better instructed by the Paraclete, who leads men indeed into all truth), believe that there is only one God . . . that this one only God has also a Son, His Word, who proceeded from Himself, by whom all things were made, and without whom nothing was made. Him we believe to have been sent by the Father into the Virgin, and to have been born of her—being both Man and God, the Son of Man and the Son of God, and to have been called by the name of Jesus Christ.

> Who sent also from heaven from the Father, according to His own promise, the Holy Ghost, the Paraclete, the sanctifier of the faith of those who believe in the Father, and in the Son, and in the Holy Ghost. That this rule of faith has come down to us from the beginning of the gospel, even before any of the older heretics, much more before Praxeas, a pretender of yesterday, will be apparent both from the lateness of date which marks all heresies, and also from the absolutely novel character of our newfangled Praxeas.

> The mystery of the dispensation is still guarded, which distributes the Unity into a Trinity, placing in their order the three Persons—the Father, the Son, and the Holy Ghost: three, however, not in condition, but in degree; not in substance, but in form; not in power, but in aspect; yet of one substance, and of one condition, and of one power, inasmuch as He is one God, from whom these degrees and forms and aspects are reckoned, under the name of the Father, and of the Son, and of the Holy Ghost.[51]

The leading modalistic Monarchian was Sabellius, a native of Libya, who taught that God appears in different faces. In history God acts in three countenances or masks as worn by actors in playing different roles: the countenance of the Father appears in His work as creator and lawgiver; the countenance of the Son appears in Redemption from the birth to the ascension of Jesus; the countenance of the Spirit appears in the work of sanctification, in warming and quickening the spiritual life of men.[52] In this way "the trinity" is developed in history. Sabellius made use of the Apostle Paul's description of the gifts of the Spirit by urging that, as there are diversities of gifts but the same Spirit, so the Father can remain One and the Same and yet extend Himself into Son and Spirit.[53]

The challenge of the Monarchians, whether dynamic or modalistic, stimulated Christian thinkers such as Tertullian, Hippolytus, and Novatian to further develop and more forcefully articulate trinitarian doctrine. In the process, interest grew in the person of the Holy Spirit, in His place in the Godhead, and in the exercise of His offices in the Church.

4. MONTANISM

About the year A.D. 155, Montanus, a pagan priest of Cybele, was converted to Christianity and baptized. Shortly thereafter, he declared that he was possessed by the Holy Spirit and had become the inspired organ of the Spirit. His critics report that he identified himself with the Paraclete promised in John 14, and claimed to be God.[54] Montanus declared that the period of revelation was coming to an end, and with its closing would come the end of the world. His followers were encouraged to gather at the community of Pepuza in Phrygia to await the descent of the New Jerusalem.

One of his critics, Eusebius, describes Montanus as a recent convert, who

> through his unquenchable desire for leadership, gave the adversary opportunity against him. And he became beside himself, and being suddenly in a sort of frenzy and ecstasy, he raved, and began to babble and utter strange things, prophesying in a manner contrary to the constant custom of the Church handed down by tradition from the beginning. Some of those who heard his spurious utterances at that time were indignant, and they rebuked him as one that was possessed, and that was under the control of a demon, and was led by a deceitful spirit, and was distracting the multitude; and they forbade him to talk, remembering the distinction drawn by the Lord and his warning to guard watchfully against the coming of false prophets. But others imagining themselves possessed of the Holy Spirit and of a prophetic gift, were elated and not a little puffed up; and forgetting the distinction of the Lord, they challenged the mad and insidious and seducing spirit, and were cheated and deceived by him. In consequence of this, he could no longer be held in check, so as to keep silence. Thus by artifice, or rather by such a system of wicked craft, the devil, devising destruction for the disobedient, and being unworthily honored by them, secretly excited and inflamed their understandings which had already become estranged from the true faith.[55]

Epiphanius of Salamis reports that Montanus pretended to have received a fuller revelation of the Spirit than that possessed by the Church. Montanus compared man to a lyre, over whom the Spirit swept like a plectrum.[56] Asterius Urbanus describes the new prophet as one who possessed an excessive lust of soul and had already left the faith in order to play the harlot with error.[57]

In time, Montanus was joined by two women, Maximilla and Priscilla, who deserted their husbands with Montanus's approval.

They too prophesied, behaving in a manner similiar to Montanus. "And he stirred up besides two women, and filled them with the false spirit, so that they talked wildly and unreasonably and strangely, like the person already mentioned."[58]

Several of Maximilla's prophecies are preserved. She is reported to have characterized herself as follows:

> I am driven away from the sheep like a wolf.
> I am not a wolf.
> I am word and spirit and power.[59]

The following utterance provides additional insight into Maximilla's state of mind:

> I was sent by the Lord
> As a partaker of this toil
> And of the Covenant
> And of the promise
> Partaker, proclaimer, and interpreter,
> Compelled, willing and not willing
> That I may learn
> The Knowledge of God.[60]

Apparently the prophetic ministry of women continued for some time among the Montanists, for Tertullian speaks of a "sister among us today" who had the gift of revelation during worship, conversed with angels and sometimes even with the Lord Himself.[61]

Among the anti-Montanist sources there is confusion regarding the place of prophecy and other ecstatic utterances among the Montanists. On the one hand, as we have seen, they are reported to have practiced such gifts. On the other hand, they are accused of wanting prophecy to end. According to Asterius Urbanus

> The Apostle deems that the gift of prophecy should abide in all the church up to the time of the final advent. But they will not be able to show the gift to be in their possession even to the present time, which is the fourteenth year only after the death of Maximilla.[62]

Irenaeus, bishop of Lyons, also indicates that the Montanists rejected the prophetic gift. They "set at nought the gift of the Spirit" by remaining aloof from the Church, not accepting the gift of prophecy as exercised in the Church.[63] It may well be that Asterius Urbanus perceives a decline in the charismata among the later Montanists and that Irenaeus is reacting against Montanist rejection of what they perceived to be "false" prophecy in the Catholic Church. Perhaps the Montanists initially saw the prophecies of Montanus and his priestesses as final and only after some decades attemped to imitate their founders. We may never know. Obviously, the picture we do have of Montanist prophecy has been warped by the sources. Nevertheless, Asterius Urbanus, Irenaeus, and Eusebius agree that the mainline Church of the late second and early third centuries had a clear understanding that the gift of prophecy was to continue until the "final coming," the parousia. Further, it seems unlikely that the Montanists would have been negatively disposed towards prophecy, since it was their exercise of the prophetic gift that aroused controversy. It may well be that they reacted against prophets outside their movement, especially if such individuals responded negatively to Montanism in the process.

What was objectionable to the Catholic Church in Montanism was not its emphasis on prophecy per se. To some extent reaction against the New Prophecy stemmed from the severity of its asceticism and internal discipline. Montanism demanded the sternest rigor in lifestyle, surpassing that of the New Testament. Second marriages were prohibited and even marriage itself. Strict fasting, unreserved preparation for martyrdom, and separation from the world also were expected of the "pneumatic," the spiritual. But these demands in and of themselves probably would not have evoked such opposition in the larger Church, which already had dealt successfully with separatist perfectionist groups, such as the Encratists. What was new and particularly galling about the Montanists was that their rigorous asceticism grew out of a series of prophecies which they considered to be a final divine revelation of truth to mankind, superseding even the teachings of Jesus and the apostles. This apocalyptic asceticism, coupled with a strong sense of exclusiveness (only the "church of the Spirit" could forgive sins, not the "church which consists of a number of bishops"[64]), and a propensity to attack without mercy the traditionalism and growing secularism in the mainline Church, proved a challenge too great to tolerate.

While all efforts to reform the Church have met stern resistance, Montanism proved to be especially threatening in that it was the first major movement which demanded such reform. And it nearly achieved its purpose. According to Tertullian, a bishop of Rome near the end of the second century was at the point of recognizing Montanus and his prophetesses and of sending letters of reconciliation to the Montanist churches of Asia Minor and Phrygia, when he was dissuaded by Praxias, himself a heretical Monarchian. In so doing, Tertullian laments, Praxeas expelled prophecy from Rome and put the Paraclete to flight and crucified the Father.[65]

There is no reason to believe that the Montanists would have been better accepted by the broader Church had their movement developed at a later time. In an age which called for martyrdom, they led the way by glorifying the martyr. And still they were rejected by mainline Christians. A century later, when the great age of persecution was past and the ideal of physical martyrdom had faded, extreme asceticism became the standard for those who reached beyond. Fasting and celibacy, which the Montanists practiced, became symbols of Christian spirituality. And the Spirit now spoke through prophetic desert types who taught that mankind could rise from glory to glory to a state of perfection—an echo of prophetic voices from Phrygia. But the Montanists continued to be rejected. They were persecuted by Constantine who enacted an edict against all heresies, depriving them of their places of worship and forbidding their religious meetings.[66] Persecution of the group continued until, under Justinian, it became so severe that they gathered their wives and children together in their places of worship, set fire to the buildings and perished there.[67]

Among those who opposed Montanism were writers who felt that the weakness in the Church lay in the Church's conception of continuing prophecy. The first representative of this viewpoint was Hippolytus of Rome, best known for his struggles against Monarchianism. Hippolytus is not convinced that he is living in the last days before the second coming of Christ.[68] He defends the process by which the institutional hierarchy is beginning to adjust to this realization. Coupled with an awareness of the delay of the parousia is a denial of the New Prophecy. Hippolytus is convinced that prophecy ended with the Apostle John. This argument strikes at the very heart of the Montanist movement. But more importantly, it strikes at the existing tradition of the Catholic Church which up to the third century accepted an ongoing tradition of prophecy. The message of Hippolytus became the orthodox position in the Church as it gradually solidified in both work and form. When prophecy was at its height there was no fixed and rigid organization in the Church. By the third century the free, spontaneous, uprushing spiritual life was giving way in a Church which was rapidly developing a fixed rule of faith and a closed canon of divine oracles, governed by an order of bishops established by an external rule of succession. The prophet ruling by revelation was giving way to the bishop ruling with authority. The free and spontaneous exercise of the charismata was being replaced by an inflexible system of form and ritual. In this environment it was impossible for the New Prophecy to exist side by side with the new order without experiencing great tension.

The final result of Montanism then was not to perpetuate the Church's awareness of the presence and functioning of the Holy

Spirit through the exercise of His gifts. Rather than looking to the future and the parousia, or to the present with the operation of the charismata, the Church looked increasingly to the past—to the apostolic canon, creed and episcopacy—to measure all movements and ideas.

Paul Tillich observes that the victory of the Christian Church over Montanism really resulted in loss:

> This loss is visible in four ways: (1) The canon was victorious against the possibility of new revelations. The solution of the Fourth Gospel that there will be new insights, always standing under the criticism of the Christ, was at least reduced in power and meaning. (2) The traditional hierarchy was confirmed against the prophetic spirit. This meant that the prophetic spirit was more or less excluded from the organized church and had to flee into sectarian movements. (3) Eschatology became less significant than it had been in the apostolic age. The ecclesiastical establishment became much more important. The expectation of the end was reduced to an appeal to each individual to be prepared for his end which can come at any moment. The idea of an end of history was not important in the church after that. (4) The strict discipline of the Montanists was lost, giving way to a growing laxity in the church. Here again something happened which has frequently happened in the history of the church. Small groups arise with a strict discipline; they are regarded with suspicion by the church; they form themselves into larger churches; then they lose their original disciplinary power in themselves.[67]

In all subsequent periods of Church history prophetic voices within the minor tradition continued to be heard. The reforming zeal of the New Prophecy, based upon a conviction that the rapid approach of the end demands greater strictness than ever, was to be witnessed again and again, not only among the desert fathers, but also with the Novations, the Donatists, the Waldensians, the radicals of the Reformation, the Wesleyan revivalists, and modern Holiness and Pentecostal/Charismatic churches. And in each case a similar opposition arose within the major tradition to remind believers that in the first century the Spirit had already led the apostles into all truth.

Notes to Chapter 3

[1]Irenaeus, *Against Heresies* i.ll.1, ANF 1:332.

[2]Elaine Pagels, "Gnosticism," *Interpreter's Dictionary of the Bible: Supplementary Volume* (New York: Abingdon, 1976), 336.

[3]Charles W. Hedrick, "Kingdom Sayings and Parables of Jesus in the Apocryphon of James: Tradition and Redaction," *New Testament Studies* 39 (January 1983): 21, note 2.

[4]*Second Treatise of the Great Seth* vii.2.56, in James M.

Robinson, ed., *The Nag Hammadi Library* (New York: Harper & Row, 1981), 332 (henceforth NHL).

[5]Justin Martyr, *First Apology* xxvi, ANF 1:171.

[6]Irenaeus, *Against Heresies* i.23.2-4, ANF 1:348.

[7]Hippolytus, *Refutation* vii.20.1-23.5, 26.8, in Werner Foerster, ed., *Gnosis: A Selection of Gnostic Texts* (Oxford: Clarendon Press, 1972), 1:64-68, 72.

[8]*Philosophumena* vii.22, quoted in Jean Doresse, *The Secret Books of the Egyptian Gnostics* (New York: The Viking Press, 1970), 294.

[9]Irenaeus, *Against Heresies* i.1.1-7.2, ANF 1:315-325. In the *Pistis Sophia* we find yet another Gnostic alternative to the traditional Incarnation story: after Jesus is born, while he is still a child, the Holy Spirit comes to visit him in Mary's house and mysteriously merges with him (i.61.11, in Carl Schmidt, ed., *Pistis Sophia* [Leiden: Brill, 1978], 121).

[10]Irenaeus, *Against Heresies* i.ll.1, ANF 1:332.

[11]*The Apocryphon of John* ii.l. 13-14, NHL 106.

[12]Irenaeus, op. cit., i.6.1-2, 7.5, ANF 1:324, 326.

[13]*The Gospel of Philip* ii.3. 77. 12-15, NHL 146.

[14]*The Gospel of Truth* i.3.42, NHL 48.

[15]*The Apocryphon of James* i.2.5, NHL 31.

[16]*The Gospel of Philip* ii.3. 65-66, NHL 139. Square brackets indicate a lacuna or blank space in the manuscript. Pointed brackets indicate a correction of a scribal omission or error.

[17]*The Teaching of Silvanus* vii.4.112, NHL 358.

[18]*The Acts of Thomas* xxvii, in Foerster, 1:359.

[19]Ibid., lxii, in Foerster, 1:363.

[20]*The Prayer of the Apostle Paul* i.l.A, NHL 27.

[21]*The Interpretation of Knowledge* xi. 1.15-17, 20, NHL 432-434.

[22]1 Corinthians 1:23.

[23]1 John 4:3.

[24]*The Interpretation of Knowledge* xi.1.ll, NHL 430-431.

[25]*The Gospel of the Egyptians* iii.2.42, 43-44, 66, NHL 196, 197, 204. On the third passage see Charles W. Hedrick, "Christian Motifs in the *Gospel of the Egyptians*," *Novum Testamentum* 23 (1981): 251-252.

[26]Irenaeus, op.cit., i.13.1-3, ANF 1:334-335.

[27]*Gospel of Philip* ii.3. 53, 67, NHL 132, 140.

[28]*The Acts of Thomas*, from the fifth act, 49, in Foerster, 1:362.

[29]*The Tripartite Tractate* i.5.57-59, NHL 58-59.

[30]*Allogenes* xi.3.66, NHL 451.

[31]*The Gospel of the Egyptians* iii.2.41-43, 59, NHL 196, 198.

[32]*Trimorphic Protennoia* xiii.i. 37, NHL 463.

[33]*Apocryphon of John* ii.1.2, NHL 99.

[34]*The Gospel of Philip* ii.3.55, NHL 134.

[35]Cited in Origen, *Commentary on John* ii.6, ANF 10:329.

[36]*The Gospel of Thomas* ii.2.49.32-50.1, NHL 128-129; *The Gospel of Philip* ii.3. 52.24-25, NHL 132.

[37]*Trimorphic Protennoia* xiii. 49.28-32, NHL 470.

[38]Irenaeus, *Against Heresies* i.21.4, ANF 1:346.

[39]Foerster, op. cit., 1:17.

[40]*The Gospel of Philip* ii.3. 57, 75, NHL 134, 145.

[41]Ibid., ii.3.64.22-30, NHL 139.

[42]Ibid., ii.3.74.12-23, NHL 144.

[43]Origen, *Against Heresies* iii.ll.9, ANF 1:429.

[44]Tertullian, *Against Marcion* v.15, ANF 3:462.

[45]Ibid., v.8, ANF 3:447.

[46]Origen, *Homilies on the Gospel of Luke* xxv, in Migne, *Patrologia graeca* (Paris, 1857-66), 13:cols. 1866-1867 (henceforth PG).

[47]Hippolytus, *The Refutation of All Heresies* vii.23, ANF 5:114-115.

[48]Malchion, *Epistle Against Paul of Samosata* iii, ANF 6:170.

[49]Ibid., ii, ANF, op. cit.

[50]Hippolytus, op. cit., x.23, ANF 5:148.

[51]Tertullian, *Against Praxeas* iii.2, ANF 3:598.

[52]Epiphanius, *Against Eighty Heresies* lxii.l, *Opera Omnia in duos Tomos distributa* (Parisis, Sumptibus Michaelis Sonnii, Claudii Morelli, et Sebastiani Cramoisy, 1622), 1:513.

[53]Athanasius, *Orations Against the Arians* iv.25, NPF Second Series 4:443.

[54]Montanus and his movement are known to us almost exclusively through the fragments of anti-Montanist writings and a few of the sayings of Montanus and his earliest followers recorded by polemicists within the Catholic Church. The only Montanist writer of significance of whom we are aware was Tertullian, who believed that the Montanist movement was the completion and perfection of early prophecy and revelation. Because all of the sources are slanted in one direction or the other, the scholar must weigh each carefully in attempting to understand and evaluate the movement and its teachings on the Holy Spirit. Modern writers dealing with Montanist pneumatology include Bernard L. Bresson, *Studies in Ecstasy* (New York: Vantage, 1966), 27-30 (a favorable reaction of a Pentecostal writer); Cecil M. Robeck, Jr., "Montanism: A Problematic Spirit Movement," *Paraclete* 15, no. 3 (Summer 1981): 24-29 (less favorable than Bresson); and R. A. Knox, *Enthusiasm* (Oxford: Clarendon Press, 1950), 25-49, who

calls the Montanists naked fanatics. M.F.G. Parmentier, "Montanisme' als etiket voor religieus enthousiasme," *Nederlands Theologisch Tijdschrift* 32, no.4 (1978): 310-317, has shown that historic Montanism often is looked upon with great respect by Charismatic writers, without giving adequate attention to its teachings and place in the early Church.

[55]Eusebius, *Church History* v.16.7-9, NPF Second Series 1:231. Also see Asterius Urbanus, *Three Books Against the Montanists* ii, ANF 7:335. Miltiades, writing in opposition to a prophet Alcibiades, is quoted by Eusebius as showing "that a prophet should not speak in ecstasy" (*Church History* v. 17.1, NPF Second Series 1:234.). This is the first known denunciation of the practice of prophesying in ecstasy.

[56]PG 40:col. 856.

[57]Asterius Urbanus, op. cit., ii, ANF 7:335-336.

[58]Eusebius, op. cit., v.16.8, NPF Second Series 1:231.

[59]Ibid., v. 16.17, NPF Second Series 1:232.

[60]PG 40:col. 875.

[61]Tertullian, *A Treatise on the Soul* ix, ANF 3:188.

[62]Asterius Urbanus, op. cit., x, ANF 7:337.

[63] Irenaeus, op. cit., xi. 9, ANF 1:429.

[64]Tertullian, *On Modesty* xxi, ANF 4:100. David F. Wright, "Why Were the Montanists Condemned?" *Themelios* 2, no.1 (1976): 15-22, disagrees with my assessment of why the larger Church opposed Montanism. He insists that the main problem was in the Montanist exercise of the charismata at a time when Christianity was emphasizing office and order. Wright's conclusions do not appear justified in the face of Irenaeus's statement that the Montanists did not accept the gift of prophecy as exercised in the Church, and the agreement of Asterius Urbanus, Irenaeus, and Eusebius that the mainline Church at the time of the Montanist movement understood that the gift of prophecy was to continue to end of the Church Era. (See notes 62 and 63 above.)

[65]Tertullian, *Against Praxeas* i, ANF 3:597.

[66]Sozomen, *Ecclesiastical History* ii.32, NPF 2nd Series 2:280-281.

[67]Procopius, *Secret History* xi, trans. Richard Atwater (Ann Arbor, MI: Ann Arbor Paperbacks, 1963), 59.

[68]Hippolytus, *Treatise on Christ and Antichrist*, ANF 5:204-219. Also see Hippolytus, *Commentary on Daniel* ii. 4-8, ANF 5:179.

[69]Paul Tillich, *A History of Christian Thought* (New York: Harper and Row, 1968), 41.

CHAPTER FOUR

THE RESPONSE OF THE POLEMICISTS AND THE LATER APOLOGISTS

In response to internal threats within the Church, Christianity came to insist on returning to certain ideals of the classical period, namely, apostolic authority. What was written at that time was valid for all later periods of time. Anything really new that came later could never be canonical. While the Scriptures became the absolute norm, the traditional interpretation of scriptural text, the *regula fidei* or rule of faith, also became decisive. In addition, a concentrated summary of the Bible and the rule of faith was needed in connection with the confession at baptism. This assumed that the bishops, the successors of the apostles, who were responsible for the rule of faith and the baptismal creed, had the gift of truth. Thus, an elaborate system of authorities emerged—the Bible, the rule of faith, the baptismal creed, the bishop, and the apostolic succession—all created in the struggle against heresy and Montanism.

The Church's doctrine of the Holy Spirit matured significantly during the late second and third centuries. In the writings of Tertullian important steps were taken toward the trinitarian distinction between the three persons. Tertullian's recognition that, despite the clear distinction between them, the three are "of one substance" paved the way for the Nicene formula. Not all Christian thinkers were so inclined, however. Origen suggested that the Spirit is called less than the Son and the Son less than the Father.

The Holy Spirit's role in salvation also was clarified. By this time baptism, the most important sacrament of the period, meant the washing away of sins and the reception of the Holy Spirit. In the teaching of the anti-Gnostic fathers, the Spirit is united with the

water, which physically extinguishes former sins. Irenaeus
recognized that the saving power is the Holy Spirit who dwells in
the Church and renews believers out of what is old into the newness
in Christ.

Finally, this is the period in which the Spirit and authority were
united officially. The bishop, according to Cyprian, was the locus
of the Spirit's prophetic ministry. Such attempted institutionaliza-
tion of the Spirit did not lesson the tension between prophecy and
order, however. As the monarchial episcopacy allowed the charismata to die, simultaneously rendering it powerless in the hands of
others, the prophetic spirit came to center in sectarian movements.
These, in turn, were immediately in tension with the institutional
church.

1. IRENAEUS

Irenaeus (ca. A.D. 130-202), bishop of Lyons in Gaul in the latter
part of the second century, was a disciple of Polycarp of Smyrna,
who had been a follower of the Apostle John. The most influential
of all the early Fathers, Irenaeus felt the Gnostic threat to the
Church, which he chose to defend by giving scientific expression to
the faith. His writings represent the first systematic exposition of
the young Church's belief.

In response to Gnostic theology of the Holy Spirit and practices
growing out of Gnostic spirituality, Irenaeus has much to say about
the person and work of the Holy Spirit. He reacts against the
Gnostic belief in emanation by speaking of the Son and the Holy
Spirit as inherent in the very life of God, rather than as proceeding
from the Father. The Spirit is identified with the divine Wisdom of
the Book of Proverbs. Wisdom, together with the Word, was
present with the Father before all creation.[1]

Irenaeus's opposition to Gnosticism leads him to stress the work
of the Son and the Holy Spirit in creation. Against the Gnostic
notion of two gods, a god of love in the New Testament, and a
demiurge creator of matter in the Old Testament, Irenaeus writes:

> There is therefore one God, who by the Word and Wisdom created
> and arranged all things.[2]

> He the creator who made those things by Himself, that is, through His
> Word and Wisdom—heaven and earth, and the seas, and all things
> that are in them.[3]

Irenaeus uses the expression, "the two hands of God," when
speaking of the work of the Word and Wisdom in creation.

> For by the hands of the Father, that is, by the Son and the Holy Spirit,
> man, and not [merely] a part of man, was made in the likeness of
> God.[4]

> And therefore throughout all time, man, having been moulded at the
> beginning by the hands of God, that is, of the Son and the Spirit, is
> made after the image and likeness of God.[5]

> Now man is a mixed organization of soul and flesh, who was formed
> after the likeness of God, and moulded by His hands, that is, by the
> Son and Holy Spirit, to whom He also said, "Let Us make man."[6]

Reacting against Marcion's depreciation of the Old Testament
—also a common trait among the Gnostics—Irenaeus emphasizes
the Spirit's role in Old Testament christological prophecy.

> The Church . . . [believes] in one God, the Father almighty . . . and
> in one Christ Jesus, the Son of God who became incarnate for our
> salvation; and in the Holy Spirit, who proclaimed through the
> prophets the dispensation of God, and the advents, and the birth from
> a virgin, and the passion and the resurrection from the dead, and the
> ascension into heaven . . . and His future manifestation from
> heaven.[7]

> Vain, too is [the effort of] Marcion and his followers when they [seek
> to] exclude Abraham from the inheritance, to whom the Spirit
> through many men, and now by Paul, bears witness.[8]

Irenaeus also refutes certain Gnostics who taught that the Old
Testament prophets uttered their predictions under the inspiration
of different gods.

> The remainder of those who are falsely termed Gnostics, and who
> maintain that the prophets uttered their prophecies under the
> inspiration of different gods, will be easily overthrown by this fact,
> that all the prophets proclaimed one God and Lord . . . while they
> moreover announced the advent of His Son.[9]

The Gnostic teaching that Jesus merely appeared to take on
human flesh prompts Irenaeus to proclaim the truth of the
Incarnation and the role of the Spirit in uniting the Word of God in
the flesh of Jesus within the womb of Mary.

> The Ebionites . . . do not choose to understand that the Holy Ghost
> came upon Mary and the power of the Most High did overshadow her:
> wherefore also what was generated is a holy thing . . . the Word of
> the Father and the Spirit of God, having become united with the
> ancient substance of Adam's formation, rendered man living and
> perfect.[10]

Irenaeus carefully distinguishes between the Incarnation and the
descent of the Holy Spirit on Jesus, the already incarnate Word, at
His baptism. Here he challenges Adoptionism, which presented
Jesus as a mere man who at the time of baptism was adopted by
God as His son and was endowed with power from above as Christ
descended upon Jesus.

> It certainly was in the power of the apostles to declare that Christ
> descended upon Jesus, or that the so-called superior Saviour [came
> down] upon the dispensational one, or he who is from the invisible
> places upon him from the Demiurge; but they neither knew nor said

anything of the kind: for, had they known it, they would have also
certainly stated it. But what really was the case, that did they record,
[namely], that the Spirit of God as a dove descended upon
Him. . . . The Lord, receiving this as a gift from His Father, does
Himself also confer it upon those who are partakers of Himself,
sending the Holy Spirit upon all the earth.[11]

For Christ did not at that time descend upon Jesus, neither was Christ
one and Jesus another: but, the Word of God—who is the Saviour of
all, and the ruler of heaven and earth, who is Jesus, as I have already
pointed out, who did take upon Him flesh, and was anointed by the
Spirit from the Father. . . . Therefore did the Spirit of God descend
upon Him, [the Spirit] of Him who had promised by the prophets that
He would anoint Him, so that we, receiving from the abundance of
His unction, might be saved.[12]

And it is the Father who anoints, but the Son who is anointed by the
Spirit, who is the unction, as the Word declares by Isaiah, "The Spirit
of the Lord is upon me, because He hath anointed me," pointing out
both the anointing Father, the anointing Son, and the unction, which
is the Spirit.[13]

The work of the Holy Spirit in the entire divine scheme of
Redemption was seen by the Gnostics as incomprehensible to all
who had not been admitted within the pleroma, having received a
special knowledge (or gnosis). Irenaeus insists that the believer is
redeemed into Christ through the regenerating power of the Holy
Spirit, without any intervention of the aeons of the Gnostic
pleroma.

There are as many schemes of "redemption" as there are teachers of
these mystical opinions. . . . This class of men have been instigated
by Satan to a denial of that baptism which is regeneration to God, and
thus to a renunciation of the whole [Christian] faith.[14]

Many nations of the world had been redeemed through their belief
in Christ, "having salvation written in their hearts by the Spirit."[15]

Irenaeus also has a deep awareness of the ongoing activity of the
Holy Spirit in the Church—an awareness far beyond other writers
of the second century, with the possible exception of Tertullian.
"For where the Church is, there is the Spirit of God; and where the
Spirit of God is, there is the Church, and every kind of grace; but
the Spirit is truth."[16] So essential to the believer are the offices of
the Spirit that Irenaeas is obliged to warn:

Those, therefore, who do not partake of Him the Spirit, are neither
nourished into life from the mother's breast, nor do they enjoy that
most limpid fountain which issues from the body of Christ; but they
dig for themselves broken cisterns out of earthly trenches . . .
rejecting the Spirit, that they may not be instructed.[17]

The Christian life is an ascent to God, and the Holy Spirit is the
ladder to facilitate that ascent:

The Holy Spirit [is] the earnest of incorruption, the means of
confirming our faith, and the ladder of ascent to God.[18]

> They ascend through the Spirit to the Son, and through the Son to the Father.[19]

> But we do now receive a certain portion of the Holy Spirit, tending towards perfection, and preparing us for incorruption, being little by little accustomed to receive and hear God.[20]

There is strong evidence that Irenaeus was supportive of the continuous activity of the Holy Spirit in the charismata given to the believer. He observes that the gifts of the Spirit are in operation among many in the Church in his day. These individuals he calls brethren, not outcasts.

> In like manner we do also hear many brethren in the Church, who possess prophetic gifts, and who through the Spirit speak all kinds of languages, and bring to light for the general benefit the hidden things of men, and declare the mysteries of God.[21]

In a more detailed statement, Irenaeus again describes the prophetic gift, as well as several other charismata listed by Paul in 1 Corinthians 12:

> Wherefore, also, those who are in truth His disciples, receiving grace from Him, do in His name perform [miracles], so as to promote the welfare of other men, according to the gift which each one has received from Him. For some do certainly and truly drive out devils, so that those who have thus been cleansed from evil spirits frequently both believe [in Christ], and join themselves to the Church. Others have foreknowledge of things to come; they see visions, and utter prophetic expressions. Others still, heal the sick by laying their hands upon them, and they are made whole. Yea, moreover, as I have said, the dead even have been raised up, and remained among us for many years. And what shall I more say? Is it not possible to name the number of gifts which the Church, [scattered] throughout the whole world, has received from God.[22]

But Irenaeus was painfully aware that certain Gnostics, especially one named Marcus, were falsely claiming to exercise gifts of the Spirit.

> There is another among these heretics, Marcus by name, who boasts himself as having improved upon his master. He is a perfect adept in magical impostures, and by this means drawing away a great number of men, and not a few women, he has induced then to join themselves to him, as to one who is possessed of the greatest knowledge and perfection. . . . It appears probably enough that this man possesses a demon as his familiar spirit, by means of whom he seems to prophesy, and also enables as many as he counts worthy to be partakers of his Charis themselves to prophesy. He devotes himself especially to women, and those such as are well-bred, and elegantly attired, and of great wealth.[23]

Of one of these women Irenaeus reports:

> Henceforth she reckons herself a prophetess, and expresses her thanks to Marcus for having imparted to her of his own Charis. She then makes the effort to reward him; not only by the gift of her own possessions . . . but also by yielding up to him her person, desiring in

every way to be united to him, that she may become altogether one with him.[24]

Because of his strong opposition to such Gnostic novelties, Irenaeus declares that the truly spiritual man holds to the apostolic tradition as handed down by the succession of Catholic bishops.

> But it has, [on the other hand, been shown], that the preaching of the Church is everywhere consistent, and continues in an even course, and receives testimony from the prophets, the apostles, and all the disciples—as I have proved—through [those in] the beginning, the middle, and the end, and through the entire dispensation of God, and that well-grounded system which tends to man's salvation, namely, our faith; which, having been received from the Church, we do preserve, and which always, by the Spirit of God, renewing its youth, as if it were some precious deposit in an excellent vessel, causes the vessel itself containing it to renew its youth also. For this gift of God has been entrusted to the Church, as breath was to the first created man, for this purpose, that all the members receiving it may be vivified; and the [means of] communion with Christ has been distributed throughout it, that is, the Holy Spirit, the earnest of incorruption, the means of confirming our faith, and the ladder of ascent to God. "For in the Church," it is said, "God hath set apostles, prophets, teachers," and all the other means through which the Spirit works; of which all those are not partakers who do not join themselves to the Church, but defraud themselves of life through their perverse opinions and infamous behaviour. For where the Church is, there is the Spirit of God; and where the Spirit of God is, there is the Church.[25]

Despite Irenaeus's strong concern for a continued movement of the Spirit in giving gifts to the Church, he actually played a powerful role in moving the interest of believers away from this gift-giving power to what seemed a more manageable understanding of the Spirit as contained in the teachings of the Church. He desired prophecy, but only within order. In his fear of abuse and his intense desire to structure the movement of the Holy Spirit within proper doctrine and the bishopric, he may have set the stage for a reduction in the Church's vitality. The Spirit, which John declared, "bloweth where it listeth," so that man "canst not tell whence it cometh, and wither it goeth" (John 3:8), was becoming institutionalized. The gifts were soon to be located in the office of the bishop. The Mass becomes the central Spirit-experience. But it was not known as such. When an act loses its name, the breadth of its significance is gone. Later outbursts of the charismata would bring apprehension in the institutional church. Prophets would be suspect, as would be all evidences of the gift-giving power of the Spirit outside the sacraments. Prophecy and order would exist in tension.

2. TERTULLIAN

According to Jerome, Tertullian was born in Carthage about

A.D. 150, the son of a centurion. He studied grammar and rhetoric and was trained as a lawyer. After moving to Rome in midlife, he was converted to Christianity. Returning to Carthage, he began an extensive literary production in support of his new faith. Early in the third century, probably in A.D. 207, he broke with the Catholics of Carthage in order to become a Montanist. Perhaps the discipline of Montanism, with its protest against the growing hierarchy and its excessive moral vigor in dealing with those in the Church who did not live up to its ideals, appealed to him. Certainly Tertullian became more exacting in the discipline he espoused as he grew older.

The Church's first important pentecostal theologian, Tertullian contributes significantly to the Christian doctrines of the Trinity and of the Holy Spirit.[26] He gives to the Church its language of "Trinity," and of "persons" in the Trinity. From his Montanist experience of the Holy Spirit, Tertullian, more than any theologian before him, is able to distinguish the personhood and work of the Spirit from that of the Father and the Son.

> What follows Philip's question, and the Lord's whole treatment of it, to the end of John's Gospel, continues to furnish us with statements of the same kind, distinguishing the Father and the Son, with the properties of each. Then there is the Paraclete or Comforter, also which He promises to pray for to the Father, and to send from heaven after He had ascended to the Father. He is called "another Comforter," indeed; but in what way He is another we have already shown. "He will receive of mine," says Christ, just as Christ Himself received of the Father's. Thus the connection of the Father in the Son, and of the Son in the Paraclete, produces three coherent Persons, who are yet distinct One from Another. These Three are one essence, not one Person, as it is said, "I and my Father are One," in respect of unity of substance, not singularity of number.
>
> Now the Spirit indeed is third from God and the Son; just as the fruit of the tree is third from the root, or as the stream out of the river is third from the fountain, or as the apex of the ray is third from the sun. Nothing, however, is alien from that original source whence it derives its own properties. . . . I testify that the Father, and the Son, and the Spirit are inseparable from each other . . . and that they are distinct from Each Other. . . . The Father is the entire substance, but the Son is a derivation and portion of the whole . . . even as we say that the Son is also distinct from the Father, so that He showed a third degree in the Paraclete, as we believe the second degree is in the Son. . . . Besides, does not the very fact that they have the distinct names of Father and Son amount to a declaration that they are distinct in personality?[27]

It is this doctrine of the Trinity that distinguishes Judaism from Christianity:

> But (this doctrine of yours bears a likeness) to the Jewish faith, of which this is the substance—so to believe in One God as to refuse to reckon the Son besides Him, and after the Son the Spirit. Now, what

difference would there be between us and them, if there were not this
distinction which you are for breaking down?[28]

The Holy Spirit hovers over the waters of the baptized, and
sanctifies them, "The spirit is corporeally washed in the waters and
the flesh is in the same spiritually cleansed."[29] He explains further:

> Not that in the waters we obtain the Holy Spirit; but in the water,
> under (the witness of) the angel, we are cleansed, and prepared for the
> Holy Spirit.

> After this, when we have issued from the font, we are thoroughly
> anointed with a blessed unction, (a practice derived) from the old
> discipline, wherein on entering the priesthood, men were wont to be
> anointed with oil from a horn, ever since Aaron was anointed by
> Moses. When Aaron is called "Christ," from the "chrism," which is
> "the unction;" which, when made spiritual, furnished an appropriate
> name to the Lord, because He was "anointed" with the Spirit by God
> the Father.

> In the next place the hand is laid on us, invoking and inviting the Holy
> Spirit through benediction. Shall it be granted possible for human
> ingenuity to summon a spirit into water, and, by the application of
> hands from above, to animate their union into one body with another
> spirit of so clear sound; and shall it not be possible for God, in the
> case of His own organ, to produce, by means of "holy hands," a
> sublime spiritual modulation?

> For just as, after the waters of the deluge, by which the old iniquity
> was purged—after the baptism, so to say, of the world—a dove was
> the herald which announced to the earth the assuagement of celestial
> wrath . . . . So by the self-same law of heavenly effect, to earth—that
> is to our flesh—as it emerges from the font, after its own sins, flies the
> dove of the Holy Spirit, bringing us the peace of God sent out from
> the heavens, where is the Church, the typified ark.[30]

For Tertullian, a new age of the Spirit had begun in his own day.
The New Prophecies were given in revelations by the Paraclete to
the Montanist prophets, especially to Montanus and to his two
female disciples, Maximilla and Priscilla. The Holy Spirit was
present, revealing God's truth and will through living prophets.
Tertullian vigorously defends what he regards as true spirituality
against the larger Church which he feels has fallen away to a state
which he describes as "psychic:"

> It is these (the psychics) which raise controversy with the Paraclete; it
> is on this account that the New Prophecies are rejected: not that
> Montanus and Priscilla and Maximilla preach another God, nor that
> they disjoin Jesus Christ (from God), nor that they overturn any
> particular rule of faith or hope, but that they plainly teach more
> frequent fasting than marrying. . . . They (the psychics) are
> constantly reproaching us with novelty.[31]

> Nor is there any other cause whence they find themselves compelled to
> deny the Paraclete more than the fact that they esteem Him to be the
> institution of a novel discipline, and a discipline which they find most
> harsh. . . . But the Paraclete . . . will begin by bearing emphatic

witness to Christ. . . . And when He has thus been recognized (as the promised Comforter). . . . He will reveal those "many things" which appertain to disciplines.[32]

Whereas the reason why the Lord sent the Paraclete was, that, since human mediocrity was unable to take in all things at once, discipline should, little by little, be directed, and ordained, and carried on to perfection, by that Vicar or the Lord, the Holy Spirit . . . . What, then, is the Paraclete's administrative office but this: the direction of discipline, the revelation of the Scriptures, the reformation of the intellect, the advancement toward the "better things?" Nothing is without stages of growth.[33]

The Spirit is central to the world and life view of Tertullian. In determining the proper discipline for life, he suggests that the pre-Christian order of faith was imperfect. Christian discipline began with the death of Christ and the manifestation of the Holy Spirit from heaven, who was sent to guide believers into all truth.[34] For Tertullian, the Spirit is "the Determiner of discipline itself."[35]

One article of discipline that Tertullian declares to be revealed by the Montanists' Paraclete, and which was particularly bothersome to non-Montanists, was that there should be no remarriage. In defense of the charge that this revelation went beyond the teachings of Jesus, Tertullian reminds his readers of John 16:12-13:

For in saying, "I still have many things to say unto you, but ye are not yet able to bear them: when the Holy Spirit shall be come, He will lead you into all truth," He sufficiently, of course, sets before us that He will bring such (teachings) as may be esteemed alike novel, as having never before been published, and finally burdensome, as if that were the reason why they were not published.[36]

The New law abrogated divorce—it has (somewhat) to abrogate; the New Prophecy (abrogates) second, (which is) no less a divorce of the former (marriage) . . . . And how long will this most shameless "infirmity" persevere in waging a war of extermination against the "better things?" The time for its indulgence was (the interval) until the Paraclete began His operations, to whose coming were deferred by the Lord (the things) which in His day "could not be endured;" which it is now no longer competent for anyone to be unable to endure, seeing that He through whom the power of enduring is granted is not wanting. How long shall we allege "the flesh," because the Lord said, "the flesh is weak?" But He has withal premised that "the Spirit is prompt," in order that the Spirit may vanquish the flesh—that the weak may yield to the stronger.[37]

But you again set up boundary-posts to God, as with regard to grace, so with regard to discipline; as with regard to gifts, so too, with regard to solemnities: so that our observances are supposed to have ceased in like manner as His benefits; and you thus deny that He still continues to impose duties. . . . It remains for you to banish Him wholly, being, as He is, so far as lies in you, so otiose.[38]

In Tertullian's understanding of the Age of the Paraclete, it is through dreams and in states of ecstasy that visions are given by the

Spirit to His prophets:

> This power we call ecstasy, in which the sensuous soul stands out of itself, in a way which even resembles madness. . . . But how, you will ask, can the soul remember its dreams, when it is said to be without any mastery over its own operations? This memory must be an especial gift of the ecstatic condition of which we are treating. . . . We are accordingly not said to be made, but to dream, in that state; to be in the full possession also of our mental faculties, if we are at any time.[39]

> But from God—who has promised, indeed, "to pour out the grace of the Holy Spirit upon all flesh, and has ordained that His servants and His handmaids should see visions as well as utter prophecies"—must all those visions be regarded as emanating, which may be compared to the actual grace of God, as being honest, holy, prophetic, inspired, instructive, inviting to virtue, the bountiful nature of which causes them to overflow even to the profane, since God, with grand impartiality, "sends His showers and sunshine on the just and on the unjust."[40]

All of Tertullian's writings give an important place to the Spirit who fills the life of the Church. Gifts of the Spirit were promised by God through the prophets and the apostles:

> Now on the subject of "spiritual gifts," I have to remark that these also were promised by the Creator through Christ; and I think that we may derive from this a very just conclusion that the bestowal of a gift is not the work of a god other than Him who is proved to have given the promise. . . . In this Christ the whole substantia of the spirit would have to rest, not meaning that it would be as it were some subsequent acquisition accruing to Him who was always, even before His incarnation, the Spirit of God . . . there would have to rest upon Him the entire operation of the Spirit of grace, which, so far as the Jews were concerned, would cease and come to an end. This result the case itself shows; for after this time the Spirit of the Creator never breathed amongst them.[41]

Tertullian's Montanist church experienced a continuation of many of the spiritual gifts described by St. Paul in his first letter to the Corinthians:

> For, seeing that we acknowledge spiritual charismata, or gifts, we too have merited the attainment of the prophetic gift, although coming after John (the Baptist). We have now amongst us a sister whose lot it has been to be favoured with sundry gifts of revelation, which she experiences in the Spirit by ecstatic vision amidst the sacred rites of the Lord's day in the church: She converses with angels, and sometimes even with the Lord; she both sees and hears mysterious communications; some men's hearts she understands, and to them who are in need she distributes remedies. Whether it be in the reading of Scriptures, or in the chanting of psalms, or in the preaching of sermons, or in the offering up of prayers, in all these religious services matter and opportunity are afforded to her of seeing visions. It may possibly have happened to us, whilst this sister of ours was rapt in the Spirit, that we had discoursed in some ineffable way about the soul. After the people are dismissed at the conclusion of the sacred services,

she is in the regular habit of reporting to us whatever things she may have seen in vision (for her communications are examined with the most scrupulous care, in order that their truth may be probed). "Amongst other things," says she, "there has been shown to me a soul in bodily shape, and a spirit has been in the habit of appearing to me; not, however, a void and empty illusion, but such as would offer itself to be even grasped by the hand, soft and transparent and of an etherial colour, and in form resembling that of a human being in every respect." This was her vision, and for her witness there was God; and the apostle most assuredly foretold that there were to be "spiritual gifts" in the church. Now, can you refuse to believe this, even if indubitable evidence on every point is forthcoming for your conviction?[42]

Gifts of the Spirit are taken by Tertullian as clear evidence of the true spirituality of the New Prophecy. He challenges the heretic Marcion to show similar evidence:

Let Marcion then exhibit, as gifts of his god, some prophets, such as have not spoken by human sense, but with the Spirit of God, such as have both predicted things to come, and have made manifest the secrets of the heart; let him produce a psalm, a vision, a prayer—only let it be by the Spirit, in an ecstasy, that is, in a rapture, whenever an interpretation of tongues has occurred to him; let him show to me also, that any woman of boastful tongue in his community has ever prophesied from amongst those specially holy sisters of his. Now all these signs (of spiritual gifts) are forthcoming from my side without any difficulty, and they agree, too, with the rules, and the dispensations, and the instructions of the Creator.[43]

The nature of the state of ecstasy is described further:

For when a man is rapt in the Spirit, especially when he beholds the glory of God, or when God speaks through him, he necessarily loses his sensation (excidat sensu), because he is overshadowed with the power of God.[44]

The Pope early had recognized the Montanists, but later withdrew his support upon the advice of Praxeas:

Not having the love of God, whose very gifts he has resisted and destroyed. For after the Bishop of Rome had acknowledged the prophetic gifts of Montanus, Prisca, and Maximilla, and, in consequence of the acknowledgment, has bestowed his peace on the churches of Asia and Phrygia, he (Praxeas), by importunately urging false accusations against the prophets themselves and their churches, and insisting on the authority of the bishop's predecessors in the see, compelled him to recall the pacific letter which he had issued, as well as to desist from his purpose of acknowledging the said gifts. By this Praxeas did a twofold service for the devil at Rome: he drove away prophecy, and he brought in heresy: he put to flight the Paraclete, and he crucified the Father.[45]

In a direct challenge to the bishop of Rome, Tertullian roars:

Exhibit therefore even now to me, apostolic sir, prophetic evidences, that I may recognise your divine virtue, and vindicate to yourself the power of remitting such sins! If, however, you have had the functions of discipline alone allotted you, and (the duty) of presiding not imperially, but ministerially; who or how great are you, that you

should grant indulgence, who, by exhibiting neither the prophetic nor
the apostolic character, lack that virtue whose property it is to
indulge?[46]

Despite these attacks on the larger Church, Tertullian always felt
that he was within Christian traditions as they had been faithfully
handed down. The New Prophecy had been built upon first-century
models. It was, in one sense, a restoration movement; but it also
served to extend early traditions.

3. THE PASSION OF THE HOLY MARTYRS PERPETUA AND FELICITAS

In A.D. 202, during the reign of Septimius Severus, five
Christians gave their lives for the faith in the arena at Carthage.
Among these were Vivia Perpetua, a twenty-two year old matron,
noble born and well educated, and her handmaiden Felicitas. Their
final hours are reported in *The Passion of The Holy Martyrs
Perpetua and Felicitas*, written by an unidentified apologist
(perhaps Tertullian), who has unmistakable Montanist leanings.

The preface contains a declaration of the importance of end-time
events in the history of the Church—a clear reference to the New
Prophecy:

But let men look to it if they judge the power of the Holy Spirit to be
one, according to the times and seasons; since some things of later
date must be esteemed of more account as being nearer to the very last
times, in accordance with the exuberance of grace manisfested to the
final periods determined for the world. For "in the last days, saith the
Lord, I will pour out of my Spirit upon all flesh; and their sons and
their daughters shall prophesy. And upon my servants and my
handmaidens will I pour out of my Spirit; and your young men shall
see visions, and your old men shall dream dreams." And thus
we—who both acknowledge and reverence, even as we do the
prophecies, modern visions as equally promised to us, and consider
the other powers of the Holy Spirit as an agency of the Church for
which also He was sent, administering all gifts in all, even as the Lord
distributed to everyone, as well needfully collect them in writing, as
commemorate them in reading to God's glory; that so no weakness or
despondency of faith may suppose that the divine grace abode only
among the ancients, whether in respect of the condescension that
raised up martyrs, or that gave revelations; since God always carries
into effect what He has promised, for a testimony to unbelievers, to
believers for a benefit.[47]

There follows a description of a vision that came to Perpetua at
the time of her baptism, in which the Spirit revealed that she should
understand her baptism as a preparation for martyrdom:

In that same interval of a few days we were baptized, and to me the
Spirit prescribed that in the water of baptism nothing else was to be
sought for than bodily endurance. After a few days, we were taken
into the dungeon, and I was very much afraid, because I had never felt
such darkness. . . . There was present there Tertius and Pomponius,

the blessed deacons who ministered to us. . . . I suckled my child, which was now enfeebled with hunger. In my anxiety for it, I addressed my mother and comforted my brother, and commended to their care my son. . . . Then my brother said to me, "My dear sister, you are already in a position of great dignity, and are such that you may ask for a vision, and that it may be known to you whether this is to result in a passion or an escape." And I, who knew that I was privileged to converse with the Lord, whose kindnesses I had found to be so great, boldly promised him: "Tomorrow I will tell you." And I asked, and this is what was shown me: I saw a golden ladder of marvellous height, reaching up even to heaven, and very narrow, so that persons could only ascend one by one, and on the sides of the ladder were fixed every kind of iron weapon. There were swords, lances, hooks, daggers; so that if any one went up carelessly, or not looking upwards, he would be torn to pieces and his flesh would cleave to the iron weapons.

And I went up, and I saw an immense extent of garden, and in the midst of the garden a white-haired man sitting in the dress of a shepherd, of large stature, milking sheep; and standing around were many thousand white-robed ones. And he raised his head, and looked upon me, and said to me, "Thou art welcome, daughter." And he called me, and from the cheese as he was milking he gave me as it were a little cake, and I received it with folded hands; and I ate it, and all who stood around said Amen. And at the sound of their voices I was awakened, still tasting a sweetness which I cannot describe. And I immediately related this to my brother, and we understood that it was to be a passion, and we ceased henceforth to have any hope in this world.[48]

Numerous other visions follow, one of which reveals to Perpetua that in her death she will triumph over the devil. Another vision is described in which her fellow martyr, Saturus, witnesses the reception of all of the Carthaginian martyrs into heaven.

Finally, the work reaches its climax in what Perpetua considers to be her ultimate moment of triumph, her martyrdom. She is led into the arena to be attacked by an enraged cow:

She was tossed, and fell on her loins; and when she saw her tunic torn from her side, she drew it over her as a veil from her middle, rather mindful of her modesty than her suffering. . . . So she rose up; and when she saw Felicitas crushed, she approached and gave her her hand, and lifted her up. And both of them stood together, and the brutality of the populace being appeased, they were recalled to the Sanavivarian gate . . . and she, as if aroused from sleep, so deeply had she been in the Spirit and in an ecstasy, began to look round her, and to say to the amazement of all, "I cannot tell when we are to be led out to that cow." And when she had heard what had already happened, she did not believe it until she had perceived certain signs of injury in her body and in her dress. . . . "Stand fast in the faith, and love one another, all of you, and be not offended at my sufferings."[49]

The work concludes with a lofty, even ecstatic, utterance of the writer's confidence that the Holy Spirit remains at work in the Church, providing strength and other virtues to believers who are summoned to martyrdom:

> O most brave and blessed martyrs! O truly called and chosen unto the
> glory of our Lord Jesus Christ! whom whoever magnifies, and
> honours, and adores, assuredly ought to read these examples for the
> edification of the Church, not less than the ancient ones, so that new
> virtues also may testify that one and the same Holy Spirit is always
> operating even until now, and God the Father Omnipotent, and His
> Son Jesus Christ our Lord, whose is the glory and infinite power for
> ever and ever. Amen.[50]

The Passion of the Holy Martyrs Perpetua and Felicitas is
particularly significant for our study because it represents a
developing trend to recognize the legitimate exercise of the
charismata in a class of believers who, in one fashion or another,
lived beyond the expectations considered normal for the ordinary
believer. These included not only martyrs, but in centuries to come
also monks and virgins.

4. CLEMENT OF ALEXANDRIA

At the end of the second and the beginning of the third centuries
A.D., Alexandria stood as one of the greatest cities of the Roman
Empire, both politically and economically. It also was the most
exciting intellectual center in the Western world. Eastern and
Western strands of religion and philosophy met and blended there.
Eclectic religions such as Hellenistic Judaism, the Gnosticism of
Basilides, the Neoplatonism of Ammonius Saccas and Plotinus,
and the esoteric and Platonic Christianity of Clement and Origen
emerged in this environment.

The first important Christian theologian to appear in
Alexandria, Clement, seems to have been born and educated in
Athens. He eventually came to Egypt where he became the head of
the "catechetical school of Alexandria" and the author of several
works which have been saved for posterity. Throughout his
writings Clement credits philosophy as being given by God to the
Greeks with the same purpose for which the Law was given to the
Jews, namely, to serve as a handmaiden to lead them to Christ.
Truth is one and comes from God.

When referring to God, Clement follows Neoplatonic doctrine
which makes heavy use of negative theology: nothing can be said
directly of God, for He cannot be defined. This does not lead
Clement to attempt any formal definition of the Trinity nor of any
Member thereof. His treatment is highly speculative:

> The flesh figuratively represents to us the Holy Spirit; for the flesh
> was created by Him. The blood points out to us the Word, for as rich
> blood the Word has been infused into life; and the union of both is the
> Lord, the food of the babes—the Lord who is Spirit and Word. The
> food—that is, the Lord Jesus—that is, the Word of God, the Spirit
> made flesh, the heavenly flesh sanctified. The nutriment is the milk of

the Father, by which alone we infants are nourished. The Word Himself, then, the beloved One, and our nourisher, hath shed His own blood for us, to save humanity; and by Him we, believing on God, flee to the Word, "the care-soothing breast" of the Father.

Let no one then think it strange, when we say that the Lord's blood is figuratively represented as milk. For is it not figuratively represented as wine? "Who washes," it is said, "His garment in wine, His robe in the blood of the grape." In His own Spirit He says He will deck the body of the Word; as certainly by His own Spirit He will nourish those who hunger for the Word.[51]

Clement, true to this theme that God has revealed truth to the Greeks, seeks to show that Plato in the *Epistle to Eratus and Coriseus* makes reference to the Father and the Son and that in the *Timaeus* there is a description of the full Trinity. The following passage from the *Timaeus* which Clement quotes demonstrates that his thinking on the Trinity has not advanced from that of Justin Martyr.

The address in the *Timaeus* calls the creator, Father, speaking thus: "Ye gods of gods, of whom I am Father; and the Creator of your works." So that when he says, "Around the king of all, all things are, and because of Him are all things; and he [or that] is the cause of all good things; and around the second are the things second in order; and around the third, the third," I understand nothing else than the Holy Trinity to be meant; for the third is the Holy Spirit, and the Son is the second, by whom all things were made according to the will of the Father.[52]

Clement's adoption of the Neoplatonic concepts of emanation and divine hierarchy is clear in this and other passages and strongly suggests a belief in subordination. Consider the following passage:

The Son is, so to speak, an energy of the Father . . . the Son, is, by the will of the Almighty Father, the cause of all good things. . . . For on one original first Principle, which acts according to the [Father's] will, the first and the second and the third depend.[53]

Clement is concerned to distinguish the "true gnostic" from the false gnostic or heretic. The true gnostic is one who has indeed gained knowledge from God. In this context, Clement has much to say about the work of the Spirit. For example, he states that the believer, made of a lesser substance, has been combined with the regal gold, the Holy Spirit, in contrast with the Jews, the silver, and the Greeks, the third element.[54] The faithful have been drawn by the Holy Spirit as by a magnet to God:

As, then, the minutest particle of steel is moved by the spirit of the Heraclean stone, when diffused over many steel rings; so also, attracted by the Holy Spirit, the virtuous are added by affinity to the first abode, and the others in succession down to the last.[55]

Believers are inspired by the Spirit.

But we assert that the Holy Spirit inspires him who has believed. The Platonists hold that mind is an effluence of divine dispensation in the

soul, and they place the soul in the body. For it is expressly said by
Joel, one of the twelve prophets, "And it shall come to pass after
these things, I will pour out of My Spirit on all flesh, and your sons
and your daughters shall prophesy." But it is not as a portion of God
that the Spirit is in each of us. But how this dispensation takes place,
and what the Holy Spirit is, shall be shown by us in the books on
prophecy, and in those on the soul.[56]

The Holy Spirit is likened to holy anointing oil.

And let woman breathe the odour of the true royal ointment, that of
Christ, not of unguents and scented powders; and let her always be
anointed with the ambrosial chrism of modesty, and find delight in the
holy unguent, the Spirit. This ointment of pleasant fragrance Christ
prepares for His disciples, compounding the ointment of celestial
aromatic ingredients.[57]

The Spirit is a guiding light to the believer who seeks true
knowledge. The more a man becomes a true gnostic, the closer he
will be to the light of the Holy Spirit.[58] All true knowledge, as
opposed to false gnosis, comes through the Holy Spirit. "But the
Lord, in His love to man, invites all men to the knowledge of the
truth, and for this end sends the Paraclete."[59]

Adorning the soul like fine jewelry, the Holy Spirit grants gifts,
which Clement describes as "radiant charms."[60] He is the first
Christian writer to refer to baptism as a charisma, by which the
punishment for sins are washed away. Being perfect, God
consequently bestows perfect gifts.[61] The perfect man or gnostic
can be distinguished by the gifts he has received.

And now we perceive where, and how, and when the divine apostle
mentions the perfect man, and how he shows the differences of the
perfect. And again, on the other hand: "The manifestation of the
Spirit is given for our profit. For the one is given the word of wisdom
by the Spirit; to another the word of knowledge according to the same
Spirit; to another faith through the same Spirit; to another the gifts of
healing through the same Spirit; to another the working of miracles;
to another prophecy; to another discernment of spirits; to another
diversities of tongues; to another the interpretation of tongues: and all
these worketh the one and the same Spirit, distributing to each one
according as He wills." Such being the case, the prophets are perfect
in prophecy, the righteous in righteousness, and the martyrs in
confession, and others in preaching, not that they are not sharers in
the common virtues, but are proficient in those to which they are
appointed.[62]

Clement seems to take for granted the exercise of the gifts in the
Church in his day. It seems unlikely that Clement would have listed
the charisms of 1 Corinthians 12 as evidence of true gnosis if those
gifts were not being practiced at the time.

5. ORIGEN

One of the greatest scholars in the ancient Church, Origen was
born about A.D. 185, probably in Alexandria. He was educated in

the various branches of Grecian learning by his father. In addition, he became a student of Clement in the catechetical school, where he eventually succeeded his mentor as head. He also was a follower of Ammonius Saccas, the founder of the Neoplatonic school at Alexandria, and was subject to the influence of many of the teachings of the Egyptian Christian Gnostics of his day. With this varied background, it readily can be understood why Origen became a philosopher as well as a theologian and why he felt it impossible for anyone to be truly pious without philosophizing. He insisted that his students examine many systems of thought, including that of the Greek philosophers. Only atheists should be avoided. Philosophy served as a preliminary to the study of religion, with the Christian Scriptures as the highest object of scholarly activity. Origen was well suited to become the first Christian to set forth a systematic theology—a balanced treatment of the whole of Christian doctrine.

In his understanding of the Trinity, Origen is deeply influenced by Neoplatonic thought. Neoplatonism recognized the One, the unspeakable being from which all other beings emanate. Further, it postulated intermediate beings between the One and the multiplicity of the world. Throughout Origen's writings one can see a tension between the recognition of the equality of members of the Trinity, and a more Neoplatonic position which distinguished between the Father and the other members of the Godhead by making the Son and the Holy Spirit subordinate beings.

Swete (p. 131) correctly has pointed out that Origen's teaching on the relationship of the Holy Spirit to the rest of the Trinity is not fully consistent throughout his writings. In his *Commentary on St. John*, Origen states that the Spirit was made through the Logos.

Now if, as we have seen, all things were made through Him, we have to enquire if the Holy Spirit also was made through Him. It appears to me that those who hold the Holy Spirit to be created, and who also admit that "all things were made through Him," must necessarily assume that the Holy Spirit was made through the Logos, the Logos accordingly being older than he. And he who shrinks from allowing the Holy Spirit to have been made through Christ must, if he admits the truth of the statements of this Gospel, assume the Spirit to be uncreated. There is a third resource besides these two (that of allowing the Spirit to have been made by the Word, and that of regarding it as uncreated), namely, to assert that the Holy Spirit has no essence of His own beyond the Father and the Son . . . . [However] there are three hypostases, the Father and the Son and the Holy Spirit; and at the same time we believe nothing to be uncreated but the Father. We therefore, as the more pious and the truer course, admit that all things were made by the Logos, and that the Holy Spirit is the most excellent and the first in order of all that was made by the Father through Christ. And this, perhaps, is the reason why the Spirit is not said to be God's own Son.[63]

This tendency toward subordination is undoubtedly a reaction to the heresy of the modalistic Monarchians, who eventually claimed that the Father, the Son, and the Holy Spirit were three temporary manifestations of the same God.

In his great treatise, *On First Principles*, Origen appears more in line with ecclesiastical tradition on matters relating to the Trinity. In part he states:

> Nothing in the Trinity can be called greater or less, since the fountain of divinity alone contains all things by His word and reason, and by the Spirit of His mouth sanctifies all things which are worthy of sanctification, as it is written in the Psalm: "By the word of the Lord were the heavens strengthened, and all their power by the Spirit of His mouth." There is also a special working of God the Father, besides that by which He bestowed upon all things that gift of natural life. There is also a special ministry of the Lord Jesus Christ to those upon whom he confers by nature the gift of reason, by means of which they are enabled to be rightly what they are. There is also another grace of the Holy Spirit, which is bestowed upon the deserving, through the ministry of Christ and the working of the Father, in proportion to the merits of those who are rendered capable of receiving it . . . . From which it most clearly follows that there is no difference in the Trinity, but that which is called the gift of the Spirit is made known through the Son, and operated by God and Father. "But all these worketh that one and the self-same Spirit, dividing to every one severally as He will."[64]

The Spirit was not created, nor does any Scripture speak of Him as a creature.

> That all things were created by God, and that there is no creature that exists but has derived from Him its being, is established from many declarations of Scripture. . . . But up to the present time we have been able to find no statement in holy Scripture in which the Holy Spirit could be said to be made or created.[65]

Neither is the Spirit inferior in knowledge, nor does He receive His knowledge from the Son.[66]

Origen struggles with the question of the Spirit's mode of existence. He asks whether the Spirit is to be regarded as "generate" like the Son, or "ingenerate" like the Father. Certainly, he says, the Word and the Wisdom were not generated by "prolation" of the Father:

> (The term "prolation" being used to signify such a generation as that of animals or men usually is), then, of necessity, both He who "prolated" and He who was "prolated" are corporeal. For we do not say, as the heretics suppose, that some part of the substance of God was converted into the Son, or that the Son was procreated by the Father out of things non-existent, [*sic*] i.e., beyond His own substance, so that there once was a time when He did not exist; but, putting away all corporeal conceptions, we say that the Word and Wisdom was begotten out of the invisible and incorporeal without any corporeal feeling, as if it were an act of the will proceeding from the understanding.[67]

It would seem that Origen is moving towards a conception of procession, but is ahead of his time and lacking in those terms and definitions necessary for adequate expression of certain of his theological insights.

The Father, the Son, and the Holy Spirit are said to transcend all time, all ages, all eternity.[68] The Spirit is associated in honor and dignity with the Father and the Son.[69] The Trinity acts together in the act of regeneration.

> Nevertheless it seems proper to inquire what is the reason why he who is regenerated by God unto salvation has to do both with Father and Son and Holy Spirit, and does not obtain salvation unless with the cooperation of the entire Trinity; and why it is impossible to become partaker of the Father or the Son without the Holy Spirit.[70]

However, the work of the Spirit also is distinct. Whereas the Father and the Son are involved in all creation ("in saints as in sinners, in rational beings and in dumb animals; nay, even in those things which are without life . . ."), the Spirit is for believers only.

> But that the operation of the Holy Spirit does not take place at all in those things which are without life, or in those which, although living, are yet dumb; nay, is not found even in those who are endued indeed with reason, but are engaged in evil courses, and not at all converted to a better life. In those persons alone do I think that the operation of the Holy Spirit takes place, who are already turning to a better life, and walking along the way which leads to Jesus Christ, i.e., who are engaged in the performance of good actions, and who abide in God.[71]

The chief function of the Holy Spirit, then, is to promote holiness among believers in Christ. Deriving their existence from the Father, their rational nature from the Logos, their holiness is from the Holy Spirit. The Spirit intercedes with the Father for the Christian when the human mind cannot pray.[72] Indeed, the Spirit turns the mind, even the imagination of man, to the things of God.[73] It then becomes the work of the Spirit to assist the faithful in apprehending spiritual truth and avoiding falsehood.

> But now there are countless multitudes of believers who, although unable to unfold methodically and clearly the results of their spiritual understandings, are nevertheless most firmly persuaded that neither ought circumcision to be understood literally, nor the rest of the Sabbath, nor the pouring out of the blood of an animal, nor that answers were given by God to Moses on these points. And this method of apprehension is undoubtedly suggested to the minds of all by the power of the Holy Spirit.[74]

Spiritual growth through the Holy Spirit is not gained in one moment of time but is progressive.

> Those who have been previously sanctified by the Holy Spirit are again made capable of receiving Christ, in respect that He is the righteousness of God; and those who have earned advancement to this grade by the sanctification of the Holy Spirit, will nevertheless obtain the gift of wisdom according to the power and working of the Spirit of God.[75]

Spiritual gifts were given by the Spirit to the apostles and are still in operation in the Church of Origen's day, although not to the extent experienced in the first century.

> But the demonstration which followed the words of the apostles of Jesus was given from God, and was accredited by the Spirit and by power. And therefore their word ran swiftly and speedily.[76]

> Moreover, the Holy Spirit gave signs of His presence at the beginning of Christ's ministry, and after His ascension He gave still more; but since that time these signs have diminished, although there are still traces of His presence in a few who have had their souls purified by the Gospel, and their actions regulated by its influence.[77]

> And there are still preserved among Christians traces of that Holy Spirit which appeared in the form of a dove. They expel evil spirits, and perform many cures, and foresee certain events, according to the will of the Logos.[78]

One of the purposes for spiritual gifts in the Church is to examine and to clarify the teachings of the apostles:

> Now it ought to be known that the holy apostles, in preaching the faith of Christ, delivered themselves with the utmost clearness on certain points which they believed to be necessary to every one, even to those who seemed somewhat dull in the investigation of divine knowledge; leaving, however, the grounds of their statements to be examined into by those who should deserve the excellent gifts of the Spirit, and who, especially by means of the Holy Spirit Himself, should obtain the gift of language, of wisdom, and of knowledge: while on other subjects they merely stated the fact that things were so, keeping silence as to the manner or origin of their existence; clearly in order that the more zealous of their successors, who should be lovers of wisdom, might have a subject of exercise on which to display the fruit of their talents,—those persons, I mean, who should prepare themselves to be fit and worthy receivers of wisdom.[79]

The pagan philosopher Celsus, in writing against Christianity, attempted to discredit the charisms exercised by individuals within the Church. Origen responds sharply:

> But as Celsus promises to give an account of the manner in which prophecies are delivered in Phoenicia and Palestine, speaking as though it were a matter with which he had a full and personal acquaintance, let us see what he has to say on the subject. First he lays it down that there are several kinds of prophecies, but he does not specify what they are; indeed, he could not do so, and the statement is a piece of pure ostentation. However, let us see what he considers the most perfect kind of prophecy among these nations. "There are many," he says, "who, although of no name, with the greatest facility and on the slightest occasion, whether within or without temples, assume the motions and gestures of inspired persons; while others do it in cities or among armies, for the purpose of attracting attention and exciting surprise. These are accustomed to say, each for himself, "I am God; I am the Son of God; or, I am the Divine Spirit; I have come because the world is perishing, and you, O men are perishing for your iniquities. But I wish to save you, and you shall see me returning

again with heavenly power. Blessed is he who now does me homage.
On all the rest I will send down eternal fire, both on cities and on
countries. And those who know not the punishments which await
them shall repent and grieve in vain; while those who are faithful to
me I will preserve eternally." Then he goes on to say: "To these
promises are added strange, fanatical, and quite unintelligible words,
of which no rational person can find the meaning: for so dark are
they, as to have no meaning at all; but they give occasion to every fool
or impostor to apply them to suit his own purposes."[80]

I am convinced, indeed, that much better arguments could be adduced
than any I have been able to bring forward, to show the falsehood of
these allegations of Celsus, and to set forth the divine inspiration of
the prophecies.[81]

Celsus asserts that it is by the names of certain demons, and by the use
of incantations, that the Christians appear to be possessed of
(miraculous) power; hinting, I suppose, at the practices of those who
expel evil spirits by incantations. And here he manifestly appears to
malign the Gospel. For it is not by incantations that Christians seem to
prevail (over evil spirits), but by the name of Jesus, accompanied by
the announcement of the narratives which relate to Him; for the
repetition of these has frequently been the means of driving demons
out of men, especially when those who repeated them did so in a
sound and genuinely believing spirit.[82]

Origen lays special emphasis on the validating force of signs and
wonders:

We have to say, moreover, that the Gospel has a demonstration of its
own, more divine than any established by Grecian dialectics. And this
diviner method is called by the apostle the "manifestation of the Spirit
and of power:" of "the Spirit," on account of the prophecies, which
are sufficient to produce faith in any one who reads them, especially in
those things which relate to Christ; and of "power," because of the
signs and wonders which we must believe to have been performed,
both on many other grounds, and on this, that traces of them are still
preserved among those who regulate their lives by the precepts of the
Gospel.[83]

It is clear from this and numerous other statements cited above
that Origen understands that the gifts of the Spirit are not for all
Christians. Rather, they are intended for those who are counted
worthy, for those who already are living a Christian life guided by
the Spirit.

Origen's teachings dominated the theology of the third century.
Because of the ambiguity in his treatment of the Trinity, when the
Arian controversy began in the early fourth century nearly all
parties claimed connections to the great Alexandrian. Athanasius
contended Origenist antecedents for his doctrine of eternal
generation, while many of the Arians, on the opposite side, were
among Origen's closest followers because of his teaching that the
Trinity was to be understood in hierarchical terms. The middle
party at the Council of Nicea (A.D. 325), represented by Eusebius

of Caesarea, was composed of moderate Origenists. Many of the most learned and ascetic monks discovered in Origen their main treasury for an understanding of the Scriptures. Even the great Cappadocian Fathers—Basil, Gregory of Nyssa, and Gregory Nazianzen— ascribed their learning to him. By the late third and early fourth centuries A.D., however, Origen also had numerous detractors. Beginning with Methodius of Olympus and Eustathius of Antioch, opposition grew until finally, at the Council of Alexandria (A.D. 400), Origenism was condemned, especially for the doctrines of the preexistence of souls and the temporary character of the body. The Fifth General Council at Constantinople (A.D. 553) listed Origen among ancient heretics.

6. NOVATIAN

One of the major controversies in the Western Church in the third century was over the question of whether the Church should excommunicate finally those who had committed grievous sins, especially apostasy. Until about A.D. 220 the penalty for idolatry, adultery and fornication, and murder was definite excommunication with no hope of restoration except for the mercy of God in the next life. By decree of Calixtus, pope from 217-222, special powers were granted to confessors in cases of sins of the flesh, thus opening the door for restoration. The Decian persecutions (249-250) caused so many Christians to deny their faith that a growing number of rigorous believers, led by Novatian of Rome, began to demand that such apostates not be welcomed back into the fellowship of the Church. The Novatians argued that the Church is the body of Christ and must be kept holy as He is holy. For all sins after baptism there is penance and forgiveness in the Church, except for idolatry and, possibly, fornication. Apostasy is a sin against the Holy Spirit, who is received by the believer at baptism and lost by this sin against God, since there is only one baptism. The Catholic Church, by restoring those who have committed such grievous sins, contaminates the Body of Christ. Novatian was certain that such sinners had lost salvation and their right to be called Christian. Within a few years Novatianism became a separate holiness movement. True to his convictions, Novatian died as a martyr during the persecution under Valerian (257-260).

Novatian was the first Latin writer of the Roman Church. His *Treatise Concerning the Trinity* was penned while he was still in communion with the Church. It reveals a doctrine of the Holy Spirit that is still not fully developed. There is no direct statement of the divine personhood of the Spirit:

> The Paraclete would not receive from Christ unless He were less than Christ. . . . If Christ were only man, Christ would receive from the Paraclete what He should say, not the Paraclete receive from Christ what He should declare.[84]

If Novatian does not expressly call the Spirit God, he certainly ascribes to Him properties and offices which could be those of God alone. While inferior to Christ, He is not referred to as a creature.

On the offices of the Holy Spirit in the Old Testament and in the life of the Church, Novatian's words are as rich as any ante-Nicene writer. What the Old Testament prophets experienced from Him in limited measure, the Church has received in the fullness of divine grace:

> He is therefore one and the same Spirit who was in the prophets and apostles, except that in the former He was occasional, in the latter always. But in the former not as being always in them, in the latter as abiding always in them; in the former distributed with reserve, in the latter liberally bestowed. . . . This is He who strengthened their hearts and minds, who marked out the Gospel sacraments, who was in them the enlightener of divine things; and they being strengthened, feared, for the sake of the Lord's name, neither dungeons nor chains, nay, even trod under foot the very powers of the world and its tortures, since they were henceforth armed and strengthened by the same Spirit, having in themselves the gifts which this same Spirit distributes and appropriates to the Church, the spouse of Christ, as he ornaments her. This is He who places prophets in the Church, instructs teachers, directs tongues, gives powers and healings, does wonderful works, offers discrimination of spirit, affords power of government, suggests counsels, and orders and arranges whatever other gifts there are of charismata; and thus makes the Lord's Church everywhere, and in all, perfected and completed.[85]

Novatian's mention of the charismata appears in the present tense, although it might be an example of the extended present. In any case, it would seem unwise to rule out the possibility that he was referring to the Church of his time. Certainly he attributes the perfection and completion of the Church to the gifts of the Spirit. Because he calls for a higher standard of perfection among Christians in his own day, it is reasonable to assume that he expects such holiness to be a product of the Spirit's involvement in the Church through His gifts.[86]

The Holy Spirit improves morality, He builds relationships among people, and He purifies the Church.

> He it is who effects with water the second birth . . . who can make us God's temple, and fits us for His house; who solicits the divine hearing for us with groanings that cannot be uttered; filling the offices of advocacy, and manifesting the duties of our defence.[87]

The fruits of the Spirit, especially moderation, are to be expected of individual believers who have been united with Christ by second birth in baptism and received a title deed of eternal inheritance through the Spirit:

> Working in us for eternity, [the Spirit] can also produce our bodies at the resurrection of immortality, accustoming them to be associated in Himself with heavenly power, and to be allied with the divine eternity of the Holy Spirit. For our bodies are both trained in Him and by Him to advance to immortality, by learning to govern themselves with moderation according to His decrees. . . . This is He who restrains insatiable desires, controls immoderate lusts, quenches unlawful fires, conquers reckless impulses, repels drunkenness, checks avarice, drives away luxurious revellings, links love, binds together affections, keeps down sects, orders the rule of truth, overcomes heretics, turns out the wicked, guards the Gospel. . . . This is he who in the apostles gives testimony to Christ; in the martyrs shows forth the constant faithfulness of their religion; in virgins restrains the admirable continency of their sealed chastity; in others guards the laws of the Lord's doctrine incorrupt and uncontaminated; destroys heretics, corrects the perverse, condemns infidels, makes known pretenders; moreover, rebukes the wicked.[88]

Where the Spirit is, the Church is "perfected and complete," "incorrupt and inviolate in the sanctity of a perpetual virginity and truth." As the leader of a "Puritan" group in the third century Church, Novatian fully expects a higher order of living from those controlled by the Holy Spirit, "an inhabitant given for our bodies and an effector of their holiness."[89]

7. HIPPOLYTUS

Hippolytus of Rome (d. 236), a student of Irenaeus, was one of the great thinkers of the Church in the early third century. He was little known in centuries following because he wrote in Greek. When the Western Church moved toward Latin later in the century, he was forgotten. It was not until the sixteenth century, when a beatiful marble statue was found which his followers had erected in his honor, that his memory was revived.

Unfortunately, Hippolytus was irascible and contentious in his dealings with other church leaders. As a presbyter at Rome he attacked his own Bishop Zephyrinus for compromising with the views of Sabellius. He also was resolutely hostile toward Zephyrinus' archdeacon, Calixtus. When Zephyrinus died and Calixtus was selected to succeed him as Bishop of Rome, Hippolytus split with him and set himself up as antipope in opposition to the "sect" of "Callistians."[90] He was devoted to maintaining the tradition handed down from the apostles and denounced with great polemical furor "that lapse or error which recently occurred through ignorance and because of ignorant men."[91] We have reason to believe that here he is referring to Zephyrinus and Calixtus.

That Hippolytus also was openly hostile to various fringe and heretical groups reflects the concern of this staunch conservative to maintain traditions established in the first and early second centuries. As they relate to our study of the Holy Spirit, we already have dealt with his polemics against the Gnostics, Marcionists, Montanists, and Monarchians.[92] Here it is our purpose to concentrate on Hippolytus's doctrine of the Holy Spirit as presented in his *Apostolic Tradition*, written about A.D. 215, two years before he broke with Calixtus and the Church of Rome. This work, which was written to perpetuate tradition against the innovations of his bishop and rival, reflects with but a few exceptions second century doctrine and practice in the Roman Church. As Gregory Dix has suggested, it is "the most illuminating source of evidence extant in the inner life and religious polity of the early Christian Church."[93]

The Apostolic Tradition opens with a reference to a now lost work entitled *peri charismaton* ("On Charismatic Gifts"), "We have duly completed what needed to be said about 'Gifts,' describing those gifts which God by His own counsel has bestowed on men, in offering to Himself His image which had gone astray."[94] It may be that *The Apostolic Tradition* is but the second part of a larger work which originally included *peri charismaton*. In any case, there is within *The Apostolic Tradition* a dominant emphasis on the Holy Spirit and His gifts,[95] which should be understood to include any gift of divine grace, gifts of official ministry, as well as those of the supporting laity. Hippolytus also recognizes the place of unstructured or extraordinary gifts of the Spirit in the Body of Christ.

The Church of Hippolytus's day is one already highly structured with various levels present in the hierarchy. At the same time, one is impressed by the degree to which Hippolytus emphasizes the Spirit's activity within structure. This really should not be surprising, however, when we consider Hippolytus's attachment to Irenaeus, who linked the Spirit and His offices directly to the Church. But Hippolytus also insists that the Spirit is not limited in operation to the ecclesiastical hierarchy, as Cyprian later would assert. The Spirit's domain reaches to all "those who believe aright," as opposed to these who lapse into error, wandering blindly and aimlessly.[96] God has bestowed gifts on men according to His own counsel or will, "for we all have the Spirit of God."[97]

The Apostolic Tradition is our most detailed and complete picture of Church at Rome at the beginning of third century. Of particular interest is Hippolytus's description of the role played by the Holy Spirit in the ordination of bishops, presbyters and deacons, and the appointment of unordained confessors.

The bishop is ordained after he has been popularly elected by all

of the people, through whom God chooses His man.[98] It is clear
that Hippolytus understands the election to be by Spirit-led laity
and clergy alike. Hands are then laid on the ordinand, first by all
the bishops, praying in silence for the descent of the Spirit.[99]
Finally one of the bishops present lays hands on him and prays:

> God and Father of our Lord Jesus Christ, Father of mercies and God
> of all comfort, who dwellest on high yet hast respect to the lowly, who
> knowest all things before they come to pass. Thou hast appointed the
> borders of thy church by the word of thy grace, predestinating from
> the beginning the righteous race of Abraham. And making them
> princes and priests, and leaving not thy sanctuary without a ministry,
> thou hast from the beginning of the world been well pleased to be
> glorified among those thou hast chosen. Pour forth now that power,
> which is thine, of thy royal Spirit, which thou gavest to thy beloved
> Servant Jesus Christ, which he bestowed on his holy apostles, who
> established the church in every place, the church which thou hast
> sanctified unto unceasing glory and praise of thy name. Thou who
> knowest the hearts of all, grant to this thy servant, whom thou hast
> chosen to be bishop, [to feed thy holy flock] and to serve as thy high
> priest without ceasing and to offer thee the gifts of thy holy church.
> And by the Spirit of high-priesthood to have authority to remit sins
> according to thy commandment, to assign the lots according to the
> authority which thou gavest to thy apostles, and to please thee in
> meekness and purity of heart, offering to thee an odour of sweet
> savour. Through thy Servant Jesus Christ our Lord, through whom be
> to thee glory, might, honour, with [the] Holy Spirit in [the] holy
> church, both now and always and world without end. Amen.[100]

The authority of the bishopric, then, is poured out from the
princely or royal Spirit whom God gave to Jesus, who in turn
bestowed Him on His apostles. Such authority exists to forgive
sins, as well as to assign lots, and to loosen every bond. None of
these functions can be exercised validly without the Holy Spirit.

The Holy Spirit also is bestowed on the presbyter at the time of
his ordination as the bishop lays his hand upon his head and prays:

> God and Father of our Lord Jesus Christ, look upon this thy servant,
> and grant to him the Spirit of grace and counsel of a presbyter, that he
> may sustain and govern thy people with a pure heart; as thou didst
> look upon thy chosen people and didst fill with thy Spirit, which thou
> gavest to thy servant. And now, O Lord, grant that there may be
> unfailingly preserved amongst us the Spirit of thy grace, and make us
> worthy that, believing, we may minister to thee in simplicity of heart,
> praising thee. Through thy Servant Jesus Christ, through whom be to
> thee glory and honour, with [the] Holy Spirit in the holy church, both
> now and always and world without end. Amen.[101]

The ordination of the deacon also involves a petition for the
granting of the Holy Spirit. However, a clear distinction is drawn
between the clergy—the bishop and the presbyter—and the deacon,
who does not share that grace of the Spirit reserved for those with
ministerial functions.[102] The bishop's prayer of deacon ordination
follows:

O God, who has created all things and hast ordered them by thy
Word, the Father of our Lord Jesus Christ, whom thou didst send to
minister thy will and to manifest to us thy desire; grant the Holy Spirit
of grace and care and diligence to this thy servant, whom thou hast
chosen to serve the church and to offer in thy holy sanctuary the gifts
that are offered to thee by thine appointed high priests, so that serving
without blame and with a pure heart he may be counted worthy of this
exalted office, by thy goodwill, praising thee continually. Through thy
Servant Jesus Christ, through whom be to thee glory and honour, with
[the] Holy Spirit, in the holy church, both now and always and world
without end. Amen.[103]

Concerning the confessor we read:

On a confessor, if he has been in bonds for the name of the Lord,
hands shall not be laid for the diaconate or the presbyterate, for he has
the honour of the presbyterate by his confession. But if he is to be
ordained a bishop, hands shall be laid upon him.

But if he is a confessor who was not brought before the authorities nor
was punished with bonds nor was shut up in prison, but was insulted
casually or privately for the name of the Lord, even though he
confessed, hands are to be laid upon him for every office of which he
is worthy.[104]

By his witness in face of the danger of death, a confessor proves
that he has the Spirit of the presbyter, and need not be ordained.
The Holy Spirit has prepared him for persecution, and he is to be
honored with the presbytry.[105] This is very much within the
tradition that the Holy Spirit gives strength to those who suffer for
Christ in martyrdom.

A similar passage follows regarding those who claim to have the
gift of healing, "If anyone says, 'I have received the gift of
healing,' hands shall not be laid upon him: the deed shall make
manifest if he speaks the truth."[106] Herein Hippolytus provides
evidence for the practice of the gift of divine healing in the Western
Church in the early third century. His advice that such a claimant
not be ordained and that the Church wait for a demonstration of
the gift seems wise, for if the gift is genuine it will be confirmed in
time.

We read of another spiritual gift—that of teaching—in *The
Apostolic Tradition* 35:3:

If a [specially gifted] teacher should come let none of you delay to
attend the place where the instruction is given, for grace will be given
to the speaker to utter things profitable to all, and thou wilt hear new
things, and thou wilt be profited by what the Holy Spirit will give thee
through the instructor; so thy faith will be strengthened by what thou
hearest, and in that place thou wilt learn thy duties at home; therefore
let everyone be zealous to go to the church, the place where the Holy
Spirit abounds.[107]

Such a teacher may be a prophet. It seems more certain that he would be a layman. Because the assembly of the faithful is the place where the Holy Spirit abounds, it is reasonable that they will hear from the Spirit there. The teacher is prompted by the Spirit and his words are profitable to his hearers. While Hippolytus does not directly address the question of judging such teaching, it is clear that any such judgment should be based upon whether it is profitable to those assembled.

Great importance is ascribed to the weekday morning assemblies in which the Spirit speaks through instruction in the Word:

> But if any instruction in the word is held, let each give first place to that, that he may attend and hear the word of God, to his soul's comfort; so let each one hasten to the church, where the Spirit abounds.[108]

> But if any instruction in God's word is held that day, everyone ought to attend it willingly, recollecting that he will hear God speaking through the instructor and that prayer in the church enables him to avoid the day's evil; any godly man ought to count it a great loss if he does not attend the place of instruction, especially if he can read.[109]

In *The Apostolic Tradition* Hippolytus links the Spirit with the Word, the Spirit with Church order, and the Spirit with the ministry of laity in such a way that one finds it reasonable to conclude with von Campenhausen that "the pneumo-charismatic and the official-sacramental conceptions are . . . still co-existing without great difficulty" in the early third century church at Rome. The Holy Spirit, while operating through the hierarchy, also is functioning through lay ministers and in the assemblies of believers. But this is the last generation in the West in which it will be recognized generally that the Spirit does indeed deal with and through the entire Church. In von Campenhausen's words, "One step—and what a long step it is!—beyond him [Hippolytus]; and in a single generation we find ourselves in the age of Cyprian."[110]

8. CYPRIAN

Perhaps the most remarkable leader of the African church between Tertullian and Augustine, Cyprian, Bishop of Carthage (A.D. 248-258), laid the doctrinal foundation for the conception of the Church in the post-Nicene Age and for the development of the Roman hierarchy in the Church. Cyprian believes that the Church is the indispensable ark of salvation. He argues that "There is no salvation out of the church. . . . He can no longer have God for his Father, who has not the Church for his mother."[111] Cyprian refuses to accept any baptism which is received from heretical or schismatic hands. For these there is no salvation, no forgiveness of sins, no true communion, no true baptism, and no direction of the Holy Spirit.[112]

Cyprian's opposition to schismatics leads him to emphasize unity. There is no truth without unity. There is no love without unity. The unity of the Church is in the episcopate. The Church was established upon the bishop. The bishop is in the Church and the Church in the bishop. Where there is no bishop there is no Church. The bishop can be judged by no one save God. To criticize the bishop is rebellion.

> Peter speaks there [John 6:67-69], on whom the Church was to be built, teaching and showing in the name of the Church, that although a rebellious and arrogant multitude of those who will not hear and obey may depart, yet the Church does not depart from Christ; and they are the Church who are a people united to the priest, and the flock which adheres to its pastor. Whence you ought to know that the bishop is in the Church, and the Church in the bishop; and if any one be not with the bishop, that he is not in the Church, and that those flatter themselves in vain who creep in, not having peace with God's priests, and think that they communicate secretly with some; while the Church, which is Catholic and one, is not cut nor divided, but is indeed connected and bound together by the cement of priests who cohere with one another.[113]

Bishop Cyprian is strongly charismatic, although he thinks that the bishop has the sole claim to prophetic gifts. As a bishop, he personally reports having numerous revelations through visions, several of which are described in his letters. The first involves a series of divine admonitions:

> You ought to know (since the Lord has condescended to show and to reveal it) that it was said in a vision, "Ask, and ye shall obtain." Then, afterwards, that the attending people were bidden to pray for certain persons pointed out to them, but that in their petitions there were dissonant voices, and wills disagreeing, and that this excessively displeased Him who had said, "Ask, and ye shall obtain," because the disagreement of the people was out of harmony. . . . For there also was shown that there sat the father of a family, a young man also being seated at his right hand, who, anxious and somewhat sad with a kind of indignation, holding his chin in his right hand, occupied his place with a sorrowful look. . . . This was shown long before the tempest of this devastation arose. And we have seen that which had been shown fulfilled. . . . For know, beloved brethren, that I was not long ago reproached with this also in a vision, that we were sleepy in our prayers, and did not pray with watchfulness . . . yet He has condescended of His goodness towards us to command: "Tell him," said He, "to be safe, because peace is coming; but that, in the meantime, there is a little delay, that some who still remain may be proved." But we are admonished by these divine condescensions both concerning a spare diet and a temperate use of drink.[114]

Cyprian felt compelled to share these revelations with the faithful:

> It was my duty not to conceal these special matters, nor to hide them alone in my own consciousness—matters by which each one of us may be both instructed and guided. And do not you for your part keep this letter concealed among yourselves, but let the brethren have it to read. For it is the part of one who desires that his brother should not be

warned and instructed, to intercept those words with which the Lord
condescends to admonish and instruct us.[115]

Such visions are for bishops and priests. With Cyprian, office and charismata are combined:

> So that first I should consult my Lord whether He would permit peace
> to be granted to you, and you to be received to the communion of His
> Church by His own showing and admonition. For I remember what
> has already been manifested to me, nay, what has been prescribed by
> the authority of our Lord and God to an obedient and fearing servant;
> and among other things which He condescended to show and to
> reveal, He also added this: "Whoso therefore does not believe Christ,
> who maketh the priest, shall hereafter begin to believe Him who
> avengeth the Priest." Although I know that to some men dreams seem
> ridiculous and visions foolish, yet assuredly it is to such as would
> rather believe in opposition to the priest, than believe the priest.[116]

To hear from God concerning His will, believers are told to wait on the bishop:

> For besides the visions of the night, by day also, the innocent age of
> boys is among us filled with the Holy Spirit, seeing in an ecstasy with
> their eyes, and hearing and speaking those things whereby the Lord
> condescends to warn and instruct us. And you shall hear all things
> when the Lord, who bade me withdraw, shall bring me back again to
> you. I shall use that power of admonition which the Lord bids me
> use.[117]

Cyprian also tells of the false ecstasy of a self-proclaimed prophetess who promised certain wonders at her own hands:

> There arose among us on a sudden a certain woman, who in a state of
> ecstasy announced herself as a prophetess, and acted as if filled with
> the Holy Ghost. And she was so moved by the impetus of the principal
> demons, that for a long time she made anxious and deceived the
> brotherhood, accomplishing certain wonderful and portentious
> things, and promised that she would cause the earth to be
> shaken. . . . [The demon] would also make that woman walk in the
> keen winter with bare feet over frozen snow, and not to be troubled or
> hurt in any degree by that walking. . . . She deceived one of the
> presbyters, a countryman, and another, a deacon, so that they had
> intercourse with that same woman, which was shortly afterwards
> detected. For on a sudden there appeared unto her one of the
> exorcists, a man approved and always of good conversation in respect
> of religious discipline: who . . . raised himself up against that wicked
> spirit to overcome it.[118]

Cyprian of Carthage culminated a trend among early Christian writers who defended the propriety of the charism of prophecy and the exercise of that gift by the bishop for their own purposes, thereby rendering it powerless in the hands of others. In the words of James L. Ash, "The charisma of prophecy was captured by the monarchical episcopate, used in its defense, and left to die an unnoticed death when true episcopate stability rendered it a superfluous tool."[119]

Notes to Chapter 4

[1]Irenaeus, *Against Heresies* iv.20.3-4, ANF 1:488. For Irenaeus on the Holy Spirit see Hans-Jochen Jaschke, *Der Heilige Geist im Bekenntnis der Kirche. Eine Studie zur Pneumatologie des Irenäus von Lyon im Aufgang von altchristliche Glaubensbekenntnis* (Munster, Verlag Aschendorff, 1976), and Heinrich Weinel, *Die wirkungen des geistes und der geister in nachapostolischen zeitalter bis auf Irenäus* (Tübingen, Druck von H. Laupp, 1898).

[2]Ibid., iv.20.4, ANF 1:488.

[3]Ibid., ii.30.9, ANF 1:406.

[4]Ibid., v.6.1, ANF 1:531.

[5]Ibid., v. 28.4, ANF 1:557. Irenaeus's concept of the two hands of God is not fully developed. For an analysis of his metaphor of the two hands and a more comprehensive treatment of the subject see Joseph Haroutunian, "The Church, the Spirit, and the Hands of God," *Journal of Religion* 54, no.2 (1974): 154-165.

[6]Ibid., iv. pref.4, ANF 1:463.

[7]Ibid., i.10.1, ANF 1:330.

[8]Ibid., iv.8.1, ANF 1:470.

[9]Ibid., ii.35.2, ANF 1:412.

[10]Ibid., v.1.3, ANF 1:527.

[11]Ibid., iii.17.1,3, ANF 1:444-445.

[12]Ibid., iii.9.3, ANF 1:423.

[13]Ibid., iii.18.3, ANF 1:446.

[14]Ibid., i.21.1, ANF 1:345.

[15]Ibid., iii.4.2, ANF 1:417.

[16]Ibid., iii.24.1, ANF 1:458.

[17]Ibid.

[18]Ibid.

[19]Ibid., v.36.2, ANF 1:567.

[20]Ibid., v.8.1, ANF 1:533.

[21]Ibid., v.6.1, ANF 1:531.

[22]Ibid., ii.32.4, ANF 1:409.

[23]Ibid., i.13.1-3, ANF 1:334-335.

[24]Ibid., i.13.3, ANF 1:335.

[25]Ibid., iii.24.1, ANF 1:458.

[26]See H. M. Evans, "Tertullian: Pentecostal of Carthage," *Paraclete* 9, no. 4 (Fall 1975): 17-21.

[27]Tertullian, *Against Praxeas* xxv, vii-ix, ANF 3:621, 603-604.

[28]Ibid., xxxi, ANF 3:627.

[29]Tertullian, *On Baptism* iv, ANF 3:671.

[30]Ibid., vi-viii, ANF 3:672-673.

[31]Tertullian, *On Fasting* i, ANF 4:102.

[32]Tertullian, *On Monogamy* ii, ANF 4:59-60.

[33]Tertullian, *On the Veiling of Virgins* i, ANF 4:27.
[34]Tertullian, *On Prescription Against Heretics* xiii, ANF 3:249.
[35]*On Modesty* xi, ANF 4:85.
[36]*On Monogamy* ii, ANF 4:59.
[37]Ibid., xiv, ANF 4:71.
[38]*On Fasting* xi, ANF 4:110.
[39]Tertullian, *A Treatise on the Soul* xlv, ANF 3:223-224.
[40]Ibid., xlvii, ANF 3:225-226.
[41]Tertullian, *Against Marcion* vii, ANF 3:445-446.
[42]*A Treatise on the Soul* ix, ANF 3:188. Swete, 7-8, suggests that the incident described is not very convincing.
[43]*Against Marcion* v.8, ANF 3:446-447.
[44]Ibid., iv.22, ANF 3:383. Tertullian's work, *On Ecstasy*, a defense of Montanism in six books, has disappeared.
[45]*Against Praxeas* i, ANF 3:597.
[46]*On Modesty* xxi, ANF 4:99.
[47]*The Passion of Perpetua and Felicitas* preface, ANF 3:699.
[48]Ibid., i.2-3, ANF 3:700.
[49]Ibid., vi.3, ANF 3:705.
[50]Ibid., vi.4, ANF 3:705-706.
[51]Clement of Alexandria, *The Instructor* i.6, ANF 2:220-221.
[52]Clement of Alexandria, *The Stromata* v.14, ANF 2:468.
[53]Ibid., vii.2, ANF 2:525.
[54]Ibid., v.14, ANF 2:467.
[55]Ibid., vii.2, ANF 2:525.
[56]Ibid., v.14, ANF 2:465.
[57]Ibid., ii.8, ANF 2:254.
[58]Ibid., iv.17, ANF 2:429.
[59]Clement of Alexandria, *Exhortation to the Heathen* ix, ANF 2:196.
[60]*The Instructor* iii.ll, ANF 2:286.
[61]Ibid., i.6, ANF 2:215.
[62]Ibid., iv.21, ANF 2:434.
[63]Origen, *Commentary on John* ii.6, ANF 10:328.
[64]Origen, *On First Principles* i.3.7, ANF 4:255.
[65]Ibid., i.3.3, ANF 4:252.
[66]Ibid., i.3.4, ANF 4:253.
[67]Ibid., iv.1.28, ANF 4:376.
[68]Ibid., iv. 1.28, 36, ANF 4:377, 381.
[69]Ibid., pref. 4, ANF 4:240.
[70]Ibid., i.3.5, ANF 4:253.
[71]Ibid.
[72]Origen, *On Oratory* ii.14, PG ll:cols. 459-460.
[73]Origen, *Against Celsus* iv.95, ANF 4:539.
[74]Origen, *On First Principles* ii.7.2, ANF 4:285.

[75]Ibid., i.3.8, ANF 4:255. See especially Joseph W. Trigg, "The Charismatic Intellectual: Origen's Understanding of Religious Leadership," *Church History* 50 (1981): 5-19.

[76]*Against Celsus* iii.68, ANF 4:491.

[77]*On First Principles* vii.8, ANF 4:614.

[78]*Against Celsus* i.46, ANF 4:415.

[79]*On First Principles* pref. 3, ANF 4:239.

[80]*Against Celsus* vii.9, ANF 4:614.

[81]Ibid., vii.ll, ANF 4:615.

[82]Ibid., i.6, ANF 4:398.

[83]Ibid., i.2, ANF 4:397-398.

[84]Novatian, *Treatise Concerning the Trinity* xvi, ANF 5:625-626.

[85]Ibid., xxix, ANF 5:640-641.

[86]See Ronald Kydd, "Novatian's *De Trinitate*, 29: Evidence of the Charismatic?" *Scottish Journal of Theology* 30 (1977): 313-318.

[87]*Treatise Concerning the Trinity* xxix, ANF 5:641.

[88]Ibid.

[89]Ibid.

[90]Hippolytus, *The Refutation of All Heresies* ix.6-7, ANF 5:128-131.

[91]Burton Scott Easton, trans., *The Apostolic Tradition of Hippolytus* (Cambridge: Cambridge University Press, 1934), 33 (henceforth *Ap Tr*). Of particular interest is the article by John E. Stam, "Charismatic Theology in the Apostolic Tradition of Hippolytus," in Gerald F. Hawthorne, ed., *Current Issues in Biblical and Patristic Interpretation* (Grand Rapids, MI: Eerdmans, 1975), 267-276.

[92]See pages 41-59.

[93]Gregory Dix, *The Treatise on the Apostolic Tradition of St. Hippolytus of Rome* (London: SPCK, 1968), iv.

[94]*Ap Tr* i.l, Easton, 33.

[95]Hippolytus, like his teacher Irenaeus, uses the terms *charis*, *charisma* and *dorea* interchangeably.

[96]*Ap Tr* i.3-4, xxxviii.3, Easton, 33, 57.

[97]*Ap Tr* i.l, xvi. 25, Easton, 33, 43.

[98]*Ap Tr* ii.l, iii.5, Easton, 33, 34.

[99]*Ap Tr* ii.l, Easton, 33.

[100]*Ap Tr* iii.1-7, Easton, 34-35.

[101]*Ap Tr* vii.2-5, Easton, 37-38. The presbyter had become the normal officiant at the Eucharist, and played a role in the ordination of a new member to the ranks. While the presbytery early formed a ruling body, by the beginning of the third century

they had been reduced to a mere council advising the bishop. In most communities the presbyter devoted much of the week to secular occupations, in contrast to the bishop and the deacons.

[102]*Ap Tr* viii.l, ix.4, Easton, 37, 38.

[103]*Ap Tr* ix. 10-12, Easton, 38-39.

[104]*Ap Tr* x.1-2, Easton, 39.

[105]Later in the third century A.D., as confessors multiplied with the intensification of persecution, the Church could no longer follow Hippolytus on this point, for the presbyterate would have been severely overloaded.

[106]*Ap Tr* xv, Easton, 41.

[107]*Ap Tr* xxxv.3, Easton, 54.

[108]*Ap Tr* xxxi.2, Easton, 60.

[109]*Ap Tr* xxxv.2, Easton, 54.

[110]Hans von Campenhausen, *Ecclesiastical Authority and Spiritual Power in the Church of the First Three Centuries* (Stanford, California: Stanford University Press, 1969), 177.

[111]Cyprian, *On the Unity of the Church* vi, ANF 5:423.

[112]Cyprian, *The Epistles of Cyprian* lxxiv.11-14, ANF 5:393. Of interest on Cyprian's understanding of the Holy Spirit are von Campenhausen, pp. 268-273, and Cecil M. Robeck, Jr., "Visions and Prophecy in the Writings of Cyprian," *Paraclete* 16, no.3 (Summer 1982): 21-25.

[113]Ibid., lxviii.8, ANF 5:374-375.

[114]Ibid., vii.3-6, ANF 5:286-287.

[115]Ibid., vii.7, ANF 5:287.

[116]Ibid., lxviii.9-10, ANF 5:375.

[117]Ibid., iv.4, ANF 5:290.

[118]Ibid., lxxiv.10, ANF 5:393.

[119]James L. Ash, Jr., "The Decline of Ecstatic Prophecy in the Early Church," *Theological Studies* 36 (June 1976): 252; Irenaeus and Hippolytus are earlier representatives of this tradition. For further discussion of this subject see Gregory Dix, *Le Ministère dans l'Eglise Ancienne (des annes 90 à 410)* (Neuchatel, Delachaux et Niestlé, 1955); Theodor Klauser, *Der Ursprung der bischöflichen Insignien und Ehrenrecht; Rede gehalten beim Antritt der Rektorats der Rheinischen Friedrich-Wilhelms-Universität zu Bonn am 11. Dez. 1948* (Krefeld, Scherpe, 1949); and Hans Fonlipps, *Ordination in den Pastoralen* (Unpublished dissertation, Heidelberg, 1974).

SECTION TWO:
FROM NICEA TO AUGUSTINE

INTRODUCTION

At the beginning of the fourth century A.D., Christians still were suffering for their faith. The efforts of third-century Roman emperors, such as Decius, to exterminate Christianity had failed. In A.D. 303 Emperor Diocletian initiated a new effort to systematically annihilate the faithful. Church buildings were destroyed, all copies of Scripture that could be located were burned publicly. Christians were removed from the protection of the laws, and, finally, death was decreed for all believers. Persecution was fierce throughout the Empire, although in the West it only lasted until A.D. 305, when Diocletian retired as Augustus. Subsequently, Galerius issued an edict (311) allowing Christians in the West to worship their own God. In the East, however, Christians continued to pay with their lives until 324, when Constantine, who had embraced Christianity, united the Empire and became its sole ruler.

Although Constantine gave to the Church privileges previously enjoyed by pagan cults, he did not impose his newly found faith on pagans. Christianity was not yet the religion of the majority of his subjects. Rather, he created a religious pluralism which lasted until A.D. 381 when Theodosius I declared the Empire to be a Christian state.

Constantine had hoped that the Church would serve as a force for unification in the Empire. In this he was to be disappointed. The Church could not hold the Empire together as long as it was itself bitterly divided. And divisive issues surfaced more frequently after Christians were freed from their struggle for survival.

Chief among those controversies which tormented the early fourth-century Church was over the relationship of Persons within the Trinity. In reaction against Monarchian and Sabellian theology, which emphasized the unity of the Godhead, Origen and certain other Neoplatonic Christian thinkers came dangerously close to the opposite extreme of subordination. The theory of emanation by degrees applied by certain of Origen's followers to the Trinity resulted in teaching that the Son was inferior to the Father, and, in turn, that the Holy Spirit was inferior to the Son. The Son had no being before He was generated or created. The Trinity was to be understood in hierarchical terms: God the Father, the highest hierarchy, is the eternal One beyond everthing; the Logos is the second hierarchy and inferior to the first; and the Spirit is the third hierarchy and inferior to the second. All immortal spirits form a fourth hierarchy, lower than the other three. A middle ground between Sabellianism and extreme Origenism was taken by the more traditional followers of Origen who saw no subordination in the Trinity. They were convinced that nothing has been added that was not present in the Godhead from the beginning. The Son is not inferior to the Father, nor the Holy Spirit to the Son.

Conflict over the relation of the Son's divinity to that of the Father eventually boiled over early in the fourth century in what is called the Arian controversy. An Alexandrian presbyter, Arius, publicly charged that his bishop, Alexander, had used Sabellian language. But in his effort to proclaim that the Son had a separate existence from the Father, Arius argued that only God the Father is eternal and unoriginated. There was a time when the Son did not exist. (Origen had stated that there was no time when the Son was not.) The Son's hypostasis is a created one. The Logos is a creature of the Father, the first and noblest of creatures, created out of nothing to serve as an instrument in the rest of creation. Whereas some of the earlier Fathers seemed to teach subordination, Arius espoused it openly and deliberately. Not only did he subordinate the Son's nature to the Father's but he denied that the Son had a divine nature or any divine attributes. The Son is neither consubstantial nor coeternal with the Father. Mary gave birth to this half-god, who is neither fully divine nor fully man. Arius's Jesus is but one of many such half-gods in the Hellenistic-Roman world. But he is not God himself.

Arius did not take the implications of his doctrine of emanation to their inevitable conclusions. Nowhere did he state that the Spirit is less divine than the Son. However, he was charged by his opponents with stating that the essences of the divine Persons are separate in nature, that they are alien and incapable of participating in each other, and ultimately that they are dissimilar in both essence and in glory.[1] He also was said to have composed the *Thalia*, a poem which may have been set to music, which addresses the matter of the relations between Persons in the Godhead. It includes the following refrains:

We praise Him as without beginning because of Him who has a beginning. And adore Him as everlasting, because of Him who in time has come to be. The Unbegun made the Son a beginning of things originated; and advanced Him as a Son to Himself by adoption. He has nothing proper to God in proper subsistence. For He is not equal, no, nor one in essence with Him. Wise is God, for He is the teacher of Wisdom. There is full proof that God is invisible to all beings; both to things which are through the Son, and to the Son He is invisible. I will say it expressly, how by the Son is seen the Invisible; by that power by which God sees, and in His own measure, the Son endures to see the Father, as is lawful. Thus there is a Triad, not in equal glories. Not intermingling with each other are their subsistences. One more glorious than the other in their glories unto immensity. Foreign from the Son in essence is the Father, for He is without beginning. Understand that the Monad was; but the Dyad was not, before it was in existence. It follows at once that, though the Son was not, the Father was God. Hence the Son, not being (for He existed at the will of the Father), is God Only-begotten, and He is alien from either.[2]

Athanasius, a deacon and secretary to the bishop of Alexandria, was the great foe of Arius. He objected to Arianism's soteriology. If the eternal Son of God did not become man in Jesus, we could not be made like God and be given immortality and eternal knowledge. This could never be accomplished by a created being, even the highest. No half-god, no limited power could be the Savior. For the time being, however, Athanasius did not attempt to define the place of the Holy Spirit in his scheme. He, like other leading voices in the early fourth century Church, did not seem to recognize that the Holy Spirit was virtually included in Arius's attack upon the equality of the Son in the Godhead.

In A.D. 325 Emperor Constantine summoned the bishops of the empire by letters of invitation to Nicea in Bithynia for the purpose of dealing with discord in the Church. After considerable debate the Council issued a creedal statement which declared that the Son is coeternal and equal in substance with the Father. But nothing is said like that about the Holy Spirit, either in the Council's discussions or in the Creed itself. Writers of the Creed content themselves on this point with the sentence, "And [we believe] in the Holy Ghost."[3] Unfortunately, Christian leaders of this era tended to react to existing heresy, rather than to anticipate areas for potential heretical growth and Church division. Their failure to deal sufficiently with the question of the Spirit at Nicea clearly left the door open for further controversy in the following decades.

Those bishops and other church leaders who stood by the Creed of Nicea finally chose to go beyond that statement when a covert attack on the person and deity of the Spirit by certain heretics in Egypt constrained them to break their silence. A group of Arians, disillusioned by irreverence in their own group, had come to admit the Nicene position regarding the Son; but then had refused to recognize the Spirit in the Godhead, declaring him to be the greatest of creatures, a ministering spirit, and differing from the angels only in rank. They came to be known as "trope-mongers" (tropes are metaphors) or "Tropici," because they dismissed Scriptures which went against their position as being merely figures of speech. The chief figure in this heretical group was the semi-Arian bishop of Constantinople, Macedonius, from whom adherents later came to be called Macedonians.[4] Athanasius also speaks of them as "enemies of the Spirit,"[5] or "Pneumatomachi."

Once again the anti-Arian champion was Athanasius, who, in response to a letter from Bishop Serapion of Thmuis, declared that the Holy Ghost is a divine person.[6] This position was affirmed by a synod at Alexandria in 362, with Athanasius presiding, which declared that the third Person is of the same substance and divinity as the other Two. The synod also required that "those who say that the Holy Spirit is a Creature and separate from the Essence of Christ" must be anathematized.[7]

Other synods at Alexandria (362), Rome (369, 373, 380), and in various locations in Asia Minor also condemned the Pneumatomachi. But the condemnations did not reach the final official and authoritative level until after one extreme Arian, Eunomius, declared that the Son was the creature of the Uncreated, and that the Spirit was the first and great work of God's greatest creature, the Son. The Spirit, then, was third in the Trinity, not only in order but also in nature.[8] This teaching shocked the Nicenes, as well as some of the more cautious Macedonians.

In 379 Theodosius replaced the Arian emperor Valens. After recovering from a serious illness that beset him shortly thereafter, Theodosius in gratitude issued an edict that all people under his authority should observe the true religion delivered by St. Peter to the Romans and that the remainder should suffer disgrace and such penalties as God and the emperor might impose. Included is a declaration of belief in the single deity of the Father, the Son, and the Holy Spirit, who "are of one majesty and virtue, of the same glory, and of one splendor."[9] Another edict followed (January 381) which extended this imperial policy to the entire Eastern empire. Theodosius then called a Church Council at Constantinople (381) to sanction his acts. No Western representatives attended, and the Macedonians who accepted the invitation left early. The Council reaffirmed the Creed of Nicea but added to the third article, "And [we believe] in the Holy Ghost," the new terminology, "the Lord and Giver-of-Life, who proceedeth from the Father, who with the Father and the Son together is worshipped and glorified, who spake by the prophets."[10] The Creed of Constantinople as found in Epiphanius's *Ancoratus*, adds that every heresy which says that "There was a time when the Son of God was not, and before he was begotten he was not, or that he was of things which are not, or that he is of a different hypostasis or substance, or pretend that he is effluent or changeable" be anathematized.[11] While not directly in words, the Creed of Constantinople in effect affirms the deity of the Holy Spirit, which the heretics had either denied or refused to assert, by requiring for Him divine dignity and worship.

By declaring that the Holy Spirit proceeds from the Father, the Arian position was rejected. However, this did not entirely settle the relation of the third Person to the Trinity. There still remained the question of His relation to the Son. The area of conflict grew out of passages in the Fourth Gospel. The Spirit proceeds from the Father (John 14:16), but He also is sent by the Son (John 15:26, 16:7), and receives from the Son (John 16:14). By the fourth century the Greek Church already was teaching a procession from the Father *through the Son*, while the Western Latin Church held that the procession was from the Father *and the Son (filioque)*. It is true that the issue was not always so clearly divided by geography or language. Stating what was to become the recognized Eastern position, Athanasius and the Cappadocians taught that the Spirit is not created by the Son but eternally proceeds directly from the Father and is mediated by the Son. But not all Eastern theologians agreed. Epiphanius and Cyril of Jerusalem derived the *Hagia Pneuma* from the Father and the Son, while Theodore of Mopsuestia went to the opposite extreme by allowing for no dependence of the Spirit on the Son.

The procession issue was not clarified in the West until Augustine's position gained general acceptance. At the Council of Toledo in 589 the *filioque* clause was inserted in the Niceno-Constantinopolitan Creed, together with an anathema against its opponents (here meaning the Arians, not the Greeks). The Eastern Church, which made the Nicene Creed, was never consulted. However, controversy did not break out immediately. Actual conflict between Greek and Latin churches developed in A.D. 867 when patriarch Photius condemned the *filioque* clause as a heretical addition to the Creed. From this point onward, it served as one of the worst causes of the friction between East and West which eventually led to schism in A.D. 1054.

Controversies over the equality of the Holy Spirit within the Godhead and over the manner of His procession were accompanied by another dispute over the relation which the Spirit bore to the incarnate Word. The central figure in this theological struggle was Nestorius, a monk at Antioch, perhaps one of Theodore of

Mopsuestia's disciples, who became patriarch of Constantinople in
A.D. 428. He was known early for his battles against the Arians,
the Novatians, and Macedonians—especially after he convinced the
emperor to enact more severe laws against these heretical groups.
His reputation worked against him when, shortly after his elevation
to the see of Constantinople, he was himself accused of heresy.

Nestorius was distressed by the popular use of the term
theotokos, "bearer of God," which was sometimes applied to the
Virgin Mary by such writers as Origen, Athanasius, Basil, and
others. Like Theodore of Mopsuestia before him, Nestorius argued
that Mary bore Jesus, not the Logos, for the Logos was
omnipresent. He preferred the expression *Christotokos*,
"Christbearer," or even *theodochos*, "God-receiving." By his
reasoning, the Spirit did not conceive the Logos but formed within
the Virgin's womb the man who was assumed by the Word.
Afterwards the Spirit came down upon Him at baptism, glorifying
Him and giving Him power to do miraculous works. The Spirit also
gave Him authority over unclean spirits and ultimately gave Him
the power to ascend to heaven.[12]

Nestorius's opponents found in his teachings not only that the
Logos did not truly become man but also that the incarnate Son
received the Spirit from without as by a superior Power. The anti-
Nestorians argued that the Spirit was the Logos's very own and that
the works done by the Son were by His own divine power. Their
position is best expressed by Cyril of Alexandria in a letter to his
opponent, Nestorius:

> We do not say that the Word of God dwelt in him as in a common
> man born of the holy Virgin, lest Christ be thought of as a Godbearing
> man; for although the Word tabernacled among us, it is also said that
> in Christ "dwelt all the fulness of the Godhead bodily." . . . One
> therefore is Christ both Son and Lord, not as if a man had attained
> only such a conjuction with God as consists in a unity of dignity alone
> or of authority. For it is not equality of nature which unites them;
> for then Peter and John, who were of equal honour with each other,
> being both Apostles and holy disciples [would have been one, and],
> yet the two are not one. Neither do we understand the manner of
> conjunction to be apposition, for this does not suffice for natural
> oneness. . . . But we do not call the Word of God the Father, the
> God nor the Lord of Christ, lest we openly cut in two the one Christ,
> the Son and Lord, and fall under the charge of blasphemy, making
> him the God and Lord of himself. For the Word of God, as we have
> said already, was made hypostatically one in flesh, yet he is God of all
> and he rules all; but he is not the slave of himself, nor his own
> Lord. . . . Yet we are not ignorant that while he remained God, he
> also became man and subject to God, according to the law suitable to
> the nature of manhood. . . . And although according to his own
> nature he was not subject to suffering, yet he suffered for us in the
> flesh according to the Scriptures, and although impassible, yet in his
> Crucified Body he made his own the sufferings of his own flesh.[13]

Emperor Theodosius II summoned the Third General Council at Ephesus in 431 to solve problems raised by the Nestorian controversy. Nestorius was deposed from his see and excommunicated. His theology was condemned, and the term *theotokos* was reaffirmed.

This decision was of critical importance to the future of the Church, not only in its understanding of the natures of Christ but also in its treatment of the Virgin Mary and of the third Person of the Trinity. Tillich has observed that from the very time that the Spirit was declared to be divine in the same sense as the Son (i.e., at the Second General Council at Constantinople in 381), the Spirit was progressively replaced in actual popular piety by the Virgin Mary.[14] If we accept Tillich's conclusion, it remains for us to determine why such a shift in piety might have occurred. While piety of the church fathers was directed towards God, who was considered to be both transcendent and immanent during this period, popular piety seems to have moved more towards that which seemed immediate. This certainly was true of those converts to Christianity from pagan religions which venerated mother goddesses and easily transferred their piety from one mother to another. The Virgin Mary was portrayed as the Mother of God, a warm and caring figure, a mother who was immediate and ever ready to assist mankind. On the other hand, while certain fourth century A.D. church fathers wrote effectively of the Spirit's vital role in the redemptive act of God, and even of His continuous operation in the Church, the overall impression left in the popular mind was one of His transcendence, not of His immanence.

One must be cautious, however, in accepting Tillich's conclusion without certain reservations. To the fourth century Christian writer, the Virgin Mary was the classic case study in how the Holy Spirit operated in human life. It would be fair to suggest that Mary was now being portrayed as the earthly locus of the Spirit. Certainly this conception was reinforced at Ephesus through the elevated position acknowledged for the Virgin as the *theotokos*. Later in the history of the Catholic Church she would be known as the spouse of the Holy Spirit.[15] After 381 the Holy Spirit was accepted as fully divine by the faithful but was understood primarily as a transcendent Being. From this point onward, the divine Spirit was never to become important for Christian piety for the vast majority of Christians.

Notes to Introduction

[1]Athanasius, *Defence of the Nicene Definition* iii.6, NPF 2nd Series 4:153-154.

²Athanasius, *Councils of Ariminium and Seleucia* ii.15, NPF 2nd Series 4:457.
³*The Nicene Creed*, NPF 2nd Series 14:3.
⁴Socrates, *Ecclesiastical History* ii.45, NPF 2nd Series 2:73-74; Sozomen, *Ecclesiastical History* iv.27, NPF 2nd Series 2:322-323.
⁵Athanasius, *Letter to Serapion* iv.1, in C.R.B. Shapland, *The Letters of Saint Athanasius Concerning the Holy Spirit* (London: The Epworth Press, 1951).
⁶Ibid., iii.5, Shapland, 174-175.
⁷Athanasius, *Letter to the Church at Antioch* iii, NPF 2nd Series 4:484.
⁸PG 29:col. 661.
⁹*The Theodosian Code* xvi.1.2-3, in Colman J. Berry, ed., *Readings in Church History* (New York: Newman Press, 1960), 1:142-143.
¹⁰*The Creed of Constantinople*, NPF 2nd Series 14:163.
¹¹Ibid., 164.
¹²Nestorius quoted in *The Third Ecumenical Council of Ephesus* ix, xi, xii, NPF 2nd Series 14:215, 217. Also see Theodoret, *Counter Statement to the Anathema IX of Cyril of Alexander*, NPF 2nd Series 14:214-216.
¹³*The Epistle of Cyril to Nestorius with the XII Anathematisms*, NPF 2nd Series 14:202-203.
¹⁴Paul Tillich, *A History of Christian Thought* (New York: Harper and Row, 1968), 78.
¹⁵E.g., John J. Wynne, (trans.), *The Great Encyclical Letters of Pope Leo XIII* (New York, Cincinnati: Benziger Brothers, 1903), 440.

CHAPTER FIVE

POST-NICENE GREEK FATHERS: ALEXANDRIA AND ANTIOCH

The end of persecution by the Roman State marked the beginning of the Golden Age of ecclesiastical literature and learning. The fourth and fifth centuries, which is the period of decline and collapse for Imperial Rome, also is a time when Christian thinkers monopolized intellectual life. This age is alive with theological controversy, featuring writers who combined the best education available with rare mental abilities and strong practical piety. These individuals justly are called "Fathers" of the Church, not only because they protected the faith against error but also because they have exercised a powerful influence on the entire history of Christianity to come through their impact on the developing ecclesiastical tradition.

The centers of theological development in the Greek East were Alexandria and Antioch. Eusebius of Caesarea, Didymus the Blind, Athanasius, and the three Cappadocians: Basil of Caesarea, Gregory of Nyssa, and Gregory of Nazianzen are prominent representatives of the Alexandrian school. Theodore of Mopsuestia and John Chrysostom belong to the school of Antioch. The two schools differed both in philosophy and in method. Alexandrians tended to be Platonists; Antiochans preferred Aristotle. Alexandrians emphasized the allegorical-mystical interpretation popularized in the third century by Origen. Antiochans were inclined toward a grammatical-historical explanation of Scripture. When faced with the continued opposition of the Arians after Nicea, the two schools reacted differently. Alexandria displayed right-wing Origenism, with its emphasis on the transcendence of God in which Word and Wisdom (Son and Holy Spirit) are viewed as intermediate beings between God and the world. Antioch generally was anti-Origenist.

The absence of a united front made it possible for the Arian leaders to continue their attack upon elements of the divided East separately. Disagreement between various anti-Arian factions continued until a new Nicene generation, led by the Cappadocians, developed formulas that made it possible to reach an understanding among the majority of bishops and theologians.

This chapter concentrates on the efforts of leading Eastern Fathers in the fourth and fifth centuries to explain and define the Holy Spirit and His offices. The efforts of the leading Alexandrians and Antiochians eventually culminated in the teachings of the three Cappadocians. Their contribution will be considered in Chapter 6.

1. EUSEBIUS

Eusebius of Caesarea (ca. 260-339), the court theologian of Emperor Constantine, is recognized by most scholars as the first great Christian historian. We know little of his early life, except that he was the pupil, perhaps the slave, of a learned priest, Pamphilus of Caesarea, after whom he called himself Eusebius Pamphili. While his mentor suffered martyrdom in the late third century, Eusebius did not share his fate. He survived the last great persecution to become bishop of Caesarea in Palestine, a position he retained until his death.

Like Pamphilus, Eusebius was a follower of Origen. This is particularly noticeable in his doctrine of the Trinity, in which the Son is subordinated to the Father. One can understand this tendency in view of the fact that the late third-century Church considered Sabellianism to be the greatest theological danger to orthodoxy. After the Arian controversy broke out, Eusebius wrote a letter to Alexander, Bishop of Alexandria, remonstrating with him for having deposed Arius. Eusebius was in agreement with Arius that the Son was himself God, but not true God. He differed with the deposed presbyter by declaring that the Son was begotten, thereby implying that He is of one substance with the Father.[1]

Such was the attitude of Eusebius when he arrived at the First Ecumenical Council at Nicea in A.D. 325, where he played a prominent role. He was seated in the first seat to the right of the emperor and delivered the inaugural address when Constantine joined the assembled bishops. When the main subject, for which the Council had been called, came under discussion, Eusebius presented the local creed of Caesarea, the creed of his baptism:

> We believe in One God, the Father Almighty, the Maker of all things visible and invisible. And in One Lord Jesus Christ, the Word of God, God from God, Light from Light, Life from Life, Son Only-begotten, first-born of every creature, before all the ages, begotten from the Father, by whom also all things were made; who for our salvation was

made flesh, and lived among men, and suffered, and rose again the third day, and ascended to the Father, and will come again in glory to judge the quick and dead. And we believe also in One Holy Ghost; believing each of These to be and to exist, the Father truly Father, and the Son truly Son, and the Holy Ghost truly Holy Ghost, as also our Lord, sending forth His disciples for the preaching, said, "Go, teach all nations, baptizing them in the Name of the Father, and of the Son, and of the Holy Ghost." Concerning whom we confidently affirm that so we hold, and so we think, and so we have held aforetime, and we maintain this faith unto the death, anathematizing every godless heresy. That this we have ever thought from our heart and soul, from the time we recollect ourselves, and now think and say in truth, before God Almighty and our Lord Jesus Christ do we witness, being able by proofs to show and to convince you, that, even in times past, such has been our belief and preaching.[2]

The Caesarean creed was pre-Arian and distinctly anti-Sabellian. It did not exclude an Arian interpretation, however. The emperor was satisfied with the orthodoxy of this creed, although he inserted the expression, "One in substance." The assembled Fathers, however, did not stop here, adding other insertions and alterations. After receiving explanations of the Council's intended meanings of such expressions as "of the same substance with the Father," "begotten, not made," and "of the same substance," Eusebius signed the creed, which contained a statement anathematizing the chief teachings of Arius. Here he demonstrates his intentions as a peacemaker. From this point on he can be described as mildly orthodox. He never again defended Arian doctrine. But he never became an Athanasian either. On occasions his hostility rose against extremists who seemed to represent a revived Sabellianism. Chief among these was Marcellus, bishop of Ancyra, against whom he composed two works: *Contra Marcellum* and *De ecclesiastica theologia*.

Marcellus taught that the Father, the Son, and the Holy Spirit are not three hypostases (persons), but rather one hypostasis under three names. Further, Marcellus did not allow for the preexistence of the Son as a distinct personality before the Incarnation.[3] Eusebius responds that Marcellus has shown himself a "downright Jew" or "a new Sabellius."[4] The Holy Spirit is different from the Son, for He comes after the Son has departed. He indwells saints whom the Son has redeemed. He sanctifies all He indwells, imparting His gifts to prophets, apostles, and their successors in the Church. However, only the Son shares the honor of the Father. The Son alone creates all things that are made, including the Holy Spirit. The Son has dominion over all things, even over the Spirit.[5]

This subordination, which is reminiscent of Origen and not Arius, is developed further in Eusebius's *Preparatio Evangelica:*

"For there is one glory of the sun, and another glory of the moon, and another glory of the stars," says the divine Apostle. . . . In this way, therefore, we must think of the order in incorporeal and intelligent Beings also, the unutterable and infinite power of the God of the universe embracing all of them together; and the second place, next to the Father, being held by the power of the Divine Word, at once creative and illuminating. . . . And next after this Being there is set, as in place of a moon, a third Being, the Holy Spirit, whom also they enroll in the first and royal dignity and honour of the primal cause of the universe, He also having been appointed by the Maker of the universe for a ruling principle of the created things which came after, those I mean which are lower in rank, and need the help which He supplies.

But this Spirit, holding a third rank, supplies those beneath out of the superior powers in Himself, notwithstanding that He also receives from another, that is from the higher and stronger, who, as we said, is second to the most high and unbegotten nature of God the King of all: from whom indeed God the Word is Himself supplied, and drawing as it were from an ever-flowing fountain which pours forth Deity, imparts copiously and ungrudgingly of the radiance of His own light to all, and especially to the Holy Spirit Himself, who is closer to Him than all and very near; and then to the intelligent and divine powers after him.

But the partial gifts He dispenses to those who are in part worthy through the ministration and mediatorship of the Second, in the measure attainable by each: and of these gifts the perfect and supremely holy have been bestowed by the Father on Him who is third from Himself, and receives the gifts through the Son, but is ruler and leader of those who follow.

Hence the whole body of Hebrew theologians, after Him who is God over all, and after Wisdom His firstborn, regard as God the third holy Power which they call Holy Spirit, and by which they were enlightened and inspired.[6]

Eusebius refers on two occasions to individuals who enjoyed unusual richness of life in the Spirit. The first involves a man named Quadratus who, along with the daughters of Philip, was renowned for prophetic gifts. Of these and numerous other "successors of the apostles," Eusebius reports that "A great many wonderful works were done through them by the power of the divine Spirit, so that at the first hearing whole multitudes of men eagerly embraced the religion of the Creator of the universe."[7] Eusebius also mentions twice Melito, Bishop of Sardis, "the Eunuch who lived altogether in the Holy Spirit."[8] Jerome quotes Tertullian's On Ecstasy (no longer extant), in which he refers to the same Melito as one whom many presumed to be a prophet. Apparently, Melito lived in the reign of Marcus Aurelius and was similarly disposed to a prophetic ministry as were the Montanists. However, he opposed Montanism and for that earned Tertullian's satire.[9]

Eusebius's own reaction to Montanism is extremely negative. The "New Prophecy" he renames "false prophecy" and "novelty."[10] He reminds his readers of the distinction Christ drew between true and false prophets.[11] The Montanists, he concludes, have been inspired by the devil, not the Holy Spirit.

> Thus by artifice, or rather by such a system of wicked craft, the devil, devising destruction for the disobedient, and being unworthily honored by them, secretly excited and inflamed their understandings which had already become estranged from the true faith.[12]

The spirit motivating the Montanists is called "the arrogant spirit which taught them to revile the entire universal Church under heaven, because the spirit of false prophecy received neither honor from it nor entrance into it."[13] Eusebius then gathers the witness of other writers against the Montanists: Asterius Urbanus, Miltiades, Apollinus, and Serapion,[14] without whose evidence our knowledge of the Phrygian enthusiasts would be much more limited.

It is clear from other Eusebian writings that his objection to the Montanists is not one directed against prophecy or any other charismata. In his commentary on Isaiah Eusebius compares the power and operations of the seraphim with the holy men of God who share most excellent charismata, such as prophecy, the healing of diseases, raising the dead, speaking in tongues, and sharing in wisdom and knowledge.[15] His discussion of Psalms 78:18 includes a comparison of the lightning accompanying a storm with the gifts of the Spirit which lighten the world.[16] In his comments on Psalm 65:4 he declares that the blessings of God's house are the charismata of the Holy Spirit, by which the Church has been adorned.[17]

Throughout the course of Christian history there have been key figures who have placed unity in the Church above all other considerations. Eusebius stands as one of the great voices for unity in the fourth century A.D. For the sake of unity, he accepted the decisions of the Nicene Council, even though they went beyond his personal doctrinal persuasion. He attacked the New Prophecy, not because he disdained the charismata, but rather because he despised the prophetic abuse of self-proclaimed practitioners operating outside the mainstream Church. His concern for unity in the Church was shared by his Emperor Constantine, who wished to advance the cause of unity in the empire by first uniting the Christian Church. Eusebius and Constantine—two great champions of order—remained mutual supporters throughout their lifetimes. After the emperor's death in 337, the historian composed a biography in which royal victories are depicted as divine successes:

> Then as if to bring a divine array against this enemy, he convoked a general council, and invited the speedy attendance of bishops from all

quarters, in letters expressive of the honorable estimation in which he held them. . . . Now when they were all assembled, it appeared evident that the proceeding was the work of God, inasmuch as men who had been widely separated, not merely in sentiment, but also personally, and by difference of country, place, and nation, were here brought together, and comprised within the walls of a single city, forming as it were a vast garland of priests, composed of a variety of the choicest flowers.[18]

At the conclusion of the Council, Constantine exhorted all assembled to obey its decrees:

Receive, then, with all willingness this truly Divine injunction, and regard it as in truth the gift of God. For whatever is determined in the holy assemblies of the bishops is to be regarded as indicative of the Divine will. As soon, therefore, as you have communicated these proceedings to all our beloved brethren, you are bound from that time forward to adopt for yourselves, and to enjoin on others the arrangements above mentioned, and the due observance of this most sacred day; and whenever I come into the presence of your love, which I have long desired, I may have it in my power to celebrate the holy feast with you on the same day, and may rejoice with you on all accounts, when I behold the cruel power of Satan removed by Divine aid through the agency of our endeavors, while your faith, and peace, and concord everywhere flourish. God preserve you, beloved brethren![19]

2. CYRIL OF JERUSALEM

According to his own testimony, Cyril of Jerusalem "was born of pious parents professing the orthodox faith and was bred up in the same in the reign of Constantine."[20] He became bishop of Jerusalem in 350, an office he held, with three intervals of exile, until his death in 386. Of his early clerical career in Jerusalem we have little information except for the comments of Jerome who was unfriendly to Cyril because of his violent quarrel with Cyril's successor and admirer, Bishop John of Jerusalem. Jerome pictures Cyril as engaged in a long period of squabbling within the ranks of the Arians. While Jerome's intent appears to be malicious, his charge that Cyril was associated with Arians and semi-Arians during his early episcopacy is not without foundation. However, late in his career Cyril gained the reputation of preserving the faith against Arianism. By the Council of 381 he openly joined the Nicenes.

The early Church had developed a process for preparing adult converts for baptism which was both long and arduous. When they were ready to receive instruction, converts were enrolled as catechumens and admitted to part of the liturgical worship of the Christian community. The "catechumen" was one who was receiving instruction from a teacher. The process of such instruction and the content thereof were known as "catechesis."

By the fourth century, the forty days before Easter, or Lent, had been designated to be used for the spiritual discipline of the faithful and for the preparation of catechumens to be baptized on Easter eve. The twenty-four catechetical lectures of Cyril were aimed, therefore, at baptizanes, not at the general public. An exceptional witness to the Church's teaching in the middle of the fourth century, they stand as Cyril's chief surviving work.

The occasion of Easter baptism called for frequent reference to the Holy Spirit, since baptism is the sacrament of the Spirit. In Lecture IV, a summary of doctrines which is divided into ten heads, Cyril provides his hearers with a brief statement on the Person and work of the Spirit:

> Believe thou also in the Holy Ghost, and hold the same opinion concerning Him, which thou hast received to hold concerning the Father and the Son, and follow not those who teach blasphemous things of Him. But learn thou that this Holy Spirit is One, indivisible, of manifold power; having many operations, yet not Himself divided; Who knoweth the mysteries, Who searcheth all things, even the deep things of God: Who descended upon the Lord Jesus Christ in form of a dove; Who wrought in the Law and in the Prophets; Who now also at the season of Baptism sealeth thy soul; of Whose holiness also every intellectual nature hath need: against Whom if any dare to blaspheme, he hath no forgiveness, neither in this world, nor in that which is to come: "Who with the Father and the Son together" is honoured with the glory of the Godhead: of Whom also thrones, and dominions, principalities, and powers have need. For there is One God, the Father of Christ; and One Lord Jesus Christ, the Only-begotten Son of the Only God; and One Holy Ghost, the sanctifier and deifier of all, Who spake in the Law and in the Prophets, in the Old and in the New Testament.

> Have thou ever in thy mind this seal, which for the present has been lightly touched in my discourse, by way of summary, but shall be stated, should the Lord permit, to the best of my power with the proof from the Scriptures.[21]

Cyril's theology of the Holy Spirit is presented in greater detail and with unusual sensitivity in Lectures XVI and XVII. He chooses to confine himself to what is said of the Spirit in Holy Writ. Anything additional is vain, even dangerous, speculation:

> Spiritual in truth is the grace we need, in order to discourse concerning the Holy Spirit; not that we may speak what is worthy of Him, for this is impossible, but that by speaking the words of the divine Scriptures, we may run our course without danger.

> It must therefore belong to Jesus Christ's grace itself to grant both to us to speak without deficiency, and to you to hear with discretion; for discretion is needful not to them only who speak, but also to them that hear, lest they hear one thing, and misconceive another in their mind. Let us then speak concerning the Holy Ghost nothing but what is written; and whatsoever is not written let us not busy ourselves about

it. . . . Now the Holy Ghost is a Power most mighty, a Being divine and unsearchable.[22]

Cyril's concern that believers should not speculatively explore the Spirit's nature and being grew in part out of his pastoral distaste for those individuals who had led others astray into irreverent speculation.

We would now say somewhat concerning the Holy Ghost; not to declare His substance with exactness, for this were impossible; but to speak of the diverse mistakes of some concerning him, lest from ignorance we should fall into them; and to block up the paths of error, that we may journey on the King's one highway.[23]

Among the "most profane" of all speculators were those who claimed to be the Holy Ghost himself. Cyril mentions Simon the Sorcerer, certain Gnostics and Valentinians, and Manes in this category. In addition, he refers to a group of heretics who had taught that the Spirit is different in the Prophets than in the New Testament. The Marcionists had torn away the sayings of the Old Testament from the New. The Cataphrygians or Phrygian Montanists had been guilty of lust and extreme cruelty to children, at the very time that Montanus was claiming to be the Holy Spirit.[24] Manes, who combined what was bad in every heresy, also declared himself to be the Comforter.[25] Cyril accuses Manes, as he does all such irreverent speculators, of having made "havoc of the Church, or rather of those outside the Church, roaming about like a lion and devouring."[26]

Having dispensed with heretics, Cyril returns to the Scriptures, to "drink waters out of our own cisterns and out of our own springing wells." "Drink we of living water, springing up into everlasting life (John 4:14); but this spake the Saviour of the Spirit, which they that believe on Him should receive (John 7:38, 39)."[27] Again and again Cyril refers to the grace of the Spirit as water. This he explains in a passage that is lofty in concept, eloquent in expression:

And why did He call the grace of the Spirit water? Because by water all things subsist; because water brings forth grass and living things; because the water of the showers comes down from heaven; because it comes down one in form, but works in many forms. For one fountain watereth the whole of Paradise, and one and the same rain comes down upon all the world, yet it becomes white in the lily, and red in the rose, and purple in violets and hyacinths, and different and varied in each several kind: so it is one in the palmtree, and another in the vine, and all in all things; and yet is one in nature, not diverse from itself; for the rain does not change itself, and come down first as one thing, then as another, but adapting itself to the constitution of each thing which receives it, it becomes to each what is suitable. Thus also the Holy Ghost, being one, and of one nature, and indivisible, divides to each His grace, according as He will: and as the dry tree, after partaking of water, puts forth shoots, so also the soul in sin, when it

has been through repentance made worthy of the Holy Ghost, brings
forth clusters of righteousness. And though He is One in nature, yet
many are the virtues which by the will of God and in the Name of
Christ He works.[28]

In this context Cyril speaks of the gifts of the Spirit:

For He employs the tongue of one man for wisdom; the soul of
another He enlightens by Prophecy, to another He gives power to
drive away devils, to another He gives to interpret the divine
Scriptures. He strengthens one man's self-command; He teaches
another the way to give alms; another He teaches to fast and discipline
himself; another He teaches to despise the things of the body; another
He trains for martyrdom; diverse in different men, yet not diverse
from Himself, as it is written [Here Cyril alludes to 1 Cor 12:7-11].[29]

Cyril's addition of chastity, virginity, and preparation for
martyrdom to scriptural gift lists is particularly interesting, for it
reveals how important such evidences of holiness were in the fourth
century. Later in the same lecture he refers again to chastity and
virginity as gifts and adds voluntary poverty:

Throughout the world He gives to one chastity, to another perpetual
virginity, to another almsgiving, to another voluntary poverty, to
another power of repelling hostile spirits. And as the light, with one
touch of its radiance sheds brightness on all things, so also the Holy
Ghost enlightens those who have eyes; for if any from blindness is not
vouchsafed His grace, let him not blame the Spirit, but his own
unbelief.[30]

As a pastor, Cyril understands the Spirit's gifts to be antidotes
for defilement of the believer brought about by wealth, rank, and
covetousness of the flesh.

And if ever, while thou has been sitting here, a thought concerning
chastity or virginity has come into thy mind, it has been His teaching.
Has not often a maiden, already at the bridal threshold, fled away, He
teaching her the doctrine of virginity? Has not often a man
distinguished at court, scorned wealth and rank, under the teaching of
the Holy Ghost? Has not often a young man, at the sight of beauty,
closed his eyes, and fled from the sight, and escaped the defilement?
Askest thou whence this has come to pass? The Holy Ghost taught the
soul of the young man. Many ways of covetousness are there in the
world; yet Christians refuse possessions: wherefore? because of the
teaching of the Holy Ghost. Worthy of honour is in truth that Spirit,
holy and good; and fitting are we baptized into Father, Son, and Holy
Spirit.[31]

Cyril is careful to distinguish between the Holy Spirit and other
forces which are called spirits. He, the Spirit, is neither an
impersonal force of nature, like the wind, nor a hostile or evil
force.

Since the name of spirit is given to different things, it is right to see
what is that which is distinctively called the Holy Spirit. For many
things are called spirits. Thus an Angel is called spirit, our soul is
called spirit, and this wind which is blowing is called spirit; and
impure practice is called spirit; and a devil our adversary is called

spirit. Beware therefore when thou hearest these things, lest from their having a common name thou mistake one for another. . . . The Holy Spirit is not pronounced by the tongue; but He is a Living Spirit, who gives wisdom of speech, Himself speaking and discoursing.

But sin also is called spirit, as I have already said; only in another sense, as when it is said, "The spirit of whoredom caused them to err." The name "spirit" is given also to the unclean spirit, the devil; but with the addition of, "the unclean;" for to each is joined its distinguishing name, to mark its proper nature. . . . For this name of spirit is common to many things; and everything which has not a solid body is in a general way called spirit.[32]

The Holy Spirit's work is uplifting, strengthening, and beneficial. His approach is gentle:

For His doings tend the contrary way; towards what is good and salutary. First, His coming is gentle; the perception of Him is fragrant; His burden most light; beams of light and knowledge gleam forth before His coming. He comes with the bowels of a true guardian; for He comes to save, and to heal, to teach, to admonish, to strengthen, to exhort, to enlighten the mind, first of him who receives Him, and afterwards of others also, through him. And as a man, who being previously in darkness then suddenly beholds the sun, is enlightened in his bodily sight, and sees plainly things which he saw not, so likewise he to whom the Holy Ghost is vouchsafed, is enlightened in his soul, and sees things beyond man's sight, which he knew not . . . for the True Enlightener is present with him. The man is within the walls of a house; yet the power of his knowledge reaches far and wide, and he sees what other men are doing.[33]

The Spirit, then, is a mighty protector against evil forces, a teacher, the Comforter who makes intercession to God for believers, and the One Who reveals the kingdom of heaven to individuals called upon for martyrdom. He works "suitably for each."[34] If anyone does not receive His grace, let him not blame the Spirit, but only his own misbelief. The prophets on earth and the archangels in heaven are not His equals, and have need of His sanctifying power, and His rule from God. In Him is the fullness of the King's spiritual bounty.[35]

After this rich exposition of the offices of the Spirit, the 16th Lecture concludes with a reminder that Christians should not attempt to venture beyond what is recorded in Scripture of His nature or substance. "It is sufficient for our salvation to know, that there is the Father, the Son, and Holy Ghost."[36]

Cyril's 17th Catechetical Lecture opens with an enumeration of the many names of the Third Person in the Godhead: the Spirit of Truth, the Comforter, the Spirit of God, the Spirit of the Father, the Spirit of the Lord, the Spirit of God and Christ, the Spirit of Jesus Christ, the Spirit of holiness, the Spirit of adoption, the Spirit of revelation, the Spirit of promise, the Spirit of grace, the Spirit of wisdom and understanding, of counsel and might, of knowledge, of godliness, and of the fear of God.[37] Cyril then directs his hearers to the work of the Spirit in the Incarnation, in the family of Zacharias, Elizabeth and John the Baptist, in the baptism of Jesus, in the descent of the Spirit on the Day of Pentecost, and in the ministry of the apostles and the early Church.

However, it is with preparation for baptism that Cyril is primarily concerned in the Catechetical Lectures. Throughout he links the sacrament of baptism with the work of the Holy Spirit.[38] The most comprehensive statement of this type occurs at the end of the 17th Lecture when he prepared his hearers for the actual moment of baptism. Cyril issues a stiff warning against hypocrisy lest the individual baptized by man fail to be baptized also by the Spirit. There follows a strong declaration of the offices of the Spirit in the remission of sins, in baptizing and in sealing the believer. We also are given a glimpse into Cyril's perception of the fullness of life in the Spirit. Here he speaks of the granting of supernatural power, the gift of prophecy, the Spirit's abiding presence and protection, and gifts of grace of all kinds, including the fruits of the Spirit as listed in Galatians 5:22-23:

> For, at the season of baptism, when thou art come before the Bishops, or Presbyters, or Deacons . . . approach the Minister of Baptism, but approaching, think not of the fact of him thou seest, but remember this Holy Ghost of whom we are now speaking. For He is present in readiness to seal thy soul, and He shall give thee that Seal at which evil spirits tremble, a heavenly and sacred seal, as also it is written, "In whom also we were sealed with the Holy Spirit of promise."

> Yet He tries the soul. He casts not His pearls before swine; if thou play the hypocrite, though men baptize thee now, the Holy Spirit will not baptize thee. But if thou approach with faith, though men minister in what is seen, the Holy Ghost bestows that which is unseen. thou art coming to a great trial, to a great muster, in that one hour, which if thou throw away, thy disaster is irretrievable; but if thou be counted worthy of the grace, thy soul will be enlightened, thou wilt receive a power which thou hadst not, thou wilt receive weapons terrible to the evil spirits; and if thou cast not away thine arms, but keep the Seal upon thy soul, no evil spirit will approach thee; for he will be cowed; for verily by the Spirit of God are the evil spirits cast out.

> If thou believe, thou shalt not only receive remission of sins, but also do things which pass man's power. And mayest thou be worthy of the gift of prophecy also! For thou shalt receive grace according to the measure of thy capacity and not of my words; for I may possibly speak of but small things, yet thou mayest receive greater; since faith is a large affair. All thy life long will thy guardian the Comforter abide with thee; He will care for thee, as for his own soldier; for thy goings out, and thy comings in, and thy plotting foes. And He will give thee gifts of grace of every kind, if thou grieve Him not by sin; for it is written, "And grieve not the Holy Spirit of God, whereby ye were sealed unto the day of redemption." What then, beloved, is it to

preserve grace? Be ye ready to receive grace, and when ye have received it cast it not away . . . that we may ever render up fruits of the Holy Ghost, love, joy, peace, long-suffering, gentleness, goodness, faith, meekness, temperance.[39]

When the newly baptized Christian came up from the baptismal water, he was anointed with scented oil while receiving the laying on of hands. The entire ceremony was called by the Greeks "chrism," of which the "unction" or anointing was always the most important. In the Latin West the term "confirmation" developed later, suggesting that greater importance was attached to the laying on of hands.

While the Catechetical Lectures were pre-baptismal, Cyril's Mystagogic Lectures were given to believers after baptism. In the 3rd Mystagogic Lecture he refers to the anointing or chrismation of the baptized:

Now ye have been made Christ's, by receiving the antitype of the Holy Ghost; and all things have been wrought in you by imitation, because ye are images of Christ. He washed in the river Jordan, and having imparted of the fragrance of His Godhead to the waters, He came up from them; and the Holy Ghost in the fulness of his being lighted on Him, like resting upon like. And to you in like manner, after you had come up from the pool of the sacred streams, there was given an Unction, the antitype of that where with Christ was anointed; and this is the Holy Ghost.[40]

The anointing balm is not common ointment, for it introduces the presence of the Holy Spirit in sanctifying power:

But beware of supposing this to be plain ointment. For as the Bread of the Eucharist, after the invocation of the Holy Ghost, is mere bread no longer, but the body of Christ, so also this holy ointment is no more simple ointment, nor (so to say) common, after in vocation, but it is Christ's gift of grace, and, by the advent of the Holy Ghost, is made fit to impart His Divine nature. Which ointment is symbolically applied to thy forehead and thy other senses; and while thy body is sanctified by the Holy and life-giving Spirit.[41]

It is not certain from Cyril's writings whether the Spirit is received at baptism or in chrism. He declares in his 17th Catechetical Lecture that the Spirit baptizes the true believer when he goes beneath the water. At this point the Holy Spirit "bestows that which is unseen." He is present to seal the believer's soul.[42] However, in the 3rd Mystagogic Lecture Cyril states:

For as Christ after His Baptism, and the visitation of the Holy Ghost, went forth and vanquished the adversary, so likewise ye, after Holy Baptism and the Mystical Chrism, having put on the whole armour of the Holy Ghost, are to stand against the power of the adversary, and vanquish it, saying, "I can do all things through Christ which strengtheneth me."[43]

Despite the scholarly debate that has attended the question of when Cyril believed that the Spirit came upon the believer, it is unlikely that any conclusive answer will be forthcoming. It may be that those who have so hotly argued this question have attempted to draw a distinction that did not exist in Cyril's mind. At more than one place in his lectures Cyril seems to treat baptism and chrism as components in one and the same vital process.

Cyril also deals with the role of the Holy Spirit in the Eucharist. In the final Mystagogic Lecture, "On the Sacred Liturgy and Communion," he informs his neophytes that in the Eucharist

> We beseech the merciful God to send forth His Holy Spirit upon the gifts lying before Him; that He may make the Bread the Body of Christ, and the Wine the Blood of Christ; for whatsoever the Holy Ghost has touched, is surely sanctified and changed.[44]

Later in this lecture, speaking of the liturgical formula which precedes the communion of the people, Cyril states:

> After this the Priest says, "Holy things to holy men." Holy are the gifts presented, having received the visitation of the Holy Ghost; the holy things therefore correspond to the holy persons. Then ye say, "One is Holy, One is the Lord, Jesus Christ." For One is truly holy, by nature holy; we too are holy, but not by nature, only by participation, and discipline, and prayer.[45]

As seen in his Catechetical and Mystagogic Lectures, Cyril was above all a pastor at heart and in practice. To be sure, he attacked a variety of heresies and doctrinal aberrations in the course of fulfilling what he considered his chief responsibility of leading the flock. But his concern was much less that of the controversialist or even the theologian than of feeding and protecting those in his trust. His biblicism, coming at a time of growing tradition and theological controversy, was misunderstood by some and exploited by others, including Jerome, who wrongly placed him within the Arian camp. We have strong evidence to the contrary. In describing Christ and His relationship to the Father, Cyril does not specifically use the term homoousios, or address himself to the question of consubstantiation. However, his statement that the Son is "in all things like to Him that begat,"[46] certainly is not that of an Arian. In addition, he is intensely hostile to adoptionism. He is equally opposed to any suggestion that Christ achieved lordship by advancement or by moral growth.[47] Christ did not become the Son at baptism. He already *was* the beloved Son.[48]

In Cyril of Jerusalem's lectures we are given an insight into pastoral teaching of neophytes in the mid-fourth century Church. Concern is shown that believers not become involved in speculative theology, especially that they avoid those individuals who declare themselves to be the Holy Spirit or claim to have new prophetic revelations about the Spirit. There is no hesitancy to encourage new believers to experience the presence and the work of the Paraclete, however. The one restriction imposed by the bishop of Jerusalem is that the faithful must not go beyond that actually authorized or mentioned in Scripture. With this in mind, Cyril portrays a rich life in the Spirit—the fullness of the King's spiritual bounty—for his hearers.

3. DIDYMUS THE BLIND

Born in A.D. 309 or 314, Didymus of Alexandria lost his sight when only four years of age. The result was that he never was taught the usual rudiments of learning.[49] However, his indomitable determination, intense desire to learn, and prayer for inner light more than compensated for his physical handicap. He studied the alphabet from wooden tablets and became acquainted with grammar, vocabulary, and literary structure by attentive listening. His memory astonished even the scholars at Alexandria. He taught himself grammar, rhetoric, logic, music, arithmetic and geometry, and became the match of all who had studied these subjects in books.[50] In addition, he attained a tremendous knowledge of the Scriptures and was appointed by Bishop Athanasius to the presidency of the catechetical school at Alexandria. Palladius reports:

> He had an excellent natural teacher—his own conscience. He was so endowed with the gift of learning that the Scriptures were literally fulfilled in him: "The Lord makes the blind wise." For he interpreted the Old and the New Testaments word by word, having such regard for doctrine, expounding his explanations so skillfully and firmly, that he surpassed all the ancients in knowledge.[51]

Asked by St. Antony of the Desert whether he was saddened by his blindness, Didymus responded that it was a great grief to him. To this Antony replied, "I am suprised that a wise man should grieve at the loss of a faculty which he shared with ants and flies and gnats, and not rejoice rather in having one of which only saints and apostles have been thought worthy." This incident is reported by Jerome who concludes that it is far "better to have spiritual than carnal vision and to possess eyes into which the mote of sin cannot fall."[52]

Didymus's writings on the Holy Scriptures include two which have relevance to our study of the Holy Spirit. The first, *On the Holy Spirit*, is a protest against Macedonianism. It was written before the Second Ecumenical Council met at Constantinople in A.D. 381 and is extant only in Jerome's Latin version.[53] The second, three books *On the Trinity*, which may have been composed after the Council of Constantinople, has survived in Greek.

Didymus's work on the Holy Spirit open with an apologia. He dwells on the reverence due to the Spirit and suggests that he would have remained silent because of the awful sanctions which guard the subject, were it not that errors are abroad, spread by deceivers of unusual temerity.[54]

The Spirit is the same in the Old as in the New Testament. He is set apart from all created beings by His very name as well as by His nature, which is holy and good and infinite. He is immutable.[55] The Spirit, therefore, is not a creature made by the Logos. He is God's great Gift to man, the culminating point of all of God's gifts to man, the common Gift of the Father and the Son. He is the first Gift, for He is love, and love is the reason for all divine gifts. In the substance of the Holy Spirit is understood the plentitude of all gifts.[56] Nothing is given by God without Him. All the advantages which are received from the favor of God's gifts flow from this Fountain-Head.[57]

In operation, the Spirit is one with the Father and the Son. This unity of operation involves a oneness of essence.[58] The Spirit is holy by essence, not by participation. His operation is as the Finger of God, stamping the divine image on the human soul. The very grace of the Father and of the Son is completed by the communication of the Holy Spirit. "By one same grace . . . which is from the Father and the Son, completed by the operation of the Holy Ghost, is proved the trinity of one substance."[59]

The Holy Spirit is a divine Person. Didymus proceeds to prove the deity of the Spirit from His inspiration of the Old Testament prophets, from the apostolic benediction, from His witness through Stephen, from the story of Ananias and Sapphira, from the sending forth of Paul and Barnabas, from Paul's comments in 1 Corinthians 3:16, and elsewhere.[60] The Spirit goes forth from the Father, sent by the Son, but still is indivisibly one with the Person who sent Him. Although He is sent, He is not separated from the Godhead. He has no subsistence except that which is given to Him by the Son.[61] The terms "sanctification" and "goodness" pertain equally to the Father, the Son, and the Holy Spirit, just as each is properly called "Spirit."[62] When Jesus called the Holy Spirit "another" Paraclete, He was not referring to a difference in nature, but rather to a difference in operation.[63]

Here Didymus appears to come very close to the Western doctrine of the *filioque*, that the Spirit proceeds from the Father *and* the Son. Whether this is due to Jerome's translation, or to textual corruption, or actually reflects Didymus's theological position we cannot determine. Didymus also deals with the matter of procession in Book Two, *On the Trinity*. He argues that the Second and the Third hypostases (the Son and the Holy Spirit) proceed from the First, not as the result of creative energy, but rather because of the nature of God. It is not appropriate to ask which Member(s) of the Godhead came after the Father, for the Trinity is not to be understood in terms of time. The Persons of the Trinity co-exist and proceed simultaneously. The Holy Spirit is the Spirit of God, and is from God, and is not posterior to the Father.[64]

In his essay on the Trinity, Didymus depicts the Spirit as the same in honor, in operation, in divine nature, and in essence with the Father and the Son.[65] The Paraclete contains all the properties of God. He fills all things, He creates, He remits sins, He inspires, and He commands. The operations of all three Members of the Trinity must be common and undivided, because this is Their nature. For example, the Incarnation involves the undivided operation of all Persons in the Godhead. It also is the work of the entire Trinity to produce sanctifying grace and justification.[66]

There is a sense in which the Holy Spirit's operation is unique, however. Quoting 1 John 2:20, Didymus declares that the believer has an unction from the Holy Ghost, just as Jesus received in His Incarnation.[67] Through this Holy Spirit unction the soul is strengthened so as to share in the life of God. The Spirit is the form of the soul and its spiritual life. The soul of the baptized Christian, in a very special way, is the temple of the same indwelling Holy Spirit. Illuminated by celestial light of the indwelling Spirit, the soul is in some measure worthy of God's presence and is permitted to drink at the everlasting fountain.

It is in baptism that the Spirit regenerates and sanctifies the soul. This is a function belonging to Him, although not in exclusion from the Father and the Son. It is uniquely His role in that He does not receive this delegation from other Persons in the Godhead. Baptism is the sacrament of the Spirit. The baptismal pool serves as a workshop of the Trinity in which the Holy Spirit regenerates the human soul. However, it is useless to those who do not believe that the Holy Spirit is God.[68] If one will approach the baptismal font with sincerity the Holy Spirit serves as the distributor of all the great gifts.

[He] renovates us in Baptism, and working with the Father and the Son, brings us back from our condition of deformity to that of pristine beauty, filling us with His grace so that we no longer allow for anything that is unworthy of our affection. He delivers us from sin, from death, and from things earthly. He makes us spiritual men, who share in His divine glory. We are sons and heirs of God and the Father. He conforms us to the image of the Son, making us co-heirs and His brothers—we who are to be glorified and to reign with Him. The Spirit gives us heaven in exchange for earth. He grants us paradise from his bounty, He makes us higher than the angels. In the waters of the baptismal pool he extinguishes the inextinguishable fire of hell.[69]

Even those with faultless lives must be regenerated by the Holy

Spirit of God and marked with the seal of His sanctification to attain His heavenly gifts. Those who are martyred before baptism are given life by the Holy Spirit, having been washed with their own blood. Thus we become like God, in as far as our human state permits, and we enjoy familiarity with Him. Only those who are made spiritually alive can understand the power and the supreme majesty of the Spirit of God.[70]

4. ATHANASIUS

The Arian controversy, a dispute about the relationship of Christ to God, arose in Alexandria in Egypt when a presbyter named Arius contended that Christ the Son, although the highest of all creatures, was still a creature. His existence had beginning. He had been made out of nothing, but he had changed and was subject to change.

Opposition to Arius eventually was led by Athanasius of Alexandria (ca. 296-373), then a deacon and secretary to the bishop of that city, who asserted that man's very salvation is at question if the Father-Son relationship is not eternal and unalterable. If Christ were merely a creature He would be a subordinate god, not fully, eternally, and unchangeably divine. Man's assurance of salvation depends upon his relationship to Christ and on Christ's unchanging relationship to God.

The First Ecumenical Council, summoned by Emperor Constantine to meet at Nicea in Asia Minor in 325, rejected any subordination of the Son to the Father. The Two are fully equal and of the same substance or being (homoousios). Christ is the very Godhead become flesh, dying for the salvation of mankind. The Father and the Son are described as two Persons sharing one being or substance.

The Council also approved the following creed presented by Athanasius:

> We believe in one only God, Father Almighty, Creator of things visible and invisible; and in the Lord Jesus Christ, for he is the Word of God, God of God, Light of Light, life of life, his only Son, the first-born of all creatures, begotten of the Father before all time, by whom also everything was created, who became flesh for our redemption, who lived and suffered amongst men, rose again the third day, returned to the Father, and will come again one day in his glory to judge the quick and the dead. We believe also in the Holy Ghost.[71]

The final sentence reveals the limited concern of the Council and Athanasius with the doctrine of the Holy Spirit in 325. The very opening of the question of the Son's place in the Trinity, however, inevitably brought the question of the place of the third Person to the foreground and, with that, a further development of the doctrine of the Holy Spirit. The Church's later understanding of the Spirit, then, grew out of a crisis within a crisis.

In 359/360 Athanasius, writing to Serapion, a fellow bishop in exile, attacked the teachings of the Tropici—Athanasius's name for a group of Egyptian theologians known for taking passages of Scripture out of context (i.e., for "troping"). The Tropici held to the doctrine of the creaturehood of the Spirit, probably derived from an earlier connection with the Arians, although they now admitted that the Son was of the same essence with the Father. In this they anticipated the Macedonians or Pneumatomachi who were anathematized in 381 at the First Council of Constantinople for their refusal to confess that the Holy Spirit, like the Son, had the same substance (homoousios) with the Father.

Athanasius's arguments for the full divinity and Godhead of the Spirit are based primarily on the divine activity of the Spirit within the Trinity.[72] The Spirit is by nature what He does. He performs and exhibits characteristics which only could be ascribed to God. The Spirit sanctifies man as He quickens, seals, and anoints. In this context nothing is said of the fruits of the Spirit, or of His witness in the believer, or His illumination of the mind and conscience. Athanasius does mention the charismata in operation in the Church of his day on several occasions. He claims to know bishops who work miracles, as well as those who do not.[73] But Athanasius does not chiefly purpose to describe the full work of the Spirit. Instead, he is concerned with His relationship in the Godhead.

According to Athanasius, sanctification is not limited to the building up of the believer to a state of divine incorruption. Rather it is an extension to all of creation what the Word has accomplished. Athanasius asserts that He who gives life to creatures cannot Himself be a creature:

He is called a quickening Spirit. For it says: "He that raised up Christ from the dead shall quicken also your mortal bodies through his Spirit that dwelleth in you." The Lord is the very life, and "author of life," as Peter put it. And as the Lord said himself: "The water that I shall give him shall become in him a well of water springing up into eternal life. . . . But this spake he concerning the Spirit which they that believed in him were to receive." But the creatures, as has been said, are quickened through him. He that does not partake of life, but who is himself partaken and quickens the creatures, what kinship can he have with things originated? How can he belong to the creatures which in him are quickened from the Word?

The Spirit is called unction and he is seal. For John writes: "As for you, and you need not that anyone teach you, but his unction"—his Spirit—"teacheth you concerning all things." In the prophet Isaiah it is written: "The Spirit of the Lord is upon me, because the Lord hath anointed me." Paul says: "In whom having also believed, ye were sealed unto the day of redemption." But the creatures are by him sealed and anointed and instructed in all things. But if the Spirit is the unction and seal with which the Word anoints and seals all things, what likeness or propriety could the unction and the seal have to the things that are anointed and sealed? Thus by this consideration also he could not belong to the "all things." The seal could not be from among the things that are sealed, nor the unction from among things that are anointed; it pertains to the Word who anoints and seals.

Further it is through the Spirit that we are all said to be partakers of God. . . . If the Holy Spirit were a creature, we should have no participation of God in him. . . . But if, by participation in the Spirit, we are made "sharers in the divine nature," we should be mad to say that the Spirit has a created nature and not the nature of God. For it is on this account that those in whom he is are made divine. If he makes men divine, it is not to be doubted that his nature is of God.[74]

To deny the full divinity of the Spirit, while recognizing His sanctifying role, is to claim that the Son, through whom all things came to be, is a creature. However, the unction of the Spirit is the breath of the Son. The seal of the Holy Spirit gives the impress of the Son.

It is clear that the Spirit is not a creature, but takes place in the act of creation. For the Father creates all things through the Word in the Spirit; for where the Word is, there is the Spirit also, and the things which are created through the Word have their vital strength out of the Spirit from the Word. Thus it is written in the thirty-second Psalm: "By the Word of the Lord the heavens were established, and by the Spirit of his mouth is all their power."

So clearly is the Spirit indivisible from the Son that what is now to be said leaves no room for doubt. When the Word came upon the prophet, it was the Spirit that the prophet used to speak the things he received from the Word. . . . The Spirit is not outside the Word, but, being in the Word, through him is in God. And so the spiritual gifts are given in the Triad.[75]

The Spirit is the instrument of the Son in both creation and sanctification. From the Son the Spirit receives His mission to create, to sanctify and to make divine. In the context of His mission the Spirit proceeds from the Father:

As the Son is an only-begotten offspring, so also the Spirit, being given and sent from the Son, is himself one and not many, nor one from among many, but Only Spirit. As the Son, the living Word, is one, so must the vital activity and gift whereby he sanctifies and enlightens be perfect and complete; which is said to proceed from the Father, because it is from the Word, who is confessed to be from the Father, that it shines forth and is sent and is given. That the Son is sent from the Father; for he says, "God so loved the world that he gave his only begotten Son." The Son sends the Spirit; "If I go away," he says, "I will send the Paraclete." The Son glorifies the Father, saying, "Father, I have glorified thee." The Spirit glorifies the Son; for he says: "He shall glorify me." The Son says: "The things I heard from the Father speak I unto the world." The Spirit takes of the Son; "He shall take of mine," he says, "and shall declare it unto you." The Son came in the name of the Father. "The Holy Spirit," says the Son, "Whom the Father will send in my name."[76]

When the Spirit is in the believer it means that the Word is in him, bestowing the Spirit.[77] The Spirit's prophetic role is a role of the Word speaking in the Spirit. The selfsame presence-in-activity of the Word and the Spirit is apparent in the Incarnation of the Word:

So too when the Word visited the holy Virgin Mary, the Spirit came to her with him, and the Word in the Spirit moulded the body and conformed it to himself; desiring to join and present all creation to the Father through himself, and in it "to reconcile all things . . . having made peace . . . whether things in the heavens or things upon the earth."[78]

The common presence-in-activity is illustrated further in the metaphors of drink, wisdom, and life:

When we are made to drink of the Spirit, we drink of Christ . . . . As the Son is Wisdom, so we, receiving the Spirit of Wisdom, have the Son and are made wise in him. . . . When we are quickened by the Spirit, Christ himself is said to live in us.[79]

The Spirit's relationship to the Son parallels the Son's relationship to the Father. The Son is sent by the Father, and the Son sends the Spirit. The Spirit takes from the Son, as the Son takes from the Father. The Son comes in the Father's name, the Spirit comes in the name of the Son.[80] The Spirit also is of the same essence with the Son and through the Son with the Godhead of the Father.

It is obvious that the Spirit does not belong to the many nor is he an angel. But because he is one, and, still more, because he is proper to the Word who is one, he is proper to God who is one, and one in essence with him.

These sayings concerning the Holy Spirit, by themselves alone, show that in nature and essence he has nothing in common with or proper to creatures, but is distinct from things originated, proper to, and not alien from, the Godhead and essence of the Son; in virtue of which essence and nature he is of the Holy Triad.[81]

In addition to his arguments for the full divinity of the Holy Spirit based upon His functions and His relationship with the Son, Athanasius also argues his case upon the Spirit's place within the Triad. In any activity involving the Spirit it is the Triad that acts. The Father and the Son are acting with the Spirit. The Father creates all things through the Word in the Spirit. The Spirit is He in whom the Father through the Word perfects and renews all things:

There is, then, a Triad, holy and complete, confessed to be God in Father, Son, and Holy Spirit, having nothing foreign or external mixed with it, not composed of one that creates and one that is originated, but all creative; and it is consistent and in nature indivisible, and its activity is one. The Father does all things through the Word in the Holy Spirit. Thus the unity of the holy Triad is preserved. Thus one God is preached in the Church, "who is over all, and through all, and in all"—"over all," as Father, as beginning, as

fountain; "through all," through the Word; "in all," in the Holy
Spirit. It is a Triad not only in name and form of speech, but in truth
and actuality. For as the Father is he that is, so also his Word is one
that is and God over all. And the Holy Spirit is not without actual
existence, but exists and has true being.[82]

The Spirit is the effective principle in the Trinity who apportions
to us what the Father accomplishes through the Son. Athanasius's
emphasis upon the absolute unity of essence contains a real
differentiation of the Father, Son, and Spirit. There is difference in
unity:

Hence in the Godhead alone the Father is and was and always is,
because he is Father in the strict sense, and Only Father. The Son is
Son in the strict sense, and Only Son. And of them it holds good that
the Father is and is called always Father, and the Son, Son; and the
Holy Spirit is always Holy Spirit, whom we have believed to be of God
and to be given from the Father through the Son.[83]

In Athanasius there is no well-developed doctrine of the Spirit's
procession from the Father and the Son. He does suggest that the
Spirit comes from the Father because the Father brings forth the
Son, from whom the Spirit shines forth. The Spirit's procession
from the Father is seen in His mission from the Son. However,
Athanasius stops at this point. He does not explain how the sending
of the Spirit by the Son can be used to establish His procession
from the Father. Athanasius's doctrine clearly is not complete in
this area. Curiously, Swete has argued that a doctrine of the Spirit's
procession from the Father and the Son is possible within the
partially constructed framework of Athanasius's thought, despite
Athanasius's statement that the Spirit is given from the Father
through the Son.[84]

Athanasius's contribution to Holy Spirit theology is of landmark
significance. He does for the Spirit what he does for the Son,
namely, to show that any rejection of the Spirit's divinity in its
fullest sense would ruin Christianity. He develops his doctrine of
the Spirit around the core issue of salvation. To deny the Spirit is to
deny the very Agent of grace Who has been provided by the Father
through the Son to sinful man. The Holy Spirit now has been
brought firmly within the problem of God in Christian theology, an
essential issue to be faced and dealt with in one manner or another.

5. THE LIFE OF ST. ANTONY

The authenticity of the *Vita S. Antoni*, which purports to be
written by Athanasius, has long been debated and is still disputed.[85]
Its effect on the post-Nicene Church is less open to question. It
clearly gave impetus to the rise of asceticism. But it also had a
significant impact on the development of Christian biography,
especially hagiography—the special category of biographical

literature which centers on those regarded as "holy."

According to the *Vita*, Antony adopted the ascetic life about A.D. 285 and remained in the desert for twenty years, by which time the first great wave of monastic settlement occurred. As persecution waned a new hero-type emerged. Monks were stepping into the shoes of the martyrs. Antony prayed to be a martyr, and when the persecution ceased he "withdrew to his cell, and was there daily a martyr to his conscience, and contending in the conflicts of faith."[86] Cassian later suggested that monks are crucified daily to this world and made living martyrs.[87] Clearly, this was Antony's purpose.

> And so for nearly twenty years he continued training himself in solitude, never going forth, and but seldom seen by any. After this, when many were eager and wishful to imitate his discipline, and his acquaintances came and began to cast down and wrench off the door by force, Antony, as from a shrine, came forth initiated in the mysteries and filled with the Spirit of God. Then for the first time he was seen outside the fort by those who came to see him.[88]

The connection between his preparation in solitude and the resulting divine enablement is drawn immediately thereafter:

> Through him the Lord healed the bodily ailments of many present, and cleansed others from evil spirits. And He gave grace to Antony in speaking, so that he consoled many that were sorrowful, and set those at variance at one, exhorting all to prefer the love of Christ before all that is in the world. . . . He persuaded many to embrace the solitary life. And thus it happened in the end that cells arose even in the mountains, and the desert was colonised by monks, who came forth from their own people, and enrolled themselves for the citizenship in the heavens.[89]

From this point onward the reader encounters a narrative overflowing with miracles, signs, and wonders. By far the largest number of these involve Antony's ability to discern evil spirits and to cast them out of the possessed. Possession by the Holy Spirit would seem to have implied the power to free those possessed by evil spirits. The following incident is typical:

> When therefore he had retired and determined to fix a time, after which neither to go forth himself nor admit anybody, Martinian, a military officer, came and disturbed Antony. For he had a daughter afflicted with an evil spirit. But when he continued for a long while knocking at the door, and asking him to come out and pray to God for his child, Antony, not bearing to open, looked out from above and said, "Man why dost thou call on me? I also am a man even as you. But if you believe on Christ whom I serve, go, and according as you believe, pray to God, and it will come to pass." Straightway, therefore, he departed, believing and calling upon Christ, and he received his daughter cleansed from the devil. Many other things also through Antony the Lord did, who saith, "Seek and it shall be given unto you."[90]

The power to discern and to cast out evil spirits is not given by the

Spirit without preparation:

> There is need of much prayer and of discipline, that when a man has
> received through the Spirit the gift of discerning spirits, he may have
> power to recognize their characteristics: which of them are less and
> which more evil; of what nature is the special pursuit of each; of what
> nature is the special pursuit of each, and how each of them is
> overthrown and cast out.[91]

Healings of a wide variety of maladies abound in the text. In many
cases, Antony does not even offer prayer for healings which are
reported. "Many of the sufferers, when he would not open his
door, slept outside his cell, and by their faith and sincere prayers
were healed."[92] Desiring solitude, Antony prefers that those who
follow after him should pray for themselves.

> But when he saw himself beset by many, and not suffered to withdraw
> himself according to his intent as he wished, fearing because of the
> signs which the Lord wrought by him, that either he should be puffed
> up, or that some other should think of him above what he ought to
> think, he considered and set off to go into the upper Thebaid, among
> those to whom he was unknown.[93]

Throughout the biography Antony's victories over evil forces
and his miraculous deeds are credited by the author to the work of
Christ in him, as one who walked after the Spirit:

> Antony . . . healed not by commanding, but by prayer and speaking
> the name of Christ. So that it was clear to all that it was not he himself
> who worked, but the Lord who showed mercy by his means and
> healed the sufferers. But Antony's part was only prayer and
> discipline, for the sake of which he stayed in the mountain.[94]

Antony also is reputed to have been clairvoyant. On one
occasion while in the mountains, he observes what is happening in
distant Egypt.[95] He also has a vision in which he sees

> The table of the Lord's House, and mules standing around it on all
> sides in a ring, and kicking the things therein, just like a herd kicks
> when it leaps in confusion. . . . These things the old man saw, and
> after two years the present inroad of the Arians and the plunder of the
> churches took place, when they violently carried off the vessels, and
> made the heathen carry them . . . and in their presence did upon the
> Table as they would. Then we all understood that these kicks of the
> mules signified to Antony what the Arians, senselessly like beasts, are
> now doing.[96]

In his *First Discourse Against the Arians*, Athanasius proclaims
that the Spirit is essential not only for the working of miracles but
also for sanctification. In the *Vita*, Antony is credited with having
received special grace from God, grace which bears strong
resemblance to certain of those fruits of the Spirit listed in
Galatians 5:22-23:

> Added to this he was tolerant in disposition and humble in spirit. For
> though he was such a man, he observed the rule of the Church most
> rigidly, and was willing that all the clergy should be honoured above
> himself. . . . And besides, his countenance had a great and

wonderful grace. This gift also he had from the Saviour. For if he were present in a great company of monks, and any one who did not know him previously, wished to see him, immediately coming forward he passed by the rest, and hurried to Antony, as though attracted by his appearance. Yet neither in height nor breadth was he conspicuous above others, but in the serenity of his manner and the purity of his soul. For as his soul was free from disturbances, his outward appearance was calm; so from the joy of his soul he possessed a cheerful countenance, and from his bodily movements could be perceived the condition of his soul, as it is written, "When the heart is merry the countenance is cheerful, but when it is sorrowful it is cast down."[97]

The reader must be reminded that anyone dealing in hagiographic material should constantly be alert to the serious problem of credibility. The *Life of Antony* is no exception. The author indiscriminately mixes that which can only be taken as incredible with types of the miraculous which have parallels in Scripture. One example is found in the story of a maiden who was healed through the prayers of Antony. The healing itself is not out of keeping with those reported in the ministry of Jesus and is compared by the writer to the account in Matthew 9:20 of the healing of the woman with the issue of blood. However, the author chooses to distort the ailment, which is described as "a terrible and hideous disorder . . . [in which] the running of her eyes, nose, and ears fell to the ground and immediately became worms."[98]

Even if one rejects all of these accounts of the miraculous, the biography remains important to our study of the Holy Spirit in the Church. Fourth-century Christians read about and wondered at the deeds of holy men and women, deeds far beyond those expected of common believers. The power behind such wonders was attributed to the Holy Spirit, whose extraordinary charismata were reserved for a special few. From the fourth century onward this select number came from among the episcopacy and the leading ascetics. Monks now were walking in the shoes of the martyrs—and they had inherited the mantle of the Spirit as well.

6. JOHN CHRYSOSTOM

John Chrysostom (347-407 A.D.), known as the "golden-mouthed," was the greatest teacher and preacher of the ancient Greek Church. After living as a hermit monk for six years, he rose to presbyter of the church at Antioch and in 397 was chosen patriarch of Constantinople. However, his impassioned sermons angered the empress Eudoxia and the patriarch of Alexandria, and he was banished from Constantinople in 404, dying in exile.

Chrysostom's sermons reflect his eloquence. His contribution to pneumatology, however, is limited to the influence of the Spirit on human ethical behavior. His understanding of the Godhead, and of the Holy Spirit's place in the inner life of God is largely a reiteration of the writings of earlier Nicenes. For example, he deals with the standard questions of the equality of the Spirit to the Father and the Son. The Son and the Spirit are invoked at baptism in addition to the Father so that all will realize their common dignity:

> This is also why the Trinity is invoked at baptism. I say this for the Father is capable of doing the whole thing, as also is the Son, and likewise the Holy Spirit. But, since no one is in doubt about the Father, though there was doubt about the Son and the Holy Spirit, They were brought into the rite of initiation in order that, by Their participation in the dispensing of those ineffable blessings, we might also realize Their common dignity.[99]

The words of Christ also affirm the coequality of the Spirit. "See how sublime His words about the Spirit were! He said: 'He is another like Me.' He declared: 'He will not leave you,' He asserted: 'He is coming to you alone, even as I have done.' He said: 'He will dwell with you.' "[100] Again, Christ stated, "If I do not go, the Advocate will not come." Chrysostom comments, "What have they to say here, who do not properly esteem the Spirit? Is it 'expedient' for the Lord to go away and for a servant to come instead? Do you perceive how great the dignity of the Spirit is?"[101] Furthermore, Chrysostom argues, the Spirit is not a creature, despite the statement by John that all things were made by Christ.[102] No creature could have the measureless operation of the Spirit:

> But He [Christ] possesses the entire operation of the Spirit, without measure and in its fullness. Now if the operation of the Spirit which He possesses is without measure, much more so is His substance. You perceive that the Spirit is without limit? Well, then, how would it be right to hold in question Him who has received the operation of the Spirit in its entirety, who knows the things of God, who said: "We speak of what we have heard, and we bear witness to what we have seen?" For He says nothing which is not of God and nothing which is not of the Spirit.[103]

The operation of the Spirit manifested immeasurably in Christ, is made available to the Christian to the extent that he is able to contain Him. The third Person is involved in every step in the great plan of Redemption, inspiring the prophets and the evangelists,[104] acting upon the womb of Mary in the Incarnation,[105] and revealing Jesus Christ.[106] His work and teachings are the same as Christ's.[107] He will give life, knowledge, and Christlikeness.[108] That which is born of the Spirit is spiritual.[109] That which is holy is given by the Holy Spirit:

> Again, if you examine the character of the holiness [described in the Old Testament]—what this is, and what that is—you will again see a great difference. For they [of the Old Dispensation] were called

"holy" when they did not commit idolatry, or fornication, or adultery; but we become "holy," not only by refraining from these actions, but also by the possession of still greater things. To begin with, we obtain this gift from the very visitation of the Spirit, and then [keep it by living] a way of life much more excellent than the Jewish one.[110]

The Spirit deals with specific human weaknesses. "If one of you has thorns, let him cast the fire of the Spirit upon them. If another has a hard and obstinate heart, using the same fire let him make it soft and pliant. If someone by the wayside is trodden on by many distractions, let him go into more sheltered places."[111] It is essential that one listens to the Spirit so that his individual needs are met:

In truth, this house [the Church] is a spiritual clinic, intended that we may there heal whatever wounds we have received outside; not that, after acquiring other wounds there also, we may depart in this condition. If, when the Holy Spirit speaks to us, we do not pay attention, not only shall we not be cleansed of former stains, but we shall receive others besides. Let us, then, approach with great eagerness the book which is being revealed to us.[112]

If a man is led by the Spirit, he is not under the Law,[113] and he is not vulnerable to the attacks of the devil.[114]

Chrysostom's sermons reflect great concern that his listeners develop a more loving and moral lifestyle. Christlikeness is to be the sign to unbelievers of the validity of the Gospel. Chrysostom calls for character (the fruits of the Spirit), rather than for the charismata (the extraordinary gifts of the Spirit). The Holy Spirit is seen more as a source of strength to live the overcoming life than as a giver of extraordinary spiritual charismation.

The Spirit dwells in earthly vessels, not in vessels made of stone. But these are earthly vessels of unusual strength because He hardens the vessels in which He dwells. The abundance of the Spirit found in such vessels is described as "a treasure," "a supply of the Spirit," and "righteousness, sanctification, redemption."

Hast thou seen a treasure more brilliant than royal treasures? O treasure which not only preserved, but also preserves the house where it is stored up. . . . He gave therefore the earnest of the Spirit . . . a small part of the whole . . . such as eye hath not seen, and ear hath not heard, neither hath entered into the heart of man.[115]

In our weakness the Spirit helps our infirmities, He searches our hearts, He makes intercession for the saints according to the will of God.[116] As partakers of the Spirit, Christians live godly lives—"the greatest of miracles, the most wonderful of signs."

Spiritual gifts played a vital role in the beginning of the Church.[117] Now they have ceased:

Let no one therefore wait for miracles. . . . If then we practise this [charity], and all the self-denial that flows from it, we shall have no need of signs; even as on the other hand, if we do not practise it, we shall gain nothing by the signs.[118]

Neither let us account ourselves worse off, in that we do not work miracles now. For that will never be any advantage to us . . . if we take heed to all virtue.[119]

Do not then therefore seek signs, but the soul's health. . . . For in truth, if we all live as we ought, workers of miracles would not be admired so much as we by the children of heathen.[120]

For if thou change from inhumanity to almsgiving . . . if thou withdraw from theatres and go to church . . . if thou draw back thine eyes from an harlot . . . if instead of satanical songs, thou has learnt spiritual psalms . . . these are the greatest miracles, these the wonderful signs.[121]

For since then [the founding of the Church] we have no need of sensible vision, faith sufficing instead of all. For signs are "not for them that believe, but for them that believe not."[122]

And in fact this [that ye should believe God without pledges], and one other thing [that individuals become vainglorious], were the reasons why God made miracles to cease.[123]

Again and again the same theme reappears: the gifts of the Spirit are no longer operative:

And otherwise he [the Spirit] ought now to have come, if he was about to come when the gifts ceased; for they have long since ceased.[124]

This statement [Romans 8:26] is not clear, owing to the cessation of many of the wonders which then used to take place.[125]

This whole place [1 Corinthians 12:1-2] is very obscure; but the obscurity is produced by our ignorance of the facts referred to, and by their cessation, being such as then used to occur, but now no longer take place.[126]

Do not then urge the fact that signs are not done now, as a proof that they were not done then. For as then they were usefully wrought, so now are they no longer so wrought.[127]

Chrysostom specifically asserts that tongues were no longer necessary after the Church had been established. So strongly does he state this argument, and in so many places,[128] that it is possible to argue, as has Harold Hunter, that Chrysostom was waging war against tongues-speech, perhaps from an experience he had as a monk.[129]

While there is little new in Chrysostom's pneumatology, his very eloquence of expression had a dramatic impact on those who heard or read his sermons. Certainly, his view that the whole range of the Spirit's extraordinary gifts were intended only for the first-century Church had an effect on Augustine and many others who were to follow. Chrysostom stands, therefore, as one of the most important early advocates of the major tradition in pneumatology, which rejected any ongoing prophetic ministry in the Church.

Notes to Chapter 5

[1]*Letter of Eusebius to Alexander of Alexandria*, NPF 2nd Series 1:70.

[2]NPF 2nd Series 1:16.

[3]*Contra Marcellum* ii.4, PG 24:cols. 811-826.

[4]Eusebius, *De ecclesiastica theologia* i.20, ii.2,3, PG 24:cols. 901-904.

[5]Ibid., iii.4-6, PG 24:cols. 1001-1016.

[6]Eusebius, *Preparation for the Gospel* vii.15, trans. Edwin H. Gifford (Oxford: Clarendon Press, 1903), 1:324-326.

[7]Eusebius, *Church History* iii.37.1-4, NPF 2nd Series 1:169. Cf. v.24.2, "Among these are Philip, one of the twelve Apostles, who fell asleep in Hierapolis; and his two virgin daughters, and another daughter, who lived in the Holy Spirit and now rests at Ephesus."

[8]Ibid., iv.26.1, v.24,5, NPF 2nd Series 1:203, 242.

[9]Jerome, *Lives of Illustrious Men* xxiv, NPF 2nd Series 3:368-369.

[10]*Church History* v.16.4, NPF 2nd Series 1:230.

[11]Ibid., 231.

[12]Ibid.

[13]Ibid., v.16.9, NPF 2nd Series 1:232.

[14]Ibid., v.16.17-19.4, NPF 2nd Series 1:232-237.

[15]Eusebius, *Commentary on Isaiah* vi:2, PG 24:cols. 125-126.

[16]Eusebius, *Commentary on Psalms* lxxvii:18, PG 23:col. 915.

[17]Ibid., lxv.4, PG 33:cols. 631-632. Eusebius quotes 1 Corinthians 12:8-10 immediately thereafter.

[18]Eusebius, *The Life of Constantine* iii.6-7, NPF 2nd Series 1:521.

[19]Ibid., iii.20, NPF 2nd Series 1:525.

[20]From the commemoration in the Synexary, quoted by William Telfer, ed., *The Library of Christian Classics* vol. IV: *Cyril of Jerusalem and Nemesius of Emesa* (Philadelphia: Westminster Press, 1955), 19-20.

[21]Cyril of Jerusalem, *Catechetical Lectures* iv.16-17, NPF 2nd Series 7:23.

[22]Ibid., xvi.1-3, NPF 2nd Series 7:115.

[23]Ibid., xvi.5, NPF 2nd Series 7:116.

[24]Ibid., xvi.6-8, NPF 2nd Series 7:116-117.

[25]Ibid., xvi.9, NPF 2nd Series 7:117.

[26]Ibid., vi.20, NPF 2nd Series 7:39.

[27]Ibid., xvi.11, NPF 2nd Series 7:117.

[28]Ibid., xvi.12, NPF 2nd Series 7:118.

[29]Ibid., On martyrdom also see xvi.20-22, NPF 2nd Series 7:121.

[30]Ibid., xvi.22, NPF 2nd Series 7:121.

[31]Ibid., xvi.19, NPF 2nd Series 7:120.

[32]Ibid., xvi.13,15, NPF 2nd Series 7:118,119.

[33]Ibid., xvi.16, NPF 2nd Series 7:119.

[34]Ibid., xvi.19-22, NPF 2nd Series 7:120-121.

[35]Ibid., xvi.23-24, NPF 2nd Series 7:121. Cf. xiii.23, NPF 2nd Series 7:88.

[36]Ibid., xvi.24, NPF 2nd Series 7:121.

[37]Ibid., xvii.5, NPF 2nd Series 7:125.

[38]Ibid., iii.4, 14, 15, iv.16, xvi.14, xx.4-6, NPF 2nd Series 7:15, 17, 18, 23, 127, 147-148.

[39]Ibid., xvii.35-38, NPF 2nd Series 7:132-133.

[40]Cyril of Jerusalem, *Mystagogic Lectures* iii.1, NPF 2nd Series 7:149.

[41]Ibid., iii.3, NPF 2nd Series 7:150.

[42]*Catechetical Lectures* xvii.35-38, NPF 2nd Series 7:132-133.

[43]*Mystagogic Lectures* iii.4, NPF 2nd Series 7:150.

[44]Ibid., v.7, NPF 2nd Series 7:154.

[45]Ibid., v.19, NPF 2nd Series 7:156.

[46]*Catechetical Lectures* iv.7, NPF 2nd Series 7:20-21.

[47]Ibid., xi.7, NPF 2nd Series 7:66.

[48]Ibid., xi.9, NPF 2nd Series VII, 66. Cf. iii.14, NPF 2nd Series 7:17.

[49]Jerome, *Lives of Illustrious Men* cix, NPF 2nd Series 3:381.

[50]Socrates, *Ecclesiastical History* iv.25, NPF 2nd Series 2:110; Sozomen, *Ecclesiastical History* iii.15, NPF 2nd Series 2:294-295; Palladius, *The Lausiac History* iv, ACW 34:35.

[51]*The Lausiac History* iv.2, ACW 34:35.

[52]Jerome, *Letter* lxviii.2, NPF 2nd Series 6:141.

[53]Printed among Jerome's writings, PL 23:cols. 101-154.

[54]Didymus the Blind, *On the Holy Spirit*, PL 23:cols. 103-105.

[55]Ibid., iv,v, ix, PL 23:cols. 106,107,111.

[56]Ibid., ix, PL 23:cols. 111.

[57]Ibid., iv, ix, xxviii, PL 23:cols. 106-107.

[58]Ibid., xvii, PL 23:cols. 119-120.

[59]Ibid., xvi, PL 23:cols. 119.

[60]Ibid., ii,viii-ix, xviii, xxiii, xxx, PL 23:cols. 105, 110-112, 120, 123, 129-130, 138.

[61]Ibid., xxxiv-xxxvii, PL 23:cols. 133-135.

[62]Ibid., lv, PL 23:col. 147.

[63]Ibid., xxvi, PL 23:col. 127.

[64]Didymus the Blind, *On the Trinity* ii.2, PL 39:cols. 454-464. Edward L. Heston, *The Spiritual Life and the Role of the Holy Ghost in the Sanctification of the Soul, as Described in the Works*

of Didymus of Alexandria (Dissertatio ad lauream in facultate theologica Pontificisae Universitatis Gregorianae, 1938), 47, suggests that there is a problem passage in *On the Trinity* ii.6, PG 39:col. 556, in which Didymus appears to suggest that the Son proceeded from the Holy Spirit, since He was anointed by the Spirit, "the uncreated and all-holy Unction," at His baptism. It seems to me, however, that this is out of character with numerous other passages in which he testifies to the Spirit's procession from the Father and the Son.

[65]*On the Trinity* ii.6.4, ii.7.4, PG 39:cols. 520, 629.
[66]Ibid., ii.6.23, ii.8.41, ii.10, PG 39:cols. 557, 629, 648.
[67]Ibid., ii.6.23, PG 29:col. 557.
[68]Ibid., ii.12,13, PG 29:cols. 668, 677, 692.
[69]Ibid., ii.11, PG 39:cols. 668-669. Author's translation.
[70]Ibid., ii.12, PG 39:col. 681.
[71]NPF 2nd Series 14:3.
[72]Of value for understanding Athanasius's doctrine of the Holy Spirit is Theodore C. Campbell, "The Doctrine of the Holy Spirit in the Theology of Athanasius," *Scottish Journal of Theology* 27 (1974): 408-443; J. MacIntyre, "The Holy Spirit in Greek Patristic Thought," *Scottish Journal of Theology* 7 (1954): 353-375; the Introduction in C. R. B. Shapland, trans., *The Letters of Saint Athanasius Concerning the Holy Spirit* (London: The Epworth Press, 1951); R. P. G. Hanson, "The Divinity of the Holy Spirit," *Church Quarterly* 1 (April 1969): 298-306; M. Damaskinos, "La disponbilité au Saint Esprit et la fidelité aux origines d' après les Pères grecs," *Istina* 19 (1974): 49-64; and Charles Kannengieser, "Athanasius of Alexandria and the Holy Spirit between Nicea I and Constantinople I," *Irish Theological Quarterly* 48 (1981): 166-180.
[73]Athanasius, *Letter to Dracontius* (354/355), Epistle xlix. 9, NPF 2nd Series 4:560.
[74]Athanasius, *Letter to Serapion* i.23-24, Shapland, 123-124, 125-127.
[75]Ibid., iii.5, Shapland, 174-175.
[76]Ibid., i.20, Shapland, 116-118.
[77]Ibid., i.31, Shapland, 145.
[78]Ibid., i.31, Shapland, 146-147.
[79]Ibid., i.19, Shapland, 112-113.
[80]Ibid., i.20, Shapland, 117-118.
[81]Ibid., i.27, Shapland, 133.
[82]Ibid., i.28, Shapland, 134-135.
[83]Ibid., iv.6, Shapland, 188.
[84]Swete, 192, insists that the *filioque* is already substantially

present in Athanasius's letters to Serapion.

[85]Those who argue that it is spurious and unhistorical tend to be Protestants who discount monastic life. In turn, its supporters come from among Roman Catholic scholars who see great value in the development of the ascetic life. For further discussion on this dispute see Archibald Robertson's Introduction to *The Life of St. Antony*, NPF 2nd Series 4:188-193.

[86]*Life of Antony* xlvi-xlvii, NPF 2nd Series 4:208-209.

[87]See Cassian, *Conferences* xxiv.2, NPF 2nd Series 9:533, and *Institutes* iv.34-35, NPF 2nd Series 11:230-231.

[88]*Life of Antony* xiv, NPF 2nd Series 4:200. Cf. Apostolos N. Athanassakis, trans., *The Life of Pachomius* (Missoula, Montana: Scholars Press, 1975), 5, where we read that God, rather than filling the earth with sorrow, chose instead to infuse it with an intoxicating spirit which especially blessed those who took to monastic life, including Pachomius (ca. A.D. 287-346), the Egyptian pioneer of cenobitic monasticism.

[89]*Life of Antony* xiv, NPF 2nd Series 4:200.

[90]Ibid., xlviii, NPF 2nd Series 4:209. Cf. with Pachomius, who was attacked on several occasions by evil spirits: *Life of Pachomius* xviii, xx, lii, Athanassakis, 25, 29, 77.

[91]Ibid., xxii, NPF 2nd Series 4:202. Cf. lviii, NPF 2nd Series 4:211.

[92]Ibid., xlviii, NPF 2nd Series 4:209.

[93]Ibid., xlix, NPF 2nd Series op. cit. Cf. with miracles attributed to Pachomus—of a woman bleeding, and a girl possessed by demons: *Life of Pachomius* xli, xliv, Athanassakis, 59, 63, 65.

[94]Ibid., lxxxiv, NPF 2nd Series 4:218. Cf. vii, lvi, NPF 2nd Series 4:197, 211.

[95]Ibid., lxxxii, NPF 2nd Series 4:217.

[96]Ibid., lxxxii, NPF 2nd Series 4:218. Cf. with Pachomius' vision concerning heresy: *Life of Pachomius* cii, Athanassakis, 143-144. Another example of Pachomius's visions may be found in *Life of Pachomius* xlviii, Athanassakis, 69, 71.

[97]Ibid., lxvii, NPF 2nd Series 4:214. Cf. Pachomius: *Life of Pachomius* lxxv, Athanassakis, 109.

[98]Ibid., lviii, NPF 2nd Series 4:211.

[99]Chrysostom, *Commentary on Saint John the Apostle and Evangelist,* trans., Sister Thomas Aquinas Goggin, in *The Fathers of the Church* (Washington, D.C.: Catholic University of America Press, 1960), 44:346 (henceforth FC).

[100]*Homily* lxxv on John, FC 41:303.

[101]*Homily* lxxviii on John, FC 41:341.

[102]*Homily* v on John, FC 33:62, 64.

[103]*Homily* xxx on John, FC 33:293.

[104]*Homily* iv on John, FC 33:45; *Homily* 1 on John, FC 41:23.

[105]*Homily* v on John, FC 33:64.

[106]*Homily* xvii on John, FC 33:165; *Homily* xxx on John, FC 44:287.

[107]*Homily* lxxviii on John, FC 44:348.

[108]*Homily* lxxviii on John, FC 44:346, 343; *Homily* xxxviii on John, FC 33:381.

[109]*Homily* xxvi on John, FC 33:253.

[110]*Homily* xiv on John, FC 33:134.

[111]*Homily* ii on John, FC 33:25.

[112]Ibid.

[113]*Homily* li on John, FC 44:34.

[114]*Homily* iii on John, FC 33:29.

[115]*Homily* ii on Eutropius, NPF 1st Series 9:260.

[116]*Homily* xiv on Romans, NPF 1st Series 11:446-447.

[117]For prophecy see *Homily* lxxviii on John, FC 44:346; for miracles see *Homily* lxxviii on John, FC 44:341, 347, and *Homily* lxxxvi on John, FC 44:453.

[118]*Homily* xlvi on Matthew, NPF 1st Series 10:291.

[119]*Homily* xxiv on Matthew, NPF 1st Series 10:168.

[120]*Homily* xxxii on Matthew, NPF 1st Series 10:218.

[121]*Homily* xxxii on Matthew, NPF 1st Series 10:219.

[122]*Homily* xii on Matthew, NPF 1st Series 10:77.

[123]*Homily* xxxii on Matthew, NPF 1st Series 10:218.

[124]*Homily* iv on 2 Thessalonians, NPF 1st Series 13:388.

[125]*Homily* xiv on Romans, NPF 1st Series 11:447.

[126]*Homily* xxix on 1 Corinthians, NPF 1st Series 12:168.

[127]*Homily* vi on 1 Corinthians, NPF 1st Series 12:31.

[128]*Homily* xxix on 1 Corinthians, NPF 1st Series 12:168; *Homily* xxxii on 1 Corinthians, NPF 1st Series 12:186-187, 189; *Homily* xxxv on 1 Corinthians, NPF 1st Series 12:209, 211; *Homily* xxxvi on 1 Corinthians, NPF 1st Series 12:217, 218, and several other locations.

[129]Harold Hunter, "Tongues-Speech: A Patristic Analysis," *Journal of the Evangelical Theological Society* 23 (June 1980): 134; Adolph Martin Ritter, *Charisma im Verständnis des Joannes Chrysostomes und seiner zeit* (Göttingen: Vandenhoeck und Ruprecht, 1972); and Andrew T. Floris, "Chrysostom and the Charismata," *Paraclete* 5, no.1 (Winter 1971): 17-22.

CHAPTER SIX
POST-NICENE GREEK FATHERS: CAPPADOCIA

While the Christian Church first was established in such great cities of the Empire as Antioch, Alexandria, and Rome, it also flourished in such unlikely places as the deserts of Egypt, the Greek isles, and the bare and forbidding uplands of Asia Minor. It was Cappadocia in what is now central Turkey which produced in a single generation three great Fathers of the Church who profoundly affected the theological course of Christianity: Basil of Caesarea, his brother Gregory of Nyssa, and their associate, Gregory of Nazianzen.

With the Cappadocians the doctrine of the Holy Spirit is brought to a new pitch of development. They were students both of Origen and Athanasius. From Athanasius came their concern to define the Spirit's homoousios—that He was of one and the *same* nature with the Father and the Son. Because of Origen's influence they realized that the homoousios was reconcilable with pluralism and that the real answer was not in weakening the term homoousios but, rather, in strengthening the doctrine of the three hypostases. The results were several. In the first place, the Cappadocians were able to reconcile many of the semi-Nicenes or Homoeans, who believed that the Son had a *similar* nature to that of the Father, with the Nicene position of Athanasius by emphasizing the presence of three hypostases within one ousia. Ousia was used to refer to the essence that is common to Members of the Godhead, and hypostasis was used to refer to the individual subsistence of each of these Members.[1] By restricting the term ousia to where the Godhead is one, and hypostasis to that wherein the Godhead is three, the Cappadocians introduced much needed clarification into trinitarian terminology. They also added the insight that each hypostasis indwells and reciprocates with the other two. In sum, they gave the

Church the great trinitarian statement which has remained the basis of orthodoxy from the time of the Council of Constantinople (381). In countering the Arian jibe that the homoousios of the Spirit seemed to involve the Father in having two sons, the Cappadocians differentiated between modes of origin of the Son and that of the Spirit. Gregory of Nyssa provides the definitive statement. The Spirit is out of God and is of Christ. He proceeds out of God and is received from the Son.[2] The Cappadocian idea of the twofold procession of the Spirit from the Father through the Son lacks all traces of subordination (as one would find in more radical Origenists such as Eusebius), because of their wholehearted recognition of the homoousios of the Spirit.

Gregory of Nazianzen even offers a theory to explain the late development of the doctrine of the Holy Spirit. In the Old Testament the Father is revealed and the Son hinted at. In the New Testament the Son is fully revealed, the Spirit adumbrated. The era of the Church has brought the doctrine of the Spirit to full development.[3]

As victors over Arianism and creators of the definitive Greek theology of the Trinity, the Cappadocians stand among the most prominent ancient Fathers in our study of the Holy Spirit. In these achievements and in their uniquely sensitive and insightful ability to expose the mysteries of the Trinity, especially the Person and offices of the Spirit, they alone are peers of the great Western champion, Augustine of Hippo.

1. BASIL

Born ca. A.D. 330 in Caesarea of Cappadocia, Basil was the third of ten children in a family of affluent landowners who counted Christian heroes of the great persecution among their ancestors. His education began at home with his father and continued in Constantinople and Athens. Having experienced a well-rounded humanistic training in Greek literature, philosophy, and oratory, Basil returned to Caesarea about 356 to teach rhetoric. However, his commitment to Christian asceticism led him to visit monastic settlements in Palestine, Syria, and Egypt, and eventually to establish the monastic system in Pontus. He attempted to involve his monks in works of social utility—providing relief to Christians, pagans, and Jews alike. On the outskirts of Caesarea he built a complex of buildings to house travelers, the sick, and the poor. At first this was called Newtown. Later it came to be known as the Basilead.

In 364 he left his seclusion to assist his bishop, who was facing opposition from radical Arians, by writing three books against

Eunomius. In 370 he was himself elected bishop of Caesarea, a role which pitted him against not only Arians and their champion, Emperor Valens, but also the Pneumatomachi ("fighters against the Spirit"), who denied the deity of the Holy Spirit. Basil vigorously upheld Nicene doctrine while helping to mediate differences between East and West. He was particularly valuable to the Church in reconciling much of the confusion over terminology.

At the time of his election to the bishopric, his supporters championed his cause with the appeal, "The Holy Ghost must win."[4] It was generally felt that the cause of true religion was at stake. Basil's reputation as a champion of the Spirit grew out of his rejection of any suggestion that the third Person in the Trinity was a created Being and his unusual insights into the relationship of the Spirit and the Church in his legislative, polemical, and dogmatic writings. His title, "Doctor of the Holy Spirit," was fully merited.[5]

To meet the challenge of heresy and to bring errant men back to the truth and the fellowship of the Catholic Church, Basil presents his doctrine of the Holy Spirit and of the Trinity. His first occasion to address these issues was in A.D. 360 when he defends his withdrawal from society to a monastery in Pontus in a letter to the Caesareans. He clearly states that the Holy Spirit is God, while attacking those who would call Him a creature and those who insist that all Trinitarians are in fact Tritheists:

> When all the while they ought to confess that the Father is God, the Son God, and the Holy Ghost God, as they have been taught by the divine words, and by those who have understood them in their highest sense. Against those who cast it in our teeth that we are Tritheists, let it be answered that we confess one God not in number but in nature. . . .If we call God one in nature how can number be charged against us, when we utterly exclude it from that blessed and spiritual nature? Number relates to quantity; and quantity is conjoined with bodily nature, for number is of bodily nature. We believe our Lord to be Creator of bodies. Wherefore every number indicates those things which have received a material and circumscribed nature. Monad and Unity on the other hand signify the nature which is simple and incomprehensible. Whoever therefore confesses either the Son of God or the Holy Ghost to be number or creature introduces unawares a material and circumscribed nature.[6]

In 364 Basil left his life of solitude to assist in the struggle against the Arians. From this point on he seems to equivocate on the deity of the Holy Spirit. This can be explained by the eagerness with which his enemies watched for any unqualified statement that the Spirit is God, so that the Arian emperor Valens might banish him from Caesarea. Basil requests that his friends not be "annoyed at his economy," "by the use of other terms and by statements which unmistakably had the same meaning."[7]

In his writing, *Against Eunomius* (Eunomius was a prominent Arian) in three books (books 4 and 5 are of dubious authenticity), Basil refutes Arian errors to protect the faith of those in the orthodox community who were endangered by Eunomius's influence. Eunomius attempted to couch Christian precepts in Aristotelian categories. Basil warns against the encroachment of philosophical ideas upon the simplicity of expression of the orthodox faith.[8] In the third book Basil attacks Eunomius's insistence that the Holy Spirit is third not only in dignity and order but also in nature, that He was made by the Son at the bidding of the Father, and that the Spirit was the first and the greatest of the works of the Son. In this teaching, the Spirit is still a creature possessing no creative power. Basil responds by proceeding to prove from liturgical evidence that the Spirit is not a creature. Even if the Spirit is third both in order and in number, it does not follow that He is third in nature. No created being could be ranked with the Father and the Son in the divine Trinity. However, Basil is careful not to refer to the Spirit as God.[9]

Two years after becoming bishop, Basil writes to the presbyters of Tarsus. Once again he avoids any mention of the divinity of the Spirit:

> Union would be effected if we were willing to accommodate ourselves to the weaker, where we can do so without injury to souls; since, then, many mouths are open against the Holy Ghost, and many tongues whetted to blasphemy against Him, we implore you, as far as in you lies, to reduce the blasphemers to a small number, and to receive into communion all who do not assert the Holy Ghost to be a creature, that the blasphemers may be left alone, and may either be ashamed and return to the truth, or, if they abide in their error, may cease to have any importance from the smallness of their numbers. Let us then seek no more than this, but propose to all the brethren, who are willing to join us, the Nicene Creed. If they assent to that, let us further require that the Holy Ghost ought not to be called a creature, nor any of those who say so be received into communion. I do not think that we ought to insist upon anything beyond this. For I am convinced that by longer communication and mutual experience without strife, if anything more requires to be added by way of explanation, the Lord Who worketh all things together for good for them that love Him, will grant it.[10]

In another letter penned in 372, Basil provides a succinct statement of the nature and the relationship of the Trinity:

> You have professed your faith in Father, Son and Holy Ghost. Do not abandon this deposit; the Father—the origin of all; the Son—Only begotten of Him, very God, Perfect of Perfect, living image, shewing the whole Father in Himself; the Holy Ghost, having His subsistence of God, the fount of holiness, power that gives life, grace that maketh perfect, through Whom man is adopted, and the mortal made immortal, conjoined with Father and Son in all things in glory and

eternity, in power and kingdom, in sovereignty and godhead: as is
testified by the tradition of the baptism of salvation.

But all who maintain that either Son or Spirit is a creature, or
absolutely reduce the Spirit to ministerial and servile rank, are far
removed from the truth. Flee their communion. Turn away from their
teaching. They are destructive to souls.[11]

Inevitably Basil's caution in labelling the Holy Spirit as divine led
to misunderstanding by small minds who did not understand that
the bishop was attempting to reconcile East and West and that he
was seeking thereby to win semi-Arians back to the Catholic
Church. One such detractor attacked Basil's orthodoxy in the
presence of Gregory of Nazianzen, who gave his friend, the bishop
of Cappadocia, an account of how he had defended him.

> There was a party here at which a great many distinguished friends of
> ours were present, and amongst them was a man who wore the name
> and dress which betoken piety (i.e. a Monk). They had not yet begun
> to drink, but were talking about us, as often happens at such parties,
> and made us rather than anything else the subject of their
> conversation. They admired everything connected with you, and they
> brought me in as professing the same philosophy; and they spoke of
> our friendship, and of Athens, and of our conformity of views and
> feelings on all points. Our Philosopher was annoyed by this. "What is
> this, gentlemen?" he said, with a very mighty shout, "What liars and
> flatterers you are. You may praise these men for other reasons if you
> like, and I will not contradict you; but I cannot concede to you the
> most important point, their orthodoxy. Basil and Gregory are falsely
> praised; the former, because his words are a betrayal of the faith, the
> latter, because his toleration aids the treason."

> What is this, said I, O vain man and new Dathan and Abiram in folly?
> Where do you come from to lay down the law for us? How do you set
> yourself up as a judge of such great matters? "I have just come," he
> replied, "from the festival of the Martyr Eupsychius, (and so it really
> was), and there I heard the great Basil speak most beautifully and
> perfectly upon the Godhead of the Father and the Son, as hardly
> anyone else could speak; but he slurred over the Spirit." And he
> added a sort of illustration from rivers, which pass by rocks and
> hollows out sand. "As for you my good sir," he said, looking at me,
> "you do now express yourself openly on the Godhead of the Spirit,"
> and he referred to some remarks of mine in speaking of God at a
> largely attended Synod, as having added in respect of the Spirit that
> expression which has made a noise, (how long shall we hide the candle
> under the bushel?) "But the other man hints obscurely, and as it were,
> merely suggests the doctrine, but does not openly speak out the truth;
> flooding people's ears with more policy than piety, and hiding his
> duplicity by the power of his eloquence."

> "It is," I said, "because I (living as I do in a corner, and unknown to
> most men who do not know what I say, and hardly that I speak at all)
> can philosophize without danger; but his word is of greater weight,
> because he is better known, both on his own account and on that of
> his Church. And everything that he says is public, and the war around

him is great, as the heretics try to snatch every naked word from Basil's lips, to get him expelled from the Church; because he is almost the only spark of truth left and the vital force, all else around having been destroyed; so that evil may be rooted in the city, and may spread over the whole world as from a centre in that Church. Surely then it is better to use some reserve in the truth, and ourselves to give way a little to circumstances as to a cloud, rather than by the openness of the proclamation to risk its destruction. For no harm will come to us if we recognize the Spirit as God from other phrases which lead to this conclusion (for the truth consists not so much in sound as in sense), but a very great injury would be done to the Church if the truth were driven away in the person of one man." The company present would not receive my economy, as out of date and mocking them; but they shouted me down as practising it rather from cowardice than for reason. It would be much better, they said, to protect our own people by the truth, than by your so-called Economy to weaken them while failing to win over the others. It would be a long business and perhaps unnecessary to tell you all the details of what I said, and of what I heard, and how vexed I was with the opponents, perhaps immoderately and contrary to my own usual temper. But, in fine, I sent them away in the same fashion. But do you O divine and sacred head, instruct me how far I ought to go in setting forth the Deity of the Spirit; and what words I ought to use, and how far to use reserve; that I may be furnished against opponents. For if I, who more than any one else know both you and your opinions, and have often both given and received assurance on this point, still need to be taught the truth of this matter, I shall be of all men the most ignorant and miserable.[12]

The following year Basil dictated a formula of faith which was submitted to Eustathius, bishop of Sebasteia. He presents a stronger statement on the Spirit's nature than at any time since being elected bishop. Here he recognizes the Holy Spirit as intrinsically holy, one with the blessed divine nature and inseparable from the Father and the Son.

> Under these circumstances we are under the necessity of putting before the men who have no pity for themselves, and shut their eyes to the inevitable threat directed by our Lord against blasphemers of the Holy Ghost, their bounden duty. They must anathematize all who call the Holy Ghost a creature, and all who so think; all who do not confess that He is holy by nature, as the Father is holy by nature, and the Son is holy by nature, and refuse Him His place in the blessed divine nature. Our not separating Him from Father and Son is a proof of our right mind, for we are bound to be baptized in the terms we have received and to profess belief in the terms in which we are baptized, and as we have professed belief in, so to give glory to Father, Son, and Holy Ghost; and to hold aloof from the communion of all who call Him creature, as from open blasphemers.[13]

In a letter to Eupaterius and his daughter (A.D. 373), Basil affirms that the Holy Spirit is no stranger to the divine nature, "We glorify the Holy Ghost together with the Father and the Son, from the conviction that He is not separated from the Divine Nature; for that which is foreign by nature does not share in the same honors."[14]

The whole question of the Spirit in the Trinity now had become of sufficient import to prompt Basil to write an entire treatise, *On the Holy Spirit*. Here he insists that the same glory, honor, and adoration given to the Father and Son must be attributed also to the Holy Spirit.[15] He must be numbered with them and not beneath them.

> What, however, they call subnumeration, and in what sense they use this word, cannot even be imagined without difficulty. It is well known that it was imported into our language from the "wisdom of the world." . . . What is it that they maintain? Look at the terms of their imposture. "We assert that connumeration is appropriate to subjects of equal dignity, and subnumeration to those which vary in the direction of inferiority." "Why," I rejoined, "do you say this? I fail to understand your extraordinary wisdom." . . . "Do you maintain that the Son is numbered under the Father, and the Spirit under the Son, or do you confine your subnumeration to the Spirit alone? If, on the other hand, you apply this subnumeration also to the Son, you revive what is the same impious doctrine, the unlikeness of the substance, the lowliness of rank, the coming into being in later time, and once for all, by this one term, you will plainly again set circling all the blasphemies against the Only-begotten. . . . If on the other hand they suppose the subnumeration to benefit the Spirit alone, they must be taught that the Spirit is spoken of together with the Lord in precisely the same manner in which the Son is spoken of with the Father. "The name of the Father and of the Son and of the Holy Ghost" is delivered in like manner, and, according to the coordination of words delivered in baptism, the relation of the Spirit to the Son is the same as that of the Son to the Father. And if the Spirit is coordinate with the Son, and the Son with the Father, it is obvious that the Spirit is also coordinate with the Father.[16]

Basil is particularly irritated by the suggestion that the Spirit does not have the rank of a servant or of a master, but that of a free being:

> He is not a slave, it is said; not a master, but free. Oh the terrible insensibility, the pitiable audacity, of them that maintain this! Shall I rather lament in them their ignorance or their blasphemy? They try to insult the doctrines that concern the divine nature by comparing them with the human, and endeavour to apply to the ineffable nature of God that common custom of human life whereby the difference of degrees is variable, not perceiving that among men no one is a slave by nature.[17]

Once again, however, Basil does not go beyond to affirm the consubstantiality of the Holy Spirit with God. He does not call Him God in fact.

On the matter of procession Basil is much more precise. In order to respond adequately to the Arians who sneeringly pretended that the homoousios of the Holy Spirit implied two sons, the bishop of Cappadocia defines two different modes of origin for the Son and the Spirit. The Spirit proceeds "out of God, not by generation, like the Son, but as Breath of His mouth."[18] Basil recognizes a certain coordination of the Son to the Father, and the Holy Spirit to the Son. When the Spirit is called the Spirit of Christ, it means that He is by nature closely related to the Son. Knowledge of God begins with the Spirit and leads through the Son to the Father.

> Thus the way of the knowledge of God lies from One Spirit through the One Son to the One Father, and conversely the natural Goodness and the inherent Holiness and the royal Dignity extend from the Father through the Only-begotten to the Spirit. Thus there is both acknowledgment of the hypostases and the true dogma of the Monarchy is not lost.[19]

Basil's grasp of the full range of the Holy Spirit's work in the life of the believer is perhaps the most exceptional in the ancient world. To gain some appreciation of this profound awareness we must turn first to his conception of the Church.

Just as the Holy Spirit is the conductor of the "symphony" of creation, so too is He the creator of the Church, which, in turn, fulfills its role through the Spirit in the sanctification of creation. In the Church there also is a "symphony" or harmony of the Spirit, who overcomes division, contradiction, and corruption.[20] The Church is the body of Christ and the fellowship of the Spirit, a brotherhood and community of love ruled and inspired by the Holy Spirit. The Spirit is the indwelling soul of the Church, as Christ is its supreme head.[21] The Church is the assembly of all those whom the Holy Spirit calls from all nations of the world with His kerygma to salvation through the prophets, the apostles, and those in later generations who are endowed with the charisma of the word and teaching.[22]

Basil visualizes the Church as a body composed of individual members each of whom is assigned a particular charisma by the Spirit:

> Since the gifts of the Spirit are different, and neither is one able to receive all nor all the same gifts, each should abide with sobriety and gratitude in the gift given him, and all should be harmonious with one another in the love of Christ, as members in a body. So that he who is inferior in gifts should not despair of himself in comparison with him that excels, nor should the greater despise the less. For those who are divided and at variance with one another deserve to perish.[23]

Edification or life and growth in the Church occurs when there exists mutual cooperation of its members in the exercise and participation of the individual charismata.[24] The Church continues to grow and expand as the Paraclete operates in its midst through the instrumentality of men endowed with the charisma of utterance and teaching.[25]

Christian preaching is not a self-chosen or self-imposed

enterprise. It is a charisma of the Holy Spirit, a sacred ministry to be exercised in the Christian comminity for the benefit of others. Those who are entrusted with the charisma of the word and teaching in the Church should loan their voices to the Spirit so that He may write words of eternal life in the hearts of believers.

> The good God, "that teacheth man knowledge," gives command by His apostle to those who are entrusted with the gift of teaching that they should continue in their teaching. And those who desire the edification of divine teachings He exhorts by Moses, saying "Ask thy father, and he will show thee; thy elders, and they will tell thee." Therefore it is necessary that we who have been entrusted with the ministry of the word should be always zealous for the perfecting of your souls. Sometimes we must needs bear witness publicly before the whole Church, at other times we may allow ourselves to be consulted privately at his pleasure by any one who may come to question us concerning that which belongs to sound faith and the true method of right conduct according to the Gospel of our Lord Jesus Christ; for by means of these two things the man of God is perfected.[26]

Those who have the gift of teaching are quickened by divine grace; their words are like arrows sharpened through the power of the Spirit.[27] Those who lead Christ's followers

> Lead them forth to the blooming and fragrant nourishment of spiritual doctrine, water them with living water with the concurrent assistance of the Spirit, raise them up and nourish them until they produce fruit; then they guide them to rest and safety from those who lay snares for them.[28]

Basil also attaches unusual weight to the spiritual charismata in determining who should exercise authority or ministry in the Church. Although there was a canonical prohibition against transferring a bishop from one church to another, he seems to have disregarded such regulations when anyone demonstrated unusual spiritual endowment. A good example of this practice is found in Letter 28 where we read of a Musonius, who, though a junior, frequently presided over episcopal assemblies because of his many charismatic gifts.[29]

In Basil's teachings a charisma is defined as a gift of the Holy Spirit, given and accepted for the benefit of others.[30] The charismata are not ends in themselves but instruments of virtue.[31] They must be used to serve one's neighbors, who in turn must be willing to accept them. Basil asks why individuals refuse to heed the spiritual word which is so profuse in the Church, gushing forth like a stream from the pious heart which is filled with the charismata of the Spirit. Why not take advantage of the benefits of divine wisdom?[32]

No man can possess all of the charismata. However, "when a number live together" a man enjoys not only his own charisma, but he multiplies it "by imparting it to others and reaps the fruits of other men's charismata as if they were his own."[33] Basil insists on "sobriety and gratitude in the charisma" received by each and on maintaining harmonious relationships with one another in the love of Christ, as members in a body.[34] Thus, Christian unity exists in the diversity of gifts, the Holy Spirit acting as a whole in parts:

> Again, the Spirit is conceived of, in relation to the distribution of gifts, as a whole in parts. For we all are "members one of another, having gifts differing according to the grace that is given us." Wherefore "the eye cannot say to the hand, I have no need of thee; nor again the head to the feet, I have no need of you," but all together complete the Body of Christ in the Unity of the Spirit, and render to one another the needful aid that comes of the gifts. "But God hath set the members in the body, every one of them, as it hath pleased Him." But "the members have the same care for one another," according to the inborn spiritual communion of their sympathy. Wherefore, "whether one member suffer, all the members suffer with it; or one member be honoured, all the members rejoice with it." And as parts in the whole so are we individually in the Spirit, because we all "were baptized in one body into one spirit."[35]

Under the rubric of charisma Basil places not only Pauline charismata, including prophecies and healings,[36] but he also includes all earthly goods and services. Together with the sharing of spiritual endowments which produce unity in the Body of Christ, the *koinonia* in material possessions contributes to edifying the Christian fellowship.[37] In seeking the common good of the Body, all are called to renounce self-love and some even to relinquish private property.[38]

Basil's understanding of the work of the Spirit in the Church through the charismata strongly influences the ordering of his cenobitic communities. He stresses the necessity of detachment from this life in order to receive the Holy Spirit.[39] Therefore, monastic spirituality and the work of the Holy Spirit are intimately connected. Petro Bilaniuk pursues this connection and concludes that the Basilian monk is, in fact, a pneumatophor—an active receptacle, carrier, and distributor of the Holy Spirit and His charisms.[40] Paul J. Fedwick is not certain as to the extent to which Basil "admitted the principle of charismatic ordering in his communities," although he surmises that "A more thorough study will almost certainly show that the ministerial structure of his brotherhoods was rather loose, flexible, and open, allowing considerably more freedom for the charismatic manifestations than one would be ready or willing to admit."[41] Fedwick shows that in Basil's teaching the Spirit is active in every stage of the growth of the soul, whether in purification, in illumination, or in perfection. This especially is true in the ideal monastic community.

Baptism is the means whereby man is introduced into life in the

Holy Spirit, into the first stage of purification or purgation. "And
as parts in the whole so are we individually in the Spirit, because we
all 'were baptized in one body into one Spirit.' "[42] Basil restates
this in other terms at another point in his treatise on the Spirit:

> Now the Spirit is not brought into intimate association with the soul
> by local approximation. How indeed could there be a corporeal
> approach to the incorporeal? This association results from the with-
> drawal of the passions which, coming afterwards gradually on the soul
> from its friendship with God. Only then after a man is purified from
> the shame whose stain he took through his wickedness, and has come
> back again to his natural beauty, and as it were cleaning the Royal
> Image and restoring its ancient form, only thus is it possible for him to
> draw near to the Paraclete.[43]

Basil then describes the subsequent illumination of believers by the
Holy Spirit in the following manner:

> And He, like the sun, will by the aid of thy purified eye show thee in
> Himself the image of the invisible, and in the blessed spectacle of the
> image thou shalt behold the unspeakable beauty of the archetype.
> Through His aid hearts are lifted up, the weak are held by the hand,
> and they who are advancing are brought to perfection. Shining upon
> those that are cleansed from every spot, He makes them spiritual by
> fellowship with Himself. Just as when a sunbeam falls on bright and
> transparent bodies, they themselves become brilliant too, and shed
> forth a fresh brightness from themselves, so souls wherein the Spirit
> dwells, illuminated by the Spirit, themselves become spiritual, and
> send forth their grace to others.[44]

Finally, the soul is lifted to a state of perfection or union with God:

> Hence comes foreknowledge of the future, understanding of
> mysteries, apprehension of what is hidden, distribution of good gifts,
> the heavenly citizenship, a place in the chorus of angels, joy without
> end, abiding in God, the being made like to God, and, highest of all,
> the being made God.[45]

Life in the Spirit involves spiritual freedom that is worked out in
a life of discipline and obedience. Any claim of independence is
seen by Basil as an exercise of the gifts for selfish purpose, rather
than for the good of the Body. He invokes the apostolic command,
"Not looking each to his own things, but each also to the things of
the others" (Phil. 2:4). Basil is particularly concerned about the
asocial anchorites who preferred solitude and, therefore, did not
exercise their gifts to meet real needs in the Church.

> Now all of us who have been received in one hope of our calling are
> one body having Christ as head, and we are severally members one of
> another. But if we are not joined together harmoniously in the close
> links of one body in the Holy Spirit, but each of us chooses solitude,
> not serving the common welfare in a way well pleasing to God but
> fulfilling the private desires of self-pleasing, how, when we are thus
> separated and divided off, can we preserve the mutual relation and
> service of the limbs one to another, or their subjection to our head,
> which is Christ? For it is impossible to rejoice with him that is
> glorified or to suffer with the sufferer when our life is thus divided,

since it is impossible for the individual monk to know the affairs of his neighbour. In the next place, no single man is sufficient to receive all spiritual gifts, but according to the proportion of the faith that is in each man the supply of the Spirit is given; consequently, in the common life the private gift of each man becomes the common property of his fellows. "For to one is given the word of wisdom, to another gifts of healing, etc." Each of which gifts the recipient has as much for other's sake as for his own. So that of necessity in the community life the working of the Holy Spirit in one man passes over to all the rest at once.[46]

Because of the charismatic structure of the Church, Basil concludes that certain people are chosen by God to lead others:

Is it not plain and incontestable that the ordering of the Church is effected through the Spirit? For He gave, it is said, "in the church, first Apostles, secondarily prophets, thirdly teachers, after that miracles, then gifts of healing, helps, governments, diversities of tongues," for this order is ordained in accordance with the division of the gifts that are of the Spirit.[47]

In the Christian community Basil detects two orders, one with the charisma of leadership and care, the other with the function "to defer and obey."[48] The term "charisma of leadership and care" is applied in Basil's works equally to ecclesiastical and ascetic leaders. It could designate either a bishop or a college of presbyters acting on his behalf or the head of an ascetic community.

In addition to the charisma of leadership, these spiritual seniors possess the gift of the discernment of spirits and that of healing of sicknesses, and the Superior par excellence has the gift of forseeing the future, for he is the eye of the body.[49]

Life in the Holy Spirit is not limited to leaders, however. The simple monk also is a pneumatophor, participating in the mystery and activity of the Spirit. He is the obedient and spiritual son of his legitimate superiors, manifesting in his life the power and presence of the Spirit. In the *Morals*, the manual for ascetics living in the world, Basil describes the monk's life in the Spirit:

What manner of men Scripture wishes Christians to be, as disciples of Christ, conformed only to the pattern of what they see in Him, or hear from Him . . . as members of Christ, in all working of the commandments of the Lord, or perfectly equipped with the gifts of the Holy Spirit according to the worthiness of the Head, which is Christ . . . as light in the world, so that both they themselves are nonreceptive of evil and illuminate those who approach them to a knowledge of the truth, and these either become what they should be or reveal what they are . . . as salt in the world, so that they who associate with them are renewed in the Spirit unto incorruptibility.[50]

But Basil does not limit the work of the Spirit or life in the Spirit to the monastic milieu. All Christians are recipients of the charisma of love, the highest of all the charismata bestowed by the Spirit, the summary of all man's obligations toward God and his neighbors.

Bilaniuk correctly observes that "thanks to St. Basil, the Eastern tradition preserved the unity of monastic lay spirituality, for there is no articulated doctrine of a separate or superior vocation for the monks."[51]

In both his role as monk and later as bishop, Basil is a true model of the pneumatophor, enunciating as few before or after him the great wealth of life in the Spirit. His confidence in the vitality of divine provision never ebbs. This is apparent in the concluding statement of his treatise on the Spirit, in which he recognizes that certain questions might still remain unanswered. However, he declares with certainty that through him or through others Christ by the Holy Spirit will grant a clarification on matters not yet settled.

> My task is now done. If you find I have said satisfactory, let this make an end of our discussion of these matters. If you think any point requires further elucidation, pray do not hesitate to pursue the investigation with all diligence, and to add to your information by putting any uncontroversial question. Either through me or through others the Lord will grant full explanation on matters which have yet to be made clear, according to the knowledge supplied to the worthy by the Holy Spirit. Amen.[52]

2. GREGORY OF NYSSA

Born in Caesarea, (ca. 335/336), the younger brother of Basil the Great, Gregory of Nyssa was from an early age highly studious, but weak in health and shy in disposition. He was totally dominated by his forceful brother, whom he referred to as "the Master." After spending a short time as a rhetorician—a secular role which Basil disapproved—Gregory broke away from the world, retiring into solitude in Pontus. He was thoroughly enamored with the ascetic life. Although he was himself married, he commended virginity as a higher grade of perfection. Virginity meant to him more than chastity; it involved purity of the whole life.

Against his will, Gregory was summoned by his brother Basil to become bishop of Nyssa. A town hitherto virtually unknown, it gained certain prominence as the bishop's reputation grew. In reaction against his efforts on behalf of the Nicene faith, his opponents, the Arians, succeeded in deposing him at a synod in 376 and forced him into exile. When the Arian emperor Valens died two years later, Gregory was allowed to return to his bishopric.

Gregory attended the Second Ecumenical Council in Constantinople in 381, influencing its decisions greatly. Ultimately, he composed the additions to the Nicene Creed that were sanctioned by the Council. Now a prominent figure in the Church, he traveled to Syria, Arabia, and Jerusalem to resolve conflicts.

In originality and intellectual ability Gregory was the most gifted of the Cappadocians. In his theological views, his idealism, and his allegorical interpretation of Scripture, Gregory was more influenced by Origen then any other teacher. Possessing a fine metaphysical mind, Gregory did lasting service to the Church in his exposition of the mystery of the Trinity and the Incarnation, as well as in his accurate distinction between essence (ousia) and personhood (hypostasis) in the Godhead.[53]

In his treatise On "Not Three Gods" Gregory explains that, while we speak of God the Father, God the Son, and God the Holy Ghost, we are not naming three Gods, for the Three share a common divine essence. We are naming three Persons. Each Person has His individual work but does not operate separately from the other Two.

> But in the case of the Divine nature we do not similarly learn that the Father does anything by Himself in which the Son does not work conjointly, or again that the Son has any special operation apart from the Holy Spirit; but every operation which extends from God to the Creation, and is named according to our variable conceptions of it, has its origin from the Father, and proceeds through the Son, and is perfected in the Holy Spirit.[54]

The three Persons must be distinguished by Their origin. The One is the "cause," and the Other Two are "caused." But there is a distinction to be drawn between the Two who are "caused."

> One is the Cause, and another is of the Cause; and again in that which is of the Cause we recognize another distinction. For one is directly from the first Cause, and another by that which is directly from the first Cause, so that the attribute of being Only-begotten abides without doubt in the Son, and the interposition of the Son, while it guards His attribute of being Only-begotten, does not shut out the Spirit from His relation by way of nature to the Father.[55]

The Spirit is thus from the Father through the Son. In this statement of relationship Gregory of Nyssa discovers what will be the definitive Eastern formula of procession. In another text he compares the process to three torches. The first communicates light to the second and, through it, lights the third.

> It is as if a man were to see a separate flame burning on three torches (and we will suppose that the third flame is caused by that of the first being transmitted to the middle, and then kindling the end torch), and were to maintain that the heat in the first exceeded that of the others; that next it showed a variation from it in the direction of the less; and that the third could not be called fire at all, though it burnt and shone just like fire, and did everything that fire does. But if there is really no hindrance to the third torch being fire, though it has been kindled from a previous flame, what is the philosophy of these men, who profanely think that they can slight the dignity of the Holy Spirit because he is named by the Divine lips after the Father and the Son?[56]

Once again, Gregory manifestly indicates that the Son is an instrument of the Father in the production of the Holy Spirit.

While the Son derives His substance immediately from the Father, the Spirit also derives from the Father but mediately through the Son. However, in all three hypostases the essence remains one and the same, untouched by differences in causation or function.

While Gregory of Nazianzen refused to define the third Person because of the mystery, Gregory of Nyssa does not evidence such reticence, claiming to offer a scientific theory based on the analogy of the breath of man's nostrils:

> Now in us the spirit (or breath) is the drawing of the air, a matter other than ourselves, inhaled and breathed out for the necessary sustainment of the body. This, on the occasion of uttering the word, becomes an utterance which expresses in itself the meaning of the word. And in the case of the Divine nature it has been deemed a point of our religion that there is a Spirit of God, just as it has been allowed that there is a Word of God.[57]

But if divine Word is accompanied by divine Breath, the Breath of God is also a living Power which has a personality or hypostasis of His own.

> We regard it [God's Spirit] as that which goes with the Word and manifests its energy, and not as a mere effluence of the breath; for by such a conception the grandeur of the Divine power would be reduced and humiliated, that is, if the Spirit that is in it were supposed to resemble ours.[58]

Having drawn his analogy of the Spirit and breath, Gregory proceeds to remind his readers that we are sorely limited in exploring the depths of the divine mystery.

> And so one who severely studies the depths of the mystery, receives secretly in his spirit, indeed, a moderate amount of apprehension of the doctrine of God's nature, yet he is unable to explain clearly in words the ineffable depth of this mystery. As, for instance, how the same thing is capable of being numbered and yet rejects numeration, how it is observed with distinctions yet is apprehended as a monad, how it is separate as to personality yet is not divided as to subject matter.[59]

In the field of speculative and mystical theology, Gregory of Nyssa surpassed both his brother, Basil, and Gregory of Nazianzen. Several modern scholars have focused on the role of the Spirit in the transformation of man into the image of God as presented in Gregory's writings. Of particular value on the sanctifying role of the Spirit are Collins's work on the Spirit and the sacraments and Jaeger's attempt to compare the role of the Spirit as the formative power in man's transformation with *paideia*—the training of the physical and mental faculties in such a way as to produce a broad enlightened mature outlook harmoniously combined with maximum cultural development—which was the transforming power in ancient Greek culture.[60] Jean Daniélou,[61] like Collins, has identified Gregory's emphasis on the sacraments or the "mysteries" of the Church as the key to understanding his mystical or speculative theology. For our purposes, it is with Gregory's treatment of the sacraments that we are able to penetrate most deeply into his perception of the work of the Holy Spirit in the life of the Christian.

Gregory is the first Christian theologian to interweave firmly the doctrine of the sacraments into a systematic theology of the Incarnation. The sacraments are a continuation of the process of the Incarnation, by which the grace of redemption reaches man. In his great compendium of Christian doctrine, *The Catechetical Oration*, the bishop of Nyssa describes the mystery involved in two of the sacraments, baptism and Eucharist. Concerning baptism he writes:

> But the descent into the water, and the trine immersion of the person in it, involves another mystery. For since the method of our salvation was made effectual not so much by His precepts in the way of teaching as by the deeds of Him Who has effected life as a living fact, so that by means of the flesh which He has assumed, and at the same time deified, everything kindred and related may be saved along with it, it was necessary that some means should be devised by which there might be, in the baptismal process, a kind of affinity and likeness between him who follows and Him Who leads the way.[62]

Regarding the Eucharist Gregory teaches that

> God who was manifested infused Himself into perishable humanity for this purpose, viz. that by this communion with Deity mankind might at the same time be deified, for this end it is that, by dispensation of His grace, He disseminates Himself in every believer through that flesh, whose substance comes from bread and wine, blending Himself with the bodies of believers, to secure that, by this union with the immortal, man, too, may be a sharer in corruption.[63]

Collins points out that in both passages "We see that the process of 'deification,' which was consummated in the humanity of Christ by the hypostatic union of the Word with it, is continuously effected in mankind through union with Christ in the sacraments."[64] It still remains, however, to clarify the role of the Holy Spirit in this process of deification. Gregory provides an answer in his efforts to counter the teachings of Eunomius, who deemphasized the sacraments in favor of dogma. The following is a passage from his *On the Baptism of Christ: A Sermon for the Day of Lights*:

> Despise not, therefore, the Divine laver, nor think lightly of it, as a common thing, on account of the use of water. For the power that operates is mighty, and wonderful are the things that are wrought thereby. For this holy altar, too, by which I stand is stone, ordinary in its nature, nowise different from the other slabs of stone that build our houses and adorn our pavements; but seeing that it was consecrated to the service of God, and received the benediction, it is a holy table, an altar undefiled, no longer touched by the hands of all, but of the priests alone, and that with reverence. The bread again is at

first common bread, but when the sacramental action consecrates it, it
is called, and becomes, the Body of Christ. So with the sacramental
oil; so with the wine: though before the benediction they are of little
value, each of them, after the sanctification bestowed by the Spirit,
has its several operation.[65]

It is the Holy Spirit, then, who transforms the various common or
material elements through His sanctifying power. In turn, man by
partaking of the sacramental provision is himself transformed by
the same blessing or sanctifying of the Spirit. It is not the elements
alone which provide the gift of spiritual rebirth. Rather, it is "the
visitation of the Spirit that comes sacramentally to set us free."[66]
Gregory indicates that the reason that the Spirit alone is not
sufficient for the completion of baptism is that man is a compound
being. "For his visible body, water, the sensible element, for his
soul, which we cannot see, the Spirit invisible, invoked by faith,
present unspeakably."[67] The three inseparable and necessary
components of baptism—water, faith, and most importantly, the
personal intervention of the Holy Spirit—together effect the
regeneration of the believer.

Gregory acknowledges that chrismation (external anointing with
holy oil) is one of the sacraments essential to Christian
initiation. (It should be noted that no mention is made of
chrismation in the Catechetical Oration.) "Whosoever is to touch
the Son by faith must needs first encounter the oil in the very act of
touching; there is not a part of Him devoid of the Holy Spirit."[68]

These destroyers of the Spirit's glory, who relegate Him to a subject
world, must tell us of what thing that unction is the symbol. Is it not a
symbol of the Kingship? . . . For the Son is King, and His living,
realized, and personified Kingship is found in the Holy Spirit, Who
anoints the Only-begotten, and so makes Him the Anointed, and the
King of all things that exist.[69]

However, in Gregory's writings the bestowal of the Spirit is not
limited to chrism. At the Eucharist, "the table of the Spirit,"[70] the
third person of the Trinity blesses and sanctifies the material
elements—which in and of themselves have little value—
transforming them into the body and blood of Christ.[71]

Gregory does not suggest that the offices exercised by the Spirit
in the sacraments are outside the operation of the remainder of the
Trinity. He stresses the operation of the Spirit in the sacraments to
prove that the Spirit is divine. However, in the economy of
redemption the entire Godhead is intimately involved as completely
in the sacraments as in the Incarnation. Gregory refers to the
baptismal formula to prove the divinity of the Spirit as well as the
involvement of the full Trinity:

Why in the name of the Father? Because He is the primal cause of all
things. Why in the name of the Son? Because He is the maker of

creation. Why in the name of the Holy Spirit? Because He is the power perfecting all. We bow ourselves therefore before the Father that we may be sanctified; before the Son also we bow that the same end may be fulfilled; we bow before the Holy Spirit that we may be made what He is in fact and in name. There is not a distinction in the sanctification in the sense that the Father sanctifies more, the Son less and the Holy Spirit in a less degree than the other Two.[72]

Baptism is not only a means of imparting grace to believers but the opening of a door to a life in the Spirit in which grace constantly flows to those who accept it.

Those who approach the Spirit with guileless intent, in perfect faith with no defilement in their conscience, the power of the Spirit cleanses according to the one who says: "For our gospel was not delivered to you in word only, but in power also; and in the Holy Spirit and in much fullness, as you know." [1 Thess. 1:5] And again: "May your spirit and soul and body be preserved blamelessly in the name of our Lord Jesus Christ," [1 Thess. 5:23] who has furnished a pledge of immortality through Baptism to those who are worthy, in order that the talent entrusted to each may, through their use of it, produce unseen wealth. For brethren, holy Baptism is important, important for the things perceptible to the mind of those who receive it with fear; for the rich and ungrudging Spirit is always flowing into those accepting grace, filled with which the holy apostles reaped a full harvest for the churches of Christ.[73]

When man has been cleansed, the Holy Spirit comes to him and dwells in him, setting his soul on fire,[74] giving him the grace of His fruits. At one point in his treatise, *Against Those Who Defer Baptism*, Gregory speaks of the Spirit symbolically as a fertile Dove, and His gifts as offspring of that Dove:

Allow time for the Dove to fly to you, that Dove which Jesus for the first brought down in figure from Heaven. That Dove is guileless, meek and very fertile. When she finds a man cleansed, like kindling wood well prepared, she dwells in him and sets his soul on fire after the manner of a bird who broods upon her eggs to hatch them. The Dove then gives birth to many excellent offsprings. These children are good actions, holy words, faith, piety, righteousness, temperance, chastity and purity. These are the children of the Spirit, but they are our possessions.[75]

Grace given by the Holy Spirit increases as one is nurtured by the same Spirit and grows to perfect manhood.

The grace of the Holy Spirit is given to everyone with the understanding that there is to be an augmenting and increase of what is received.

One who accepts the coin does so on terms of interest, that is, the grace of the Holy Spirit is given to everyone with the understanding that there is to be an augmenting and increase of what is received. It is necessary for the soul which has been born again by the power of God to be nurtured by the Spirit in proportion to its age of intelligibility, refreshed by the water of virtue and the abundance of grace. Just as the nature of the child newly-born does not continue in the tenderness of age, but when it is nourished by food according to the law of nature it takes its measure in proportion to what is given it, so it is fitting for the recently-born soul whose participation in the Spirit restores to its nature its former beauty, after it has destroyed the sickness which comes over it through disobedience, not to remain always like a child, inactive, leisurely, sleeping unmoved in the state of its birth, but to nourish itself by its own food, and, in proportion to what its nature demands, to rear itself by means of every virtue and labor so that it fortifies itself through the power of the Spirit by its own virtue against the unseen robber attacking it with many devices. It is necessary, therefore, for us to bring ourselves to perfect manhood.[76]

Gregory then refers to those who "hold in high esteem the seal of the Spirit through baptism." It is the desire of the Apostle Paul that these reach the age of intelligence and grow through the additional help of the Spirit. Gregory relates Paul's wish that the Ephesians be granted the Spirit of wisdom and of revelation in the deep knowledge of Christ, that they might know the riches of the glory of His inheritance in the saints and the exceeding greatness of His power towards those who believe (Eph. 1:15-19). The Spirit exercised His mighty power by raising Jesus from the dead. Those who participate in communion with Him have the same assurance that He also will quicken them. At this point Gregory deals with the progress of the inner man as the Spirit strengthens, that "you may be able to comprehend with all the saints what is the breadth and length and height and depth, and to know Christ's love which surpasses knowledge, in order that you may be filled unto all the fullness of God" (Eph. 3:14-19).[77]

The bishop next turns to the matter of gifts, still in the context of the growth of Christian life. Having quoted 1 Corinthians 13:1-8, he comments:

Even if someone receives the other gifts which the Spirit furnishes (I mean the tongues of angels and prophecy and knowledge and the grace of healing), but has never been entirely cleansed of the troubling passions within him through the charity of the Spirit, and has not received the final remedy of salvation in his soul, he is still in danger of failing if he does not keep charity steadfast and firm among his virtues.

Do not acquiesce in His gifts, thinking that because of the wealth and ungrudging grace of the Spirit nothing else is needed for perfection. When these riches come to you be modest in thought, ever submissive and thinking of love as the foundation of the treasure of grace for the soul. . . . The "new creation" is the apostolic rule. . . . A new creature he called the indwelling of the Holy Spirit in a pure and blameless soul removed from evil and wickedness and shamefulness.[78]

Such an individual was Macrina, Gregory's saintly sister, who made the decision not to marry after the death of her betrothed. She lived a contemplative and rigorously ascetic life and exercised great influence over her two famous brothers. Gregory wrote a personal portrait of Macrina not long after 380, the year of her death. On one occasion near the end of her life, Gregory records that ill though she was:

> She tried to cover up her groans and to conceal somehow the difficulty she had in breathing, and, through it all, she adjusted herself to the brighter side. She initiated suitable topics of conversation and gave me an opportunity to speak by asking me questions. As we spoke, we recalled the memory of the great Basil and my soul was afflicted and my face fell and tears poured from my eyes. But she was so far from being downcast by our sorrow that she made the mentioning of the saint a starting point towards the higher philosophy. She rehearsed such arguments, explaining the human situation through natural principles and disclosing the divine plan hidden in misfortune, and she spoke of certain aspects of the future life as if she was inspired by the Holy Spirit, so that my soul almost seemed to be lifted up out of its human sphere by what she said and, under the direction of her discourse, take its stand in the heavenly sanctuaries.[79]

To those who follow the ascetic life, there is no gain in fasting, prayer, and vigils if the fruits of the grace of the Holy Spirit are absent.[80] But for the Christian who, "through faith and the toils of virtue, has received goods from the grace of the Spirit" beyond his nature, has advanced "to the measure of the age of reason, after grace is given to him," and has endured insult and shame because of his faith in God, the final result will be glory, pleasure, and enjoyment, greater than any human pleasure.[81] The advance to perfect manhood will be completed. With this end in view Gregory advises his followers:

> So, govern yourselves thus as you are about to ascend to the highest power and glory through your cooperation with the Spirit; endure every suffering and trial with joy with a view toward appearing to be worthy of the dwelling of the Spirit within you and worthy of the inheritance of Christ.[82]

3. GREGORY OF NAZIANZEN

Gregory of Nazianzen was born about A.D. 330 in Arianzum in southwestern Cappadocia. His father had belonged to the Hypsistarians, a strictly monotheistic sect that rejected both polytheism and trinitarianism. The elder Gregory later was converted to Catholicism by the influence of his wife, Nonna, and soon after was consecrated bishop of Nazianzus. He sent his son, Gregory, to Christian schools in Caesarea in Palestine where he met St. Basil, who was to become a lifelong friend. Later Gregory studied in Alexandria and, finally, in Athens, where his friendship with Basil grew. He remained in Athens for approximately eighteen years, returning to Cappadocia at the age of thirty.

Gregory was strongly attracted to a life of solitude, and lived for a brief period of time with his friend Basil in Pontus in solitary exile. However, seclusion from the world did not seem to be his vocation. He chose instead to live in the world, assisting his elderly father, but under a strict ascetic rule. After being ordained to the priesthood by his father against his will, he fled back to Pontus and Basil. However, he soon returned to Nazianzus to deliver a "Defense of His Flight to Pontus and His Return" on Easter day, 362. About 371 Basil, now archbishop of Caesarea, established several new bishoprics to strengthen his position against Anthimius, Metropolitan of Cappadocia Secunda. To one of these, Sasima, which Gregory described as a miserable little village, [83] Basil consecrated his reluctant friend, Gregory, as bishop. Gregory never resided in Sasima, however, preferring to help his father in Nazianzus.

Gregory's father and mother both died in 374, leaving him free to withdraw into solitude in Seleucia. However, five years later the Church of Constantinople, which had been oppressed by a succession of Arian archbishops and had been hard pressed by Eunomians, Macedonians, and other heresies, begged Gregory to come to their assistance. Gregory agreed after a considerable delay. In Constantinople the Christian Demosthenes, as he now was known, delivered five Theological Orations, which gained for him the additional title "Theologian." When the new emperor, Theodosius, took control of the city in 380 he installed Gregory as archbishop of the Imperial City. His appointment was recognized by the Second Ecumenical Council convoked in 381 in the capital. His nomination was opposed by late arriving bishops from Egypt, however, and he resigned in disgust within a few days. He then went home to Nazianzus to live out the rest of his years in seclusion.

Several of Gregory's most eloquent orations and homilies, delivered on major feast days, are concerned with the Holy Spirit. Of these the most important for our purposes are the Fifth Theological Oration and his sermon on Pentecost. The former, entitled *On the Holy Spirit*, was delivered in Constantinople on the eve of the Second Ecumenical Council, called to reaffirm the Nicene faith. It is considered by some modern scholars to be the greatest of all sermons on the Holy Spirit. [84]

Gregory begins by describing certain men who have wearied in their disputations concerning the Son and have turned with even greater intensity to struggle against the Spirit. They rail, "From whence are you bringing in upon us this strange God, of whom Scripture is silent?" [85] This is nothing new, for the Sadducees denied the existence of the Holy Spirit. The Greeks referred to Him as the Mind of the World or the Eternal Mind. Some Christian wise men have not agreed whether He is an activity, a creature, or God.

Some have been uncertain what to call Him, and they claim that out of reverence for Scripture, it is better to leave the matter unresolved. There are still others who suggest that three entities exist: one is infinite in essence and power, the second in power but not in essence, and the third circumscribed in both. Christians must recognize, Gregory continues, that the Holy Spirit is either a substantive or a contingent existence. He cannot be the latter because Scripture speaks of Him as having a capacity to work without assistance, yet with the actions of a person. If a person, He is either a creature or God. If He is a creature, how do we believe in Him? How are we made perfect in Him? If He is God, He is neither a creature nor a servant. Neither can He be described by any other lowly appellation.

Gregory then deals forcibly with the suggestion that if all things were made by the Son, the Spirit must be one of them. Further, he refuses to accept the argument that, if the Spirit is God, there must be two "Sons" in the Godhead. If we reject both that the Holy Spirit is generate and ingenerate, it still remains that He proceeds from the Father.

> For tell me, what position will you assign to that which proceeds, which has started up between the two terms of your division, and is introduced by a better Theologian than you, our Saviour Himself? Or perhaps you have taken that word out of your Gospels for the sake of your Third Testament, The Holy Ghost, which proceedeth from That Source, is no Creature; and inasmuch as he is not Begotten is no Son; and inasmuch as He is between the Unbegotten and the Begotten is God. And thus escaping the toils of your syllogisms, He has manifested himself as God, stronger than your divisions. What then is Procession? Do you tell me what is the Unbegottenness of the Father, and I will explain to you the physiology of the Generation of the Son and the Procession of the Spirit, and we shall both of us be frenzy-stricken for prying into the mystery of God. And who are we to do these things, we who cannot even see what lies at our feet, or number the sand of the sea, or the drops of rain, or the days of Eternity, much less enter into the Depths of God, and supply an account of that Nature which is so unspeakable and transcending all words?[86]

Gregory then asks what is lacking in the Spirit which prevents His being a Son:

> We assert that there is nothing lacking—for God has no deficiency. But the difference of manifestation, if I may express myself or rather of their mutual relations one to another, has caused the difference of their Names. . . . The Three are One in Godhead, and the One Three in Properties; so that neither is the Unity a Sabellian one, nor does the Trinity countenance the present evil distinction.[87]

Is the Spirit, then, God? Gregory answers, "Most certainly."[88] It follows that He is consubstantial because He is God. But there still remains the problem that nowhere in Scripture can be found worship or prayer addressed to the Spirit. Gregory replies that it is the Spirit *in* whom we worship and *through* whom we pray.

> For Scripture says, God is a Spirit, and they that worship Him must
> worship Him in Spirit and in truth. And again, We know not what we
> should pray for as we ought; but the Spirit Itself maketh intercession
> for us with groanings which cannot be uttered; and I will pray with the
> Spirit and I will pray with the understanding also; that is, in the mind
> and in the Spirit. Therefore to adore or to pray to the Spirit seems to
> me to be simply Himself offering prayer or adoration to Himself. And
> what godly or learned man would disapprove of this, because in fact
> the adoration of One is the adoration of the Three, because of the
> equality of honour and Deity between the Three?[89]

Gregory's assumption that to pray to the Spirit is "to be simply
Himself offering prayer or adoration to Himself" is not necessary
to his argument on behalf of the deity of the Spirit. There is no
need to offer prayer to the Spirit because He is there before we pray
to make good the deficiencies of our prayer. Gregory's matter-of-
fact manner of dealing with prayer in the Spirit does suggest that
this was generally understood and practiced in his day.

Certain of the Macedonians who worshipped the Son revolted
from the Spirit, insisting that the Catholic Church was teaching
Tritheism. In response, Gregory argues that if he is a Tritheist, his
opponents are Ditheists, worshipping the Father and the Son.[90]

Again, the statement by his opponents that the Scriptures are
silent regarding the deity of the Spirit brings a strong retort from
Gregory:

> This, then is what may be said by one who admits the silence of
> Scripture. But now the swarm of testimonies shall burst upon you
> from which the Deity of the Holy Ghost shall be shewn to all who are
> not excessively stupid, or else altogether enemies to the Spirit, to be
> most clearly recognized in Scripture. Look at these facts: Christ is
> born; the Spirit is His Forerunner. He is baptized; the Spirit bears
> witness. He is tempted; the Spirit leads Him up. He works miracles;
> the Spirit accompanies them. He ascends; the Spirit takes His place.
> What great things are there in the idea of God which are not in His
> power? What titles which belong to God are not applied to Him,
> except only Unbegotten and Begotten? For it was needful that the
> distinctive properties of the Father and the Son should remain peculiar
> to Them, lest there should be confusion in the Godhead which brings
> all things, even disorder itself, into due arrangement and good order.
> Indeed I tremble when I think of the abundance of the titles, and how
> many Names they outrage who fall foul of the Spirit. He is called the
> Spirit of God, the Spirit of Christ, the Mind of Christ, the Spirit of the
> Lord, and Himself The Lord, the Spirit of Adoption, of Truth, of
> Liberty; the Spirit of Wisdom, of Understanding, of Counsel, of
> Might, of Knowledge, of Godliness, of the fear of God. For He is the
> Maker of all these, filling all with His Essence, containing all things,
> filling the world in His Essence, yet incapable of being comprehended
> in His power by the world; good, upright, princely, by nature not by
> adoption; sanctifying, not sanctified: measuring, not measured;
> shared, not sharing; filling, not filled; containing, not contained;

inherited, glorified, reckoned with the Father and the Son; held out as a threat; the Finger of God; fire like God; to manifest, as I take it, His consubstantiality; the Creator-Spirit, Who by Baptism and by Resurrection creates anew; the Spirit That knoweth all things, That teacheth, That bloweth where and to what extent He listeth; That guideth, talketh, sendeth forth, separateth, is angry or tempted; That revealeth, illumineth, quickeneth, or rather is the very Light and Life; That maketh Temples; That deifieth; That perfecteth so as even to anticipate Baptism, yet after Baptism to be sought as a separate gift; That doeth all things that God doeth; divided into fiery tongues; dividing gifts, making Apostles, Prophets, Evangelists, Pastors, and Teachers; understanding manifold, clear, piercing, undefiled, unhindered, which is the same thing as Most wise and varied in His actions; and making all things clear and plain; and of independent power, unchangeable, Almighty, all-seeing, penetrating all spirits that are intelligent, pure, most subtle (the Angel Host I think); and also all prophetic spirits and apostolic in the same manner and not in the same places; for they lived in different places; thus showing that He is uncircumscript.

They who say and teach these things, and moreover call Him another Paraclete in the sense of another God, who know that blasphemy against Him alone cannot be forgiven, and who branded with such fearful infamy Ananias and Sapphira for having lied to the Holy Ghost, what do you think of these men? Do they proclaim the Spirit God, or something else? Now really, you must be extraordinarily dull and far from the Spirit if you have any doubt about this and need some one to teach you. So important then, and so vivid are His Names.[91]

Figures of speech and imagery borrowed from the world of nature are not adequate to depict relationship within the Trinity. Pictures of eye, fountain, and river, of sun, ray, and light are imperfect.

In a word, there is nothing which presents a standing point to my mind in these illustrations from which to consider the Object which I am trying to represent to myself, unless one may indulgently accept one point of the image while rejecting the rest. Finally, then, it seems best to me to let the images and the shadows go, as being deceitful and very far short of the truth; and clinging myself to the more reverent conception, and resting upon few words, using the guidance of the Holy Ghost, keeping to the end as my genuine comrade and companion the enlightenment which I have received from Him, and passing through this world to persuade all others also to the best of my power to worship Father, Son, and Holy Ghost, the one Godhead and Power.[92]

Gregory's resolve to depend upon "few words" is amplified in several discourses. Everywhere he insists upon the unity of divine essence and the uniqueness of the three Persons therein. One example is found in his *Oration on the Holy Lights*, in which he speaks of

But One God, the Father, of Whom are all things, and One Lord Jesus Christ, by Whom are all things, and One Holy Ghost, in Whom are all things; yet these words, of, by, in Whom, do not denote a difference

of nature (for if this were the case, the three prepositions, or the order
of the three names would never be altered), but they characterize the
personalities of a nature which is one and unconfused.[93]

This desire for an economy of terms is coupled with a distaste for
irreverent inquiry, for those who become "frenzy-stricken for
prying into the mystery of God."[94]

Gregory devotes another sermon to the doctrine of the Holy
Spirit, *The Oration on Pentecost*. Again, his theme is to establish
the deity of the Spirit but by different arguments than we have seen
in his Fifth Theological Oration, *On the Holy Spirit*. Here we find a
masterful account of the supernatural work of the Spirit leading up
to the climax of Pentecost. Among the most beautiful passages
deals with the creativity of the Spirit, both in forming the universe
and in bringing individuals in the Old and the New Testaments to
their ultimate potential in God:

> This Spirit shares with the Son in working both the Creation and the
> Resurrection, as you may be shewn by this Scripture; By the Word of
> the Lord were the heavens made, and all the power of them by the
> breath of His Mouth; and this, The Spirit of God that made men, and
> the Breath of the Almighty that teacheth me; and again, Thou shalt
> send forth Thy Spirit and they shall be created, and Thou shalt renew
> the face of the earth. And He is the Author of spiritual regeneration.
> Here is your proof: None can see or enter into the Kingdom, except he
> be born again of the Spirit, and be cleansed from the first birth, which
> is a mystery of the Light, by a remoulding of the day and of the Light,
> by which every one singly is created anew. This Spirit, for He is most
> wise and most loving, if He takes possession of a shepherd makes him
> a Psalmist, subduing evil spirits by his word, and proclaims him King;
> if he possess a goat herd and scraper of sycamore fruit, He makes him
> a Prophet. Call to mind David and Amos. If He possess a goodly
> youth, He makes him a Judge of Elders, even beyond his years, as
> Daniel testifies, who conquered the lions in their den. If he takes
> possession of Fishermen, He makes them catch the whole world in the
> nets of Christ, taking them up in the meshes of the Word. Look at
> Peter and Andrew and the Sons of Thunder, thundering the things of
> the Spirit. If of Publicans, He makes gain of them for discipleship,
> and makes them merchants of souls; witness Matthew, yesterday a
> Publican, today an Evangelist. If of zealous persecutors, He changes
> the current of their zeal, and makes them Pauls instead of Sauls, and
> as full of piety as He found them of wickedness.[95]

Gregory fully understands that he is living in the real age of the
Spirit:

> We are keeping the feast of Pentecost and of the Coming of the Spirit,
> and the appointed time of the Promise, and the fulfilment of our
> hope. And how great, how august, is the Mystery. The dispensations
> of the Body of Christ are ended; or rather, what belongs to His Bodily
> Advent (for I hesitate to say the Dispensation of His Body, as long as
> no discourse persuades me that it is better to have put off the body),
> and that of the Spirit is beginning.[96]

The work of the Spirit within the believer is as He wills, not as we
command:

As to the things of the Spirit, may the Spirit be with me, and grant me speech as much as I desire; or if not that, yet as is in due proportion to the season. Anyhow He will be with me as my Lord; not in servile guise, nor awaiting a command, as some think. For He bloweth where He wills and on whom He wills, and to what extent He wills. Thus we are inspired both to think and to speak of the Spirit.[97]

But the Spirit also operates in ecclesiastical context, especially in the sacrament of baptism. In his *Oration on the Holy Lights,* preached on the Festival of the Epiphany 381, one day before that of baptism, Gregory compares the baptism by John with baptism by Christ. The latter he sees as the perfect baptism because it is in the Spirit.

John also baptized; but this was not like the baptism of the Jews, for it was not only in water, but also "unto repentence." Still it was not wholly spiritual, for he does not add "And in the Spirit." Jesus also baptized, but in the Spirit. This the perfect Baptism.[98]

The Spirit serves as the Giver of the gift and hope of grace, the Consecrator of the Christian who approaches the waters of baptism with faith in the regenerating work of the divine Spirit of God.[99] He deifies the believer by baptism. "Indeed from the Spirit comes our New Birth, and from the New Birth our new creation, and from the new creation our deeper knowledge of the dignity of Him from Whom it is derived."[100] The Spirit shows us the Son who takes us to the Father.[101] He assists us in prayer when we fall short.[102] He indwells the redeemed. While we might have expected a fuller exposition of the meaning of the *koinonia* of the Spirit, Gregory does give us glimpses into the Spirit's work in his own life and in several of those close to him. The indwelling operation of the Spirit is seen as essential to his own functioning as a priest:

How could I dare to offer to Him the external sacrifice, the antitype of the great mysteries, or clothe myself with the garb and name of priest, before my hands had been consecrated by holy works; before my eyes had been accustomed to gaze safely upon created things, with wonder only for the Creator, and without injury to the creature; before my ear had been sufficiently opened to the instruction of the Lord, and He had opened mine ear to hear without heaviness, and had set a golden earring with precious sardius, that is, a wise man's word in an obedient ear; before my mouth had been opened to draw in the Spirit, and opened wide to be filled with the spirit of speaking mysteries and doctrines; and lips bound, to use the words of wisdom, by divine knowledge, and, as I would add, loosed in due season; before my tongue had been filled with exultation, and become an instrument of Divine melody, awaking with glory, awaking right early, and laboring till it cleave to my jaws; before my feet had been set upon the rock, made like hart's feet, and my footsteps directed in godly fashion so that they should not well-nigh slip, nor slip at all; before all my members had become instruments of righteousness, and all mortality had been put off, and swallowed up of life, and had yielded to the Spirit?[103]

In obedience not to man but to the Spirit's beckoning, he lives, he moves, he speaks, or is silent. He lives in the Spirit!

> I opened my mouth, and drew in the Spirit, and I give myself and all to the Spirit, my action and speech, my inaction and silence, only let Him hold me and guide me, and move both hand and tongue whither it is right, and expedient. I am an instrument of God, a rational instrument, an instrument tuned and struck by that skillful artist, the Spirit. Yesterday His work in me was silence. I mused on abstinence from speech. Does He strike upon my mind today? My speech shall be heard, and I will muse on utterance. I am neither so talkative, as to desire to speak, when He is bent on silence; nor so reserved and ignorant as to set a watch before my lips when it is the time to speak: but I open and close my door at the will of that Mind and Word and Spirit, Who is One kindred Deity.[104]

Gregory's father had experienced divine healing while he was bishop. The story is related in Gregory's oration commemorating the later death of his father in A.D. 374. The incident is remarkable, not only because of the elder Gregory's physical recovery, but also because of his recognition, through the power of the Spirit, of the divine intervention on his behalf.

> His whole frame was on fire with an excessive, burning fever, his strength had failed, he was unable to take food, his sleep had departed from him, he was in the greatest distress, and agitated by palpitations. Within his mouth, the palate and the whole of the upper surface was so completely and painfully ulcerated, that is was difficult and dangerous to swallow even water. The skill of physicians, the prayers, most earnest though they were, of his friends, and every possible attention were alike of no avail. He himself in this desperate condition, while his breath came short and fast, had no perception of present things, but was entirely absent, immersed in the objects he had long desired, now made ready for him. We were in the temple, mingling supplications with the sacred rites, for, in despair of all others, we had betaken ourselves to the Great Physician, to the power of that night, and to the last succour, with the intention, shall I say, of keeping a feast, or of mourning; of holding festival, or paying funeral honours to one no longer here? O those tears! which were shed at that time by all the people. O voices, and cries, and hymns blended with the Psalmody! From the temple they sought the priest, from the sacred rite the celebrant, from God their worthy ruler, with my Miriam to lead them and strike the timbrel not of triumph, but of supplication; learning then for the first time to be put to shame by misfortune, and calling at once upon the people and upon God; upon the former to sympathize with her distress, and to be lavish of their tears, upon the latter, to listen to her petitions, as, with the inventive genius of suffering, she rehearsed before Him all His wonders of old time.

> What then was the response of Him who was the God of that night and of the sick man? A shudder comes over me as I proceed with my story. And though you, my hearers, may shudder, do not disbelieve; for that would be impious, when I am the speaker, and in reference to him. The time of the mystery was come, and the reverend station and

order, when silence is kept for the solemn rites; and then he was raised up by Him who quickeneth the dead, and by the holy night. At first he moved slightly, then more decidedly; then in a feeble and indistinct voice he called by name one of the servants who was in attendance upon him, and bade him come, and bring his clothes, and support him with his hand. He came in alarm, and gladly waited upon him, while he, leaning upon his hand as upon a staff, imitates Moses upon the mount, arranges his feeble hands in prayer, and in union with, or on behalf of, his people eagerly celebrates the mysteries, in such few words as his strength allowed, but, as it seems to me, with a most perfect intention. What a miracle! In the sanctuary without a sanctuary, sacrificing without an altar, a priest far from the sacred rites: yet all these were present to him in the power of the spirit recognised by him, though unseen by those who were there. Then, after adding the customary words of thanksgiving and after blessing the people, he retired again to his bed and after taking a little food, and enjoying a sleep he recalled his spirit and his health being gradually recovered on the new day of the feast as we call the first Sunday after the festival of the Resurrection, he entered the temple and inaugurated his life which had been preserved, with the full complement of clergy, and offered the sacrifice of thanksgiving. To me this seems no less remarkable than the miracle in the case of Hezekiah, who was glorified by God in his sickness and prayers with an extension of life.[105]

Immediately following this account, Gregory relates a similar miracle affecting his mother, who was unable to eat but experienced healing through a dream in which she ate from a basket of pure white loaves. He also describes a sea voyage taken early in his adult life, before his baptism, during which he sailed into a terrible storm. His parents, who were many miles away, experienced a vision during the night at the very time the storm was at its peak. Their prayers for his deliverance were answered, and the miracle was confirmed upon his return home.[106]

Gregory reasons that the Spirit's presence brings men into harmony. While at the Tower of Babel God chose to confuse tongues, the Spirit has chosen presently to provide a diversity of gifts to many men, bringing them together in a unity of the Spirit:

But as the old Confusion of tongues was laudable, when men who were of one language in wickedness and impiety, even as some now venture to be, were building the Tower; for by the confusion of their language the unity of their intention was broken up, and their undertaking destroyed; so much more worthy of praise is the present miraculous one. For being poured from One Spirit upon many men, it brings them again into harmony. And there is a diversity of Gifts, which stands in need of yet another Gift to discern which is the best, where all are praiseworthy.[107]

In his *Oration On Pentecost* "the Theologian" Gregory summarizes his doctrine of the Spirit. Most noteworthy is his declaration that the Spirit is known by the Spirit only. What little

we know is revealed to us by the Spirit through the Scriptures. Why
discuss it further?

> The Holy Ghost, then, always existed, and exists, and always will
> exist. He neither had a beginning, nor will He have an end; but He was
> everlastingly ranged with and numbered with the Father and the Son.
> For it was not ever fitting that either the Son should be wanting to the
> Father, or the Spirit to the Son. For then Deity would be shorn of Its
> Glory in its greatest respect, for It would seem to have arrived at the
> consummation of perfection as if by an afterthought. Therefore He
> was ever being partaken, but not partaking; perfected; sanctifying,
> not being sanctified; deifying, not being deified; Himself ever the
> same with Himself, and with Those with Whom He is ranged;
> invisible, eternal, incomprehensible, unchangeable, without quality,
> without quantity, without form, impalpable, self-moving, eternally
> moving, with free-will, self-powerful, All-powerful (even though all
> that is of the Spirit is referable to the First Cause, just as is all that is
> of the Only-begotten); Life and Lifegiver; Light and Lightgiver;
> absolute Good, and Spring of Goodness; the right, the Princely Spirit;
> the Lord, the Sender, the Separator; Builder of His own Temple;
> leading, working as He wills; distributing His own Gifts; the Spirit of
> Adoption, of Truth, of Wisdom, of Understanding, of Knowledge, of
> Godliness, of Counsel, of Fear (which are ascribed to Him) by Whom
> the Father is known and the Son is glorified; and by Whom alone He
> is known; one class, one service, worship, perfection, sanctification.
> Why make a long discourse of it?[108]

Notes to Chapter 6

[1]Adolph von Harnack, *History of Dogma* (New York: Russell
and Russell, 1958), 4:84-88, accuses the Cappadocians of having
twisted the doctrine of Nicea, of playing a practical joke on the
Church by achieving the universal acceptance of the homoousios,
but in the sense of the homoousios. Harnack's position assumes
that the bishops of Nicea were primarily concerned with the unity
of God, and that the Cappadocian fomula "three hypostases and
one ousia" was a veiled tritheism and, therefore, a betrayal of the
Nicene faith. Harnack's argument does not appear justified for the
following reasons: (1) the Nicenes' use of the homoousios was to
affirm the divine nature of the Son, not to proclaim the unity of the
divine substance or to deny uniqueness among Persons in the
Godhead; (2) the Cappadocians asserted the common essence
which the three divine Persons share as well as the particular
subsistence of each; (3) the movement encouraged by the
Cappadocians was of the semi-Nicenes to Nicenism, not vice versa
as Harnack would suggest.

[2]Gregory of Nyssa, *On "Not Three Gods,"* NPF 2nd Series
5:336.

[3]Gregory of Nazianzen, *The Fifth Theological Oration on the*

Holy Spirit xxvi, NPF 2nd Series 7:326.

⁴Gregory of Nazianzen, *Oration* xliii.37, NPF 2nd Series 7:408.

⁵Basil's theology of the Holy Spirit has been studied from a variety of perspectives by such scholars as R.P.C. Hanson, "Basil's doctrine of tradition in relation to the Holy Spirit," *Vigiliae Christianae* 22 (December 1968): 241-255; Petro B. T. Bilaniuk, "The Monk as Pneumatophor in the Writings of St. Basil the Great," *Diakonia* 15, no.1 (1980): 48-63; Paul Jonathan Fedwick, *The Church and the Charisma of Leadership in Basil of Caesarea* (Toronto: Pontifical Institute of Mediaeval Studies, 1979); Reinhart Staats, "Die Basilianische Verherrlichung des Heiligen Geistes auf dem Konzil zu Konstantinopel 381," *Kerygma und Dogma* 25 (Oct.-Dec. 1979): 232-253; K. Yamamura, "Development of the doctrine of the Holy Spirit in patristic philosophy: St. Basil and St. Gregory of Nyssa," *St. Vladimers Theological Quarterly* 18, no.1 (1974): 3-21; Jean Gribomont, "Saint Basile et le monachisme enthousiaste," *Irenikon* 52, no.2 (1980): 123-144; Anthony Meredith, "The Pneumatology of the Cappadocian Fathers and the Creed of Constantinople," *Irish Theological Quarterly* 48 (1981): 196-211; and Jose Maria Yanguas, "La divinidad del Espiritu Santo en S. Basilio," *Scripta Theologica* 9, no.2 (1977): 485-539.

⁶Basil, *Letter* viii.2, NPF 2nd Series 8:116.

⁷Gregory Nazianzen, *The Penagyric on St. Basil*: *Oration* xlviii.68, NPF 2nd Series 7:418.

⁸Basil, *Against Eunomius* i.1.5, 9, PG 29:cols. 497ff, 516ff, 532.

⁹Ibid., iii.1, PG 39:cols. 497ff.

¹⁰*Letter* cxiii, NPF 2nd Series 8:189-190.

¹¹*Letter* cv, NPF 2nd Series 8:186.

¹²Gregory Nazianzen, *Letter* lviii, NPF 2nd Series 7:455.

¹³Basil, *Letter* cxxv.3, NPF 2nd Series 8:195.

¹⁴*Letter* clix.2, NPF 2nd Series 8:212.

¹⁵Basil, *On the Holy Spirit* x.24-26, NPF 2nd Series 8:16-17.

¹⁶Ibid., vii.41-43, NPF 2nd Series 8:26-27.

¹⁷Ibid., xx.51, NPF 2nd Series 8:32.

¹⁸Ibid., xviii.46, NPF 2nd Series 8:29.

¹⁹Ibid., xviii.47, NPF 2nd Series 8:29-30.

²⁰Ibid., xvi.38, NPF 2nd Series 8:24-25.

²¹*Letter* xc.1, NPF 2nd Series 8:176; Basil, *Homily on the Psalms* xlv.4, PG 31:col, 421; *De jud.* iii, PG 31:col. 660; *Homily on the Psalms* xlviii.1, PG 31:col. 433.

²²*Homily on the Psalms* xlviii.1, PG 31:col. 433; *The Morals* lxxx.4, 12, PG 31:col. 864, W.K.L. Clarke, trans., *The Ascetic Works of Saint Basil* (London: SPCK, 1925), 127-128.

[23] *The Morals* lx.1, Clarke, 117.

[24] Basil, *The Longer Rules* vii.2, PG 31:col. 932.

[25] *Homily on the Psalms* xlviii.1, PG 31:col. 433.

[26] *The Shorter Rules*, preface, Clarke, 229; *Homily on the Psalms* xliv.3, PG 31:col. 396.

[27] *Homily on the Psalms* xliv.4, 6, PG 31:cols. 396-397, 404.

[28] *Homily on the Psalms* xxviii.2, PG 31:col. 284.

[29] *Letter* xxviii.1, NPF 2nd Series 8:132.

[30] *The Small Asceticism* iii, PL CIII, col. 495.

[31] *Homily on the Psalms* xi.5, PG 31:col. 381.

[32] Ibid., xi.5, PG 31:col. 384.

[33] *The Longer Rules* vii.2, PG 31:col. 932, Clarke, 165.

[34] *The Morals* lx.1, PG 31:col. 793, Clarke, 117.

[35] *On the Holy Spirit* xxvi.61, NPF 2nd Series 8:38-39.

[36] Ibid., xxvi.61, NPF 2nd Series 8:38.

[37] *Homily on the Psalms* xi.5, PG 31:cols. 381ff.

[38] *Letter* ccxxxvi.7, NPF 2nd Series 8:278-279; *Homily on the Psalms* vi.7, PG 31:col. 267.

[39] *Shorter Rules* cciv, Clarke, 304: "So long then as we do not keep all the commandments of the Lord and are not such as to be testified of by Him that 'ye are not of this world,' let us not expect to be counted worthy of the Holy Spirit."

[40] Bilaniuk, loc. cit.

[41] Fedwick, 39.

[42] *On the Holy Spirit* xxvi.61, NPF 2nd Series 8:39.

[43] Ibid., xxvi.61, NPF 2nd Series, loc. cit.

[44] Ibid.

[45] Ibid., ix.23, NPF 2nd Series 8:16.

[46] *The Longer Rules* vii, Clarke, 164-165.

[47] *On the Holy Spirit* xvi.39, NPF 2nd Series 8:25.

[48] *The Morals* lx-lxi, Clarke, 117; *Shorter Interrogation* 235, PG 31:col. 1240. Fedwick pursues the matter of church leadership in Basil's writings.

[49] *The Longer Rule* xxiv, xxxv, xlii, lv, Clarke, 190-191, 203, 216, 224-228.

[50] *The Morals* lxxx.1, 4, 9-10, Clarke, 127-128.

[51] *Homily on the Psalms* xxxii.1, PG 31:col. 324; *Letter* lxv, NPF 2nd Series 8:163; Bilaniuk, 51.

[52] *On the Holy Spirit* xxx.79, NPF 2nd Series 8:50.

[53] Among the more important writings on Gregory of Nyssa and the Holy Spirit are James J. Collins, "The Holy Spirit's Transforming Activity in Gregory of Nyssa's Sacramental Theology," *Diakonia* (Fordham) 12, no.3 (1977): 234-243; Werner Jaeger,

Early Christianity and Greek Paideia (Cambridge, MA: Belknap Press of Harvard University Press, 1961); Andrew T. Floris, "Two Fourth-Century Witnesses on the Charismata," *Paraclete* 4, no.4 (Fall 1970): 17-22; and K. Yamamura, 3-21.

[54]Gregory of Nyssa, On *"Not Three Gods,"* NPF 2nd Series 5:334.

[55]Ibid., 336.

[56]Gregory of Nyssa, *On the Holy Spirit*, NPF 2nd Series 5:317.

[57]Gregory of Nyssa, *The Great Catechism* ii, NPF 2nd Series 5:477.

[58]Ibid.

[59]*The Great Catechism* iii, NPF 2nd Series 5:477.

[60]See note 53 above.

[61]Jean Daniélou, *Platonisme et Theologie Mystique* (Paris: Aubier, 1944).

[62]*The Great Catechism* xxxv, NPF 2nd Series 5:502; also see Gregory of Nyssa, *Commentary on the Canticle of Canticles*, PG 44:col. 944.

[63]*The Great Catechism* xxxvii, NPF 2nd Series 5:506.

[64]Collins, 235.

[65]Gregory of Nyssa, *On the Baptism of Christ*, NPF 2nd Series 5:519. The Day of Lights is the Festival of the Epiphany or Theophany, during which the Eastern Church commemorates especially the Baptism of Jesus.

[66]Ibid.

[67]Ibid.

[68]*On the Holy Spirit*, NPF 2nd Series 5:321.

[69]Ibid.

[70]Gregory of Nyssa, *On the Ascension of Christ*, in W. Jaeger, ed., *Gregorii Nysenni Opera* (Leiden: Brill, 1952), 9:324.

[71]*On the Baptism of Christ*, NPF 2nd Series 5:519.

[72]Ibid., 520.

[73]Gregory of Nyssa, *On the Christian Mode of Life*, in Virginia Woods Callahan, trans., *The Fathers of the Church* (Washington, D.C.: The Catholic University of America Press, 1967), 58:129 (henceforth FC).

[74]PG 44:cols. 866-867. English translation by Herbert Musurello in Jean Daniélou, *From Glory to Glory* (New York: Scribner's, 1961), 184-185.

[75]Gregory of Nyssa, *Against Those Who Defer Baptism*, PG 46:col. 421; trans. by Collins, 238. Also see PG 44:cols. 868-869.

[76]*On the Christian Mode of Life*, FC 58:129-130.

[77]Ibid., FC 58:139-140.

[78]Ibid., FC 58:141-142.

[79]Gregory of Nyssa, *The Life of St. Macrina*, FC 58:175.

[80]*On the Christian Mode of Life*, FC 58:155.

[81]On the subject of ecstasy, which Gregory of Nyssa refers to as "sober inebriation," see his *On Virginity* x, NPF 2nd Series 5:354-355 for David, and PG 44:cols. 940-941 for Abraham.

[82]*On the Christian Mode of Life*, FC 58:157-158.

[83]Gregory of Nazianzen, *Carm. de vita sua*, 439, quoted in NPF 7:195, note 16.

[84]For example, Swete, 24. See also M. Edmund Hussey, "The Theology of the Holy Spirit in the Writings of St. Gregory of Nazianzus," *Diakonia* (Fordham) 14, no.3 (1979): 224-233; and Andrew T. Floris, "Two Fourth-Century Witnesses on the Charismata," *Paraclete* 4, no.4 (Fall 1970): 17-22.

[85]Gregory of Nazianzen, *On the Holy Spirit* i, NPF 2nd Series 7:318.

[86]Ibid., vii, NPF 2nd Series 7:320. In his *Oration on the Holy Lights*, Gregory recognizes that he has helped to clarify the matter by coining the expression "procession," although he again is content to show that the Spirit was not generated since by Christ's own teaching (John 15:26) He proceeds from the Father, and does not raise the question of the relationship of the Spirit to the Son. *Oration* xxxix: *On the Holy Lights* xii, NPF 2nd Series 7:356.

[87]*On the Holy Spirit* ix, NPF 2nd Series 7:320-321.

[88]Ibid., x, NPF 2nd Series 7:321. Also see *Oration* xii.6, NPF 2nd Series 7:247.

[89]*On the Holy Spirit* xii, NPF 2nd Series 7:321.

[90]Ibid., xii, NPF 2nd Series 7:322.

[91]Ibid., xxix-xxx, NPF 2nd Series 7:327.

[92]Ibid., xxxiii, NPF 2nd Series 7:328.

[93]*Oration on the Holy Lights* xii, NPF 2nd Series 7:356.

[94]*On the Holy Spirit* viii, NPF 2nd Series 7:320.

[95]*On Pentecost* xiv, NPF 2nd Series 7:384.

[96]Ibid., v, NPF 2nd Series 7:380.

[97]Ibid., v, NPF 2nd Series 7:381.

[98]*Oration on the Holy Lights* xvii, NPF 2nd Series 7:358.

[99]Gregory of Nazianzen, *Oration on Holy Baptism* xliv, NPF 2nd Series 7:376.

[100]*On the Holy Spirit* xxviii, NPF 2nd Series 7:327.

[101]Gregory of Nazianzen, *Oration on Peace*, quoted in NPF 2nd Series 7:193.

[102]*On the Holy Spirit* xvii, NPF 2nd Series 7:321.

[103]Gregory of Nazianzen, *In Defence of His Flight To Pontus* xvc, NPF 2nd Series 7:223-224.

[104]Gregory of Nazianzen, *Oration* xii: *To His Father* i, NPF 2nd

Series 7:245.

[105]Gregory of Nazianzen, *On the Death of His Father* xxviii-xxix, NPF 2nd Series 7:263-264.

[106]*On the Death of His Father* xxxi, NPF 2nd Series 7:264.

[107]*On Pentecost* xvi, NPF 2nd Series 7:384-385.

[108]Ibid., ix, NPF 2nd Series 7:382.

CHAPTER SEVEN
LATIN THEOLOGIANS OF THE FOURTH AND FIFTH CENTURIES

Long before Nicea, Tertullian had developed the trinitarian formula which was to continue throughout the history of the Western Church: three persons with one substance. This long-established trinitarian tradition in the West, together with the emphasis of Latin Christianity on practical, nonspeculative theology, and the influence of Stoicism, with its stress on divine immanence (in contrast to the Eastern Neoplatonic concern with divine transcendence), helped to save the Western Church from much of the devastation experienced in the East growing out of its struggles against Arianism. In time the West also was challenged by Arian heretics, with the result that it further developed its unique expression of trinitarian doctrine. Until the coming of Augustine of Hippo, however, this expression remained couched in the language of Tertullian and that of the Greek Fathers.[1]

In the second half of the fourth century, Hilary of Poitiers, having returned from exile in the East (356-359), wrote twelve books *On the Trinity*, in which he borrowed heavily from Eastern contemporaries. He was quite ready to concede the propriety of either homoousion, which safeguards the unity of essence, or homoiousion, which preserves the distinctness of the three hypostases. He recognized that the homoousion, unless safeguarded by a proper stress on the distinction between the Persons of the ingenerate Father and the generate Son, lent itself to Sabellian interpretations. Because of this insight and his flexibility, Hilary was successful in converting the great body of homoeans to acceptance of the homoousion.

Bishop Ambrose of Milan was no more original than Hilary, depending heavily on Basil's writings on the Holy Spirit. However, he, together with Hilary, laid the foundation for Augustine of

Hippo, who accomplished for the West what the Cappadocians had for the Greek East: a synthesis of trinitarian doctrine. It is with Augustine that the Western Church showed its originality and depth. His writing *On the Trinity* immediately suggested major distinctions between Eastern and Western trinitarian theologies. Augustine begins with the unity of God and proceeds to the Persons, while his Eastern predecessors began with the three hypostases and moved then to the divine unity. He never granted the diversity of Persons the importance found in the Cappadocians, perhaps because of his reaction against his predecessor in the West, Marius Victorinus, who spoke of God as a "triple being."[2] In addition, Augustine saw no need to offer proofs of the divinity of the Son and the Holy Spirit, or to demonstrate their essential unity with the Father, as the Cappadocians had done before him. Finally, Augustine's understanding of the procession of the Spirit from both the Father and the Son set the stage for the early Medieval struggle with the East regarding the *filioque* clause.

1. HILARY OF POITIERS
Our knowledge of the personal life of Hilary of Poitiers is very limited. We do have evidence that, after serving as bishop of Poitiers in France, he was exiled to Phrygia by the Arian Emperor, Constantius II. While in exile he came in contact with Eastern theologians and their writings. Subsequently, he became a source in Western Christian thought of Eastern ideas. He argued in defense of Nicene orthodoxy and Athanasius, and in so doing summarized for the West the issues at stake in the Arian controversy.

Hilary's great writing on the nature and the relationship of the Trinity, originally titled *On the Faith* and eventually known as *On the Trinity*, was composed before A.D. 362 at a time when the doctrine of the Holy Spirit was still undeveloped. Most scholars agree that this writing served as one of Augustine's chief sources of information about the orthodox consensus of the Fathers, both Greek and Latin, on the dogma of the Holy Spirit.[3]

During the same period when Athanasius was insisting on the divinity of the Spirit in the East, Hilary was championing similar doctrine in the West. The Holy Spirit is at the same time the Spirit of God as well as the Spirit of Christ. He has the same nature as God and Christ.

> But if it is understood that Christ dwells in us through the Holy Spirit, we must yet recognize this Spirit of God as also the Spirit of Christ. And since the nature dwells in us as the nature of one substantive Being, we must regard the nature of the Son as identical with that of the Father, since the Holy Spirit Who is both the Spirit of Christ and the Spirit of God is proved to be a Being of one nature.[4]

In the Father, Son, and Holy Spirit, all are One. There is equality of nature, of perfection, and of dignity.

> For God the Father is One, from whom are all things; and our Lord Jesus Christ the Only-begotten, through Whom are all things, is One; and the Spirit, God's Gift to us, Who pervades all things, is also One. Thus all are ranged according to powers possessed and benefits conferred; the One Power from Whom all, the One Offspring through Whom all, the One Gift Who gives us perfect hope. Nothing can be found lacking in that supreme Union which embraces, in Father, Son and Holy Spirit, infinity in the eternal. His likeness in His express Image, our enjoyment of Him in the Gift.[5]

The doctrine of equality in the Godhead is confirmed in the baptismal formula: "The Lord said that the nations were to be baptized 'in the Name of the Father, and of the Son, and of the Holy Ghost.' "[6]

Although He shares in the same divine nature, the Spirit remains distinct from the Father and the Son. He is a real person within the Trinity.

> (Quoting from a copy of the creed composed at Sirnium by Eastern theologians to oppose Photinus) If any may deny that, as the Lord has taught us, the Paraclete is different from the Son; for He said, "And the Father shall send you another Comforter, Whom I shall ask," let him be anathema.[7]

In attempting to understand and to express the nature and the function of the Trinity, Hilary finds human cognition and language wholly inadequate. But in so doing his intellect and language soar to heights rarely found in the writings of the Fathers:

> I can see no limit to my venture of speaking concerning God in terms more precise than He Himself has used. He has assigned the Names—Father, Son and Holy Ghost, which are our information of the Divine nature. Words cannot express or feeling embrace or reason apprehend the results of inquiry carried further; all is ineffable, unattainable, incomprehensible. Language is exhausted by the magnitude of the theme, the splendour of its effulgence blinds the gazing eye, the intellect cannot compass its boundless extent. . . . Let imagination range to what you suppose is God's utmost limit, and you will find Him present there; strain as you will there is always a further horizon towards which to strain. . . . Words will fail you, but His being will not be circumscribed. . . . Gird up your intellect to comprehend Him as a whole; He eludes you. God, as a whole, has left something within your grasp, but this something is inextricably involved in His entirety. Thus you have missed the whole, since it is only a part which remains in your hands. . . . Reason, therefore cannot cope with Him, since no point of contemplation can be found outside Himself and since eternity is eternally His. . . . It is easier for me to feel this concerning the Father than to say it. I am well aware that no words are adequate to describe His attributes. We must feel that He is invisible, incomprehensible, eternal.[8]

Hilary is hesitant to speculate theologically about the Trinity beyond what Scripture specifies. For example, he does not use the word "coessential," preferring to be silent where Scripture is silent. At one point he states that he will say nothing about the Holy Spirit except that "He is Thy Spirit."[9] Again, he declares, "I cannot describe Him, whose pleas for me I cannot describe."[10] Time and again he quotes Colossians 2:8, "See to it that no one makes a prey of you by philosophy and vain deceit."[11] By this he intends to warn his readers against speculative heresy. The proper alternative to speculation as a means of understanding God is worship:

> For me, who hold that God cannot be known except by devotion, even to answer such objections seems no less unholy than to support them. What presumption to suppose that words can adequately describe His nature, when thought is often too deep for words, and His nature transcends even the conceptions of thought![12]

> We must believe, must apprehend, must worship, and such acts of devotion must stand in lieu of definition.[13]

On the subject of the procession Hilary asserts a position very much like the Western doctrine of the *filioque*, although his scheme of the Trinity is incomplete and his language is somewhat confusing.[14]

> Accordingly He [the Holy Spirit] receives from the Son, Who is both sent by Him, and proceeds from the Father. Now I ask whether to receive from the Son is the same thing as to proceed from the Father. But if one believes that there is a difference between receiving from the Son and proceeding from the Father, surely to receive from the Son and to receive from the Father will be regarded as one and the same thing.[15]

Hilary's formula is *ex Patre per filium*. The Spirit is through (*per*) Him through Whom are all things (i.e., the Son), and from (*ex*) Him from Whom are all things (i.e., the Father). However, Hilary discounts any difference between receiving from the Son and proceeding from the Father. Therefore, his views are consistent with the *filioque* doctrine.

Curiously, in his discussion of the work of the Trinity in creation, Hilary does not mention the Spirit, identifying both Word and Wisdom with Christ.[16] However, he has as complete an awareness of the role of the Spirit in the Incarnation and in the everyday life of the believer as any of the Fathers:

> For the Virgin conceived, what she conceived, from the Holy Ghost alone, and though for His birth in the flesh she supplied from herself that element, which women always contribute to the seed planted in them, still Jesus Christ was not formed by an ordinary human conception. In His birth, the cause of which was transmitted solely by the Holy Ghost, His mother performed the same part as in all human conceptions: but by virtue of His origin He never ceased to be God.

> This deep and beautiful mystery of His assumption of manhood the Lord Himself reveals in the words, "No man hath ascended into heaven, but He that descended from heaven, even the Son of Man which is in heaven." "Descended from heaven" refers to His origin from the Spirit: for though Mary contributed to His growth in the

womb and birth all that is natural to her sex, His body did not owe to
her its origin. . . . By the virtue of the Spirit and the power of God
the Word, though He abode in the form of a servant, He was ever
present as Lord of all, within and beyond the circle of heaven and
earth.[17]

Hilary speaks with great conviction about the work of the Spirit
in sanctifying and in enlightening the believer:

Let us hear from our Lord's own words what is the work of the Holy
Ghost within us. He says, "I have yet many things to say unto you,
but ye cannot bear them now. For it is expedient for you that I go: if I
go I will send you the Advocate. And again, I will ask the Father and
He shall send you another Advocate, that He may be with you for
ever, even the Spirit of truth. He shall guide you into all truth, for He
shall not speak from Himself, but whatsoever things He shall hear He
shall speak, and He shall declare unto you the things that are to come.
He shall glorify Me, for He shall take of Mine." These words were
spoken to show how multitudes should enter the kingdom of heaven;
they contain an assurance of the goodwill of the Giver, and of the
mode and terms of the Gift. They tell how, because our feeble minds
cannot comprehend the Father or the Son, our faith which finds
God's incarnation hard of credence shall be illumined by the gift of
the Holy Ghost, the Bond of union and the Source of light.

The next step naturally is to listen to the Apostle's account of the
powers and functions of this Gift. He says, "As many as are led by the
Spirit of God, these are the children of God. For ye received not the
Spirit of bondage again unto fear, but ye received the Spirit of
adoption whereby we cry, Abba, Father; and again, For no man by
the Spirit of God saith anathema to Jesus, and no man can say, Jesus
is Lord, but in the Holy Spirit;" and he adds, "Now there are
diversities of gifts, but the same Spirit, and diversities of
ministrations, but the same Lord, and diversities of workings, but the
same God, Who worketh all things in all. But to each one is given the
enlightenment of the Spirit, to profit withal. Now to one is given
through the Spirit the word of wisdom, to another the word of
knowledge according to the same Spirit, to another gifts of healings in
the One Spirit, to another workings of miracles, to another prophecy,
to another discerning of spirits, to another kinds of tongues, to
another interpretation of tongues. But all these worketh the One and
same Spirit." Here we have a statement of the purpose and results of
the Gift; and I cannot conceive what doubt can remain, after so clear a
definition of His Origin, His action and His powers.[18]

Hilary then encourages believers to make full use of God's Gift,
the Holy Spirit:

Let us therefore make use of this great benefit, and seek for personal
experience of this most needful Gift. For the Apostle says, in words I
have already cited, "But we have not received the spirit of this world,
but the Spirit which is of God, that we may know the things that are
given unto us by God." We receive Him, then, that we may know.
Faculties of the human body, if denied their exercise will lie dormant.
The eye without light, natural or artificial, cannot fulfill its office; the
ear will be ignorant of its function unless some voice or sound be
heard; the nostrils unconscious of their purpose unless some scent be

breathed. Not that the faculty will be absent, because it is never called into use, but that there will be no experience of its existence. So, too, the soul of man, unless through faith it have appropriated the gift of the Spirit, will have the innate faculty of apprehending God, but be destitute of the light of knowledge. That Gift, which is in Christ, is One, yet offered, and offered fully, to all; denied to none, and given to each according to the measure of his willingness to receive; its stores the richer, the more earnest the desire to earn them. This gift is with us unto the end of the world, the solace of our waiting, the assurance, by the favours which He bestows, of the hope that shall be ours, the light of our minds, the sun of our souls. This Holy Spirit we must seek and must earn, and then hold fast by faith and obedience to the commands of God.[19]

Making full use of the gift of the Spirit includes exercise of the various charismata:

For the gift of the Spirit is manifest, where wisdom makes utterance and the words of life are heard, and where there is the knowledge that comes of God-given insight, lest after the fashion of beasts through ignorance of God we should fail to know the Author of our life; or by faith in God, lest by not believing the Gospel of God, we should be outside His Gospel; or by the gift of healings, that by the cure of diseases we should bear witness to His grace Who bestoweth these things; or by the working of miracles, that what we do may be understood to be the power of God, or by prophesy, that through our understanding of doctrine we might be known to be taught of God; or by discerning of spirits, that we should not be unable to tell whether any one speaks with a holy or a perverted spirit; or by kinds of tongues, that the speaking in tongues may be bestowed as a sign of the gift of the Holy Spirit; or by the interpretation of tongues, that the faith of those that hear may not be imperilled through ignorance, since the interpreter of a tongue explains the tongue to those who are ignorant of it. Thus in all these things distributed to each one to profit withal there is the manifestation of the Spirit, the gift of the Spirit being apparent through these marvelous advantages bestowed upon each.[20]

That Hilary is speaking of the ongoing function of the gifts of the Spirit in the Church of his own day is evident from his frequent use of the personalized "we." Indeed, it is the unbelievers and the heretics who lack the Holy Spirit, and, therefore, are led into error.[21] In his *Life of St. Honoratus* Hilary describes the monastery of the saint in terms which reflect his concept of the ideal—the full working out of the plan and operation of the Spirit in the Church:

Here the grace of the Holy Spirit was diffused throughout his monastery, and remains there still by his prayers, strengthened by the example and the lesson of so great a teacher, revealed in varied charismatic gifts, in humility and meekness, in charity unfeigned, and in the one glory of the head in the diversity of the members.[22]

2. AMBROSE

Ambrose, bishop of Milan, was born in Treves about A.D. 340, the son of Ambrosius, prefect of Spain, Britain, Cis- and Trans-

Alpine Gaul. Shortly after his father's death, the family moved to Rome where Ambrose devoted himself to legal studies. His success as a lawyer led to rapid advancement. When in A.D. 370 he was appointed governor of Liguria and Aemilia by the Praetorian Prefect Probus, he was told to "Go and act, not as a judge, but as a bishop." He followed this advice to the extent that he came to be known as a father rather than as a judge.

Four years later the intended Arian bishop of Milan, Auxentius, died. The assembly called to appoint his successor proceeded to elect Ambrose by acclamation to the bishopric, even though he was still but a catechumen, and ineligible canonically. His biographer, Paulinus, insists that he attempted to escape this unexpected honor, but to no avail. When the emperor Valentinian ratified his election, he proceeded to be baptized by a Catholic priest. Eight days later, December 8, 374, he was consecrated bishop of Milan.

After divesting himself of worldly property, Ambrose devoted himself to his new episcopal duties. He also began theological studies, emphasizing Scripture and such Church writers as Athanasius, Basil of Caesarea, and Didymus of Alexandria. It is hardly surprising that in his own writings he is not original, owing much to these Eastern greats, since he had not previously studied theology and now found it necessary to compose a wide variety of sermons, together with dogmatic, exegetical, and polemical works. It does not appear fair to label him as a plagiarist and as a spoiler of the good things he had stolen from the Greeks, as did his contemporary, Jerome.[23] Given his newness to Christian theology, one must agree with Swete[24] that Ambrose showed humility and wisdom in using the writings of his great Eastern contemporaries. In so doing, Ambrose actually provided a valuable service as carrier of the rich doctrine of the Eastern Church, laying solid grounds for the Western doctrinal synthesis of his great follower, Augustine.

Bishop Ambrose proved to be a champion of orthodoxy against both Arianism and heathenism in the declining Roman West. More than one emperor was forced to accept the Church's discipline because of him, and numerous illustrious figures, including Augustine, were won to the faith by his character and teachings.

Holy Scripture is for Ambrose an immense sea which does not reveal its secrets to the superficial observer. The human soul is constantly searching for the true meaning of God's word. Only as one seeks to discern the layers of meaning which lie in each verse, only as he seeks the mystery can he hope to attain to a higher intelligence. Mysteries within Scripture must be revealed through the Holy Spirit, since "the things of God knoweth no man save the Spirit of God" (1 Corinthians 2:11). To the knowledge of the literal sense must be added by way of allegorical interpretation a mystical understanding of a higher significance.[25] The Holy Spirit Himself is to be understood through the category of mystery. The images of the Spirit and water are joined from Genesis 1:2, "The Spirit moved upon the waters," to Exodus 15:10, "Thou sentest Thy Spirit, and the sea covered them." These passages, coupled with Paul's statement in 1 Corinthians 10:1-2, "For all our fathers were under the cloud, and all passed through the sea, and were baptized to Moses in the cloud and in the sea," are taken by Ambrose as prefiguring baptism. By Psalm 46:4, "The stream of the river makes glad the city of God," he understands the Holy Spirit to be the abundant river watering the mystical Jerusalem.

> So, then, the Holy Spirit is the River, and the abundant River, which according to the Hebrews flowed from Jesus in the lands, as we have received it prophesied by the mouth of Isaiah. This is the great River which flows always and never fails. And not only a river, but also one of copious stream and overflowing greatness, as also David said: "The stream of the river makes glad the city of God."

> For neither is that city, the heavenly Jerusalem, watered by the channel of any earthly river, but that Holy Spirit, proceeding from the Fount of Life, by a short draught of Whom we are satiated, seems to flow more abundantly among those celestial Thrones, Dominions and Powers, Angels and Archangels, rushing in the full course of the seven virtues of the Spirit. For if a river rising about its banks overflows, how much more does the Spirit, rising above every creature, when He touches the as it were low-lying fields of our minds, make glad that heavenly nature of the creatures with the larger fertility of His sanctification.

> And let it not trouble you that either here it is said "rivers," or elsewhere "seven Spirits," for by the sanctification of these seven gifts of the Spirit, as Isaiah said, is signified the fulness of all virtue; the Spirit of wisdom and understanding, the Spirit of counsel and strength, the Spirit of knowledge and godliness and the Spirit of the fear of God. One, then, is the River, but many the channels of the gifts of the Spirit. This River, then goes forth from the Fount of Life.[26]

This stream proceeding from the living Fount of God is indeed the grace of the Spirit, promised by the prophet Joel (2:28), "I will pour My Spirit upon all flesh."[27] He is poured into souls, He flows into the senses, in order that He may quench the burning of this world's thirst.[28] He is "a river of peace, and like a stream overflowing the glory of the Gentiles."[29] Ambrose completes his allegorical treatment of the Spirit and water by affirming that it is in water that one experiences the grace and baptism of the life-giving Spirit.

> Good, then, is this water, even the grace of the Spirit. Who will give this Fount to my breast? Let it spring up in me, let that which gives eternal life flow upon me. Let that Fount overflow upon us, and not

flow away. . . . How shall I preserve my vessel, lest any crack of sin penetrating it, should let the water of eternal life exude?[30]

Because of his vision that man must strive to lift the layers of the mystery of salvation, Ambrose utilizes the same allegorical method throughout his writings, willfully seeking to rise above the literal interpretation of Scripture to a higher level of significance. Because such mysteries only can be comprehended through the action and guidance of the Spirit, Ambrose is particularly concerned to provide his readers with a careful and thorough explication of the nature and the offices of the third Person. Of several writings which treat the Spirit, his most important effort is the treatise, *Of the Holy Spirit*, the first separate work of any size by a Western author on the subject.

Ambrose is concerned first with the nature of the Spirit. He states that the Spirit who spoke through the prophets and breathed upon the apostles is the same One who is referred to as the Spirit of God and of Christ.[31] The Holy Spirit is not a creature because He is not circumscribed by any measure or limitation. Not only is He not made, the Spirit is not to be numbered among created things.[32] He is higher than created beings for He sanctifies angels, having already been involved in the divine partnership which created them. In the same way He sanctifies man, making him equal to the angels.[33] He is the great Dispenser of God's blessing to the human race.

What, then, is more divine than the working of the Holy Spirit, since God Himself testifies that the Holy Spirit presides over His blessings, saying: "I will put My Spirit upon thy seed and My blessings upon thy children." For no blessing can be full except through the Inspiration of the Holy Spirit.[34]

The Holy Spirit possesses certain properties from which Ambrose argues that He is equal with the Father and the Son. These include divine power, creativity, life, and light.[35] The Spirit is the Author of spiritual renewal and the ointment of Christ, or the oil of gladness.[36] He is without sin; indeed He forgives sin.[37] He receives worship and does not offer it.[38] In short, the Holy Spirit is divine as Jesus himself witnessed (John 3:6).

Ambrose also addresses the Person of the Spirit in the context of the essential unity of the Godhead. Three Persons are one in divine operation and cannot be conceived of one without the other:

And as he who is blessed in Christ is blessed in the Name of the Father, and of the Son, and of the Holy Spirit, because the Name is one and the Power one; so, too, when any divine operation, whether of the Father, or of the Son, or of the Holy Spirit, is treated of, it is not referred only to the Holy Spirit, but also to the Father and the Son, and not only to the Father, but also to the Son and the Spirit.[39]

The Three also are one in power and in counsel. "For as the Father

is Power, so, too, the Son is Power, and the Holy Spirit is Power.
. . . And as the Son is the Angel of great counsel, so, too, is the
Holy Spirit the Spirit of Counsel, that you may know that the
Counsel of the Father, the Son, and the Holy Spirit is One.''[40] It
follows, Ambrose argues, that if there is unity in divine operation,
in power, and in counsel, then the substance must be one.

> But if the Holy Spirit is of one will and operation with God the Father,
> he is also of one substance, since the Creator is known by His works.
> So, then, it is the same Spirit, he says, the same Lord, the same God.
> And if you say Spirit, He is the same; and if you say Lord, He is the
> same; and if you say God, He is the same. Not the same, so that
> Himself is Father, Himself Son, Himself Spirit [one and the selfsame
> Person]; but because both the Father and the Son are the same Power.
> He is, then, the same in substance and in power, for there is not in the
> Godhead either the confusion of Sabellius nor the division of Arius,
> nor any earthly and bodily change.[41]

While united in substance, each member of the Godhead consti-
tutes a separate Person. Of the Holy Spirit Ambrose writes:

> He exists then, and abides always, Who is the Spirit of His mouth, but
> He seems to come down when we receive Him, that He may dwell in
> us, that we may not be alien from His grace. To us He seems to come
> down, not that he does come down, but that our mind ascends to
> Him.[42]

The Spirit is distinct and is not to be confused with the Father and
the Son. "We hold the distinction, not the confusion, of Father,
Son and Holy Spirit; a distinction without separation; a distinction
without plurality. . . . We know that fact of distinction, we know
nothing of the hidden mysteries.''[43] The Spirit has personal
characteristics which indicate His personality. For example, He is
said to be grieved and tempted.[44]

On the position of the Holy Spirit with reference to the Son,
Ambrose seems to waver between procession of the Holy Spirit
"from the Father through the Son" and "from the Father and the
Son." The matter had not been settled yet. The common position
in the East was that the Spirit proceeded from the Father through
the Son. Before Augustine the Western Church generally followed
the East. It was in response to Augustine's teaching that the Latin
Church ultimately adopted the position that the Spirit proceeded
from both the Father and the Son.

In several passages Ambrose seems to follow the formula of the
Greeks. In each case, however, he is concerned with the
communication of divine knowledge. It can be argued that by
analogy Ambrose also would have accepted this formula with
reference to the procession of divine life. In one such passage he is
speaking of the Holy Spirit as the Giver of revelation:

> For our knowledge proceeds from one Spirit, through one Son to one
> Father; and from one Father through one Son to one Holy Spirit is

delivered goodness and sanctification and the sovereign right of
eternal power.[45]

In other texts Ambrose appears to favor the formula of Augustine that the Holy Spirit proceeded from the Father and the Son.
In each of these, however, the author deals with the mission of the
Spirit. Scholars are not in agreement whether they actually refer to
the procession of the Holy Spirit. In one such passage Ambrose
refers to the Spirit's mission to all men: "The Spirit is not, then,
sent as it were from a place, nor does He proceed as from a place,
when He proceeds from the Son, as the Son Himself, when He
says, 'I came forth from the Father, and am come into the
world.' "[46] The one text that seems to anticipate the position
subsequently formulated by Augustine and at the same time to be
free from difficulty refers to Psalm 36:9, "With You is the fountain
of life":

> Learn now that as the Father is the Fount of Life, so, too, many have
> stated that the Son is dignified as the Fount of Life; so that, he says,
> with Thee, Almighty God, Thy Son is the Fount of Life. That is the
> Fount of the Holy Spirit, for the Spirit is Life.[47]

The Spirit's operation is viewed across the span of time elapsing
from creation to the Church of the fourth century as part of the
grand design of Redemption. As with Basil, Ambrose recognizes
that every creative activity which the Father operates through the
Son receives its fulfillment and completion in the action of the
Spirit. The whole universe, including man, receives its actuality and
perfection from the Spirit. That which He creates He also renews:

> And who can deny the creation of the earth is the work of the Holy
> Spirit, Whose work it is that it is renewed? For if they desire to deny
> that it was created by the Spirit, since they cannot deny that it is
> renewed by the Spirit, they who desire to sever the Persons must
> maintain that the operation of the Holy Spirit is superior to that of the
> Father and the Son, which is far from the truth; for there is no doubt
> that the restored earth is better than it was created.[48]

The creative Spirit also is the Giver of revelation and the Author of
the Incarnation. In both He reveals the things of God, the mystery
of His design for redemption.[49] But His role in the plan of salvation
is not fulfilled until Pentecost when He descends with complete
power.[50] The Spirit then becomes the primary link binding Christ
with the Church. The Church is built by the Spirit, uniting Gentiles
and Jews.[51] Without the infusion of the Holy Spirit there can be no
complete blessing.[52] He infuses His gifts to individual souls:

> And the Wisdom of God said: "I will send prophets and apostles."
> And "To one is given," as it is written, "through the Spirit, the word
> of wisdom; to another, the word of knowledge, according to the same
> Spirit; to another faith, in the same Spirit; to another, the gift of
> healings, in the one Spirit; to another, the working of miracles; to
> another, prophecy." Therefore, according to the Apostle, prophecy is

not only through the Father and the Son, but also through the Holy
Spirit, and therefore the office is one, and the grace one. So you find
that the Spirit also is the author of prophecies.[53]
While the Spirit seems to descend to the believer, in fact the human
mind ascends to Him.[54] He provides all things relating to life and
godliness: "Of the Spirit also, as being formed by Him,
strengthened by Him, established in Him, we receive the gift of
eternal life."[55]

In his treatment of life in the Spirit, Ambrose begins with the
sacraments, for which the Holy Spirit, together with the Father and
the Son, is the Source. The efficacy of the sacraments only is
derived by the action of the Spirit. "Damasus cleansed not, Peter
cleansed not, Ambrose cleansed not, Gregory cleansed not; for
ours is the ministry, but the sacraments are Thine."[56] In baptism
the water is not productive unto salvation without the presence of
the Holy Spirit. The water is consecrated through the invocation of
the Spirit.[57] In baptism the water, the blood, and the Spirit play
essential roles. The water is to wash, the blood is to redeem, and the
Holy Spirit is to renew the mind and to resurrect.

> Hear how they are witnesses: The Spirit renews the mind, the water is
> serviceable for the laver, and the blood refers to the price. For the
> Spirit made us children by adoption, the water of the sacred Font
> washed us, the blood of the Lord redeemed us. So we obtain one
> invisible and one visible testimony in a spiritual sacrament, for "the
> Spirit Himself beareth witness to our spirit." Though the fulness of
> the sacrament be in each, yet there is a distinction of office; so where
> there is distinction of office, there certainly is not equality of
> witness.[58]

Ambrose associates baptism with the Incarnation as part of the
total divine plan of redemption:

> If, then, the Holy Spirit coming down upon the Virgin wrought the
> conception, and effected the work of generation, surely we must not
> doubt but that, coming down upon the Font, or upon those who
> receive Baptism, He effects the reality of the new birth.[59]

Again, in the Eucharist the Holy Spirit actualizes the mystery of
salvation. "Whenever you drink you receive remission of your sins,
and you are inebriated by the Holy Spirit. For this reason the
Apostle states, 'be not drunk with wine, but be filled with the
Spirit.' "[60] The Incarnation, a work of the Holy Spirit, is
actualized through the Eucharist. At the same time, the Eucharist
anticipates the Resurrection, which is also a work of the Spirit. As
Belval suggests, "The Eucharist is thus the zone of the Spirit which
is situated between the Incarnation and the Resurrection."[61]

In the sacrament of confirmation the Spirit seals the soul of the
believer and provides His sevenfold gift:

> And then remember that you received the seal of the Spirit; the spirit
> of wisdom and understanding, the spirit of counsel and strength, the

> spirit of knowledge and godliness, and the spirit of holy fear, and
> preserved what you received. God the Father sealed you, Christ the
> Lord strengthened you, and gave the earnest of the Spirit in your
> heart.[62]

In ordination the Holy Spirit provides power to the priest to
forgive sins. The very office of the priesthood is considered a gift of
the Spirit of God.

> Consider, too, the point that he who has received the Holy Ghost has
> also received the power of forgiving and of retaining sin. For thus it is
> written: "Receive the Holy Spirit: whosesoever sins ye forgive, they
> are forgiven unto them, and whosesoever sins ye retain, they are
> retained." So, then, he who has not received power to forgive sins has
> not received the Holy Spirit. The office of the priest is a gift of the
> Holy Spirit, and His right it is specially to forgive and to retain sins.
> How, then, can they claim His gift who distrust His power and His
> right?[63]

Grace comes from the agency of the Holy Spirit exclusively. All
creatures must depend on Him for sanctification, whether they be
angels, dominions, powers, or men. "Where the Spirit is, there is
also life, and where life is, there also is the Holy Spirit."[65] He is the
source of living water which washes the soul and purges the
emotions.[66] He is the oil of gladness which brightens the innermost
heart.[67] At times He descends like a burning bush to reveal and to
refine.[68]

The Spirit also illuminates the human mind, imparting two
characteristics of His own mind: purity and creativity.

> For if a river rising above its banks overflows, how much more does
> the Spirit, rising above every creature, when He touches the as it were
> low-lying fields of our minds, make glad that heavenly nature of the
> creatures with the larger fertility of His sanctification.[69]

Mankind is led by the Spirit into all truth to the extent that he is
able to receive. "We receive so much as the advancing of our mind
acquired, for the fulness of the grace of the Spirit is indivisible, but
is shared in by us according to the capacity of our own nature."[70]
By His grace we are lifted above our animal natures; we are
elevated from earth to heaven:

> We then were wild beasts, and therefore the Lord said: "Beware of
> false prophets, which come in sheep's clothing, but inwardly are
> ravening wolves." But now, through the Holy Spirit, the rage of lions,
> the spots of leopards, the craft of foxes, the rapacity of wolves, have
> passed away from our feelings; great, then, is the grace which has
> changed earth to heaven, that the conversation of us, who once were
> wandering as wild beasts in the woods, might be in heaven.[71]

It is the nature of the Holy Spirit to infuse holiness in others.
Through Him we attain to the image and likeness of God and
become partakers of the divine nature.

> Good, then, is the Spirit, but good, not as though acquiring but as
> imparting goodness. For the Holy Spirit does not receive from

creatures but is received; as also He is not sanctified but sanctifies; for the creature is sanctified, but the Holy Spirit sanctifies. In which matter, though the word is used in common, there is a difference in the nature. For both the man who receives and God Who gives sanctity are called holy, as we read: "Be ye holy, for I am holy."[72]

Who, then, can dare to say that the Holy Spirit is separated from the Father and the Son, since through Him we attain to the image and likeness of God, and through Him, as the Apostle Peter says, are partakers of the divine nature? In which there is certainly not the inheritance of carnal succession, but the spiritual connection of the grace of adoption. And in order that we may know that this seal is rather on our hearts than on our bodies, the prophet says: "The light of Thy countenance has been impressed upon us, O Lord, Thou hast put gladness in my heart."[73]

Ambrose's treatment of the Person and the offices of the Spirit, while not original, is comprehensive and incisive. Had his ministry not resulted in the conversion of Augustine, his writings might well have become the doctrinal foundation for the Christian West. But this was not to be. Instead, we now recognize the bishop of Milan to be the fountainhead for much of the theology of his great protégé from Hippo.

3. AUGUSTINE OF HIPPO

Augustine of Hippo was the greatest theologian and teacher of the ancient Christian Church. From his autobiography, *The Confessions*, we know that he was born in A.D. 354 to a pagan father and a Christian mother, Monica. Raised as a Christian, he nevertheless was not baptized until well into adult life. His youthful indiscretions left him with a strong consciousness of the sinful nature of man. His own spiritual turmoil led him to a study of the classics, and, at an early age, to embrace the creed of the Manichaeans. Before long he was disillusioned by the simplicity of their explanation of evil. He sailed to Rome where he stayed until he obtained a post as professor of rhetoric. Still groping for ultimate answers, he attached himself to the Neoplatonists for a short period, and as his frustrations increased, he turned to skepticism.

Because of his great interest in rhetoric, Augustine went to the church in Milan to study the oratory of the celebrated bishop, Ambrose. Being deeply impressed that a man of such intellect was, at the same time, a devout Christian, and having heard the voice of child at play say, "Take up and read," Augustine turned to a study of the New Testament. Paul's Letter to the Romans, chapter 13, which warns against reveling and drunkenness, debauchery and licentiousness, quarreling and jealousy, and admonishes man "to put on the Lord Jesus," deeply impressed him. Augustine was baptized by Ambrose in Milan at Easter A.D. 387. He returned soon after to North Africa where he was ordained. In 396 he became bishop of Hippo, an office he held until his death in 430. Augustine's great contribution was to build on the Nicene foundation a theology which carried great appeal to the thought of the Christian West. His genius combined the mystical warmth and intellectual depth of the East with the pragmatism of the Latin mind. He drew richly from the past. Although he appropriated much from classical writers such as Cicero and the Stoics, and from the Neoplatonic vision of God, Augustine is best remembered for having revived the teachings of the Apostle Paul as no one had done in the intervening centuries. The implications of Pauline writings on the relationship of man and God, sin and grace, predestination, and the Church as the institution for man's salvation were spelled out with great clarity. Augustine, like Paul, formed the habit of seeing everything in relation to God. His was a unique gift of dealing with abstract questions and practical issues with equal facility. Traditional doctrines, such as that of the Trinity, were made intelligible by use of analogy. But above all, Augustine gave definitive shape to Western theology. His theological synthesis was of such spiritual vitality that each succeeding generation in the Western Church, whether Catholic or Protestant, has felt its universal influence.[74]

Of the many distinctive features of Western Christianity set in motion by, or channeled through, the bishop of Hippo, none is more significant than his treatment of the inner life of God. While Eastern Fathers focused on the ontological unity (unity of essence) of the Trinity, Augustine concentrates on the relationship between three equal persons.

Much of Augustine's writings, especially after he became bishop, was devoted to an effort to show the truth of Christianity against such errors as Manichaeism, Donatism, Pelagianism, and semi-Pelagianism. This certainly is true in treating the subject of the Holy Spirit, whose full deity was rejected by the Sadducees, Photinians, Arians, Eunomians, Macedonians, and Sabellians.

> For the Sadducees indeed denied the Holy Ghost; but the Pharisees maintained His existence against their heresy, but they denied that He was in the Lord Jesus Christ, who they thought cast out devils through the prince of the devils, whereas He did cast them out through the Holy Ghost. And hence, both Jews and whatsoever heretics there are who confess the Holy Ghost, but deny that He is in the Body of Christ, which is His One Only Church, none other than the One Catholic Church, are without doubt like the Pharisees who at that time although they confessed the existence of the Holy Ghost, yet denied that He was in Christ, whose works in casting out devils they attributed to the prince of devils. I say nothing of the fact that some

heretics either boldly maintain that the Holy Ghost is not the Creator but a creature, as the Arians, and Eunomians, and Macedonians, or so entirely deny His existence, as to deny that God is Trinity, but assert that He is God the Father only, and that He is sometimes called the Son, and sometimes the Holy Ghost; as the Sabellians, whom some call Patripassians, because they hold the Father suffered; and forasmuch as they deny that He has any Son, without doubt they deny His Holy Spirit also. The Photinians again who say that the Father only is God, and the Son a mere man, deny altogether that there is any third Person of the Holy Ghost.[75]

For Augustine the Holy Spirit is "at once God and the Gift of God."[76] Moreover, the relationship within the Trinity is between three equal Persons. "In all Three the Divinity is equal, and the Unity inseparable."[77] Nowhere is this better expressed than in the following excerpt from Sermon LV:

But when thou hast gotten the three loaves, that is, to feed on and understand the Trinity, thou hast that whereby thou mayest both live thyself, and feed others. Now thou needest not fear the stranger who comes out of his way to thee, but by taking him in mayest make him a citizen of the household: nor needest thou fear lest thou come to the end of it. That Bread will not come to an end, but it will put an end to thine indigence. It is Bread, God the Father, and it is Bread, God the Son, and it is Bread, God the Holy Ghost. The Father Eternal, the Son Coeternal with Him, and the Holy Ghost Coeternal. The Father Unchangeable, the Son Unchangeable, the Holy Ghost Unchangeable. The Father Creator, and the Son, and the Holy Ghost. The Father the Food and Bread eternal, and the Son, and the Holy Ghost. Learn, and teach; live thyself, and feed others. God who giveth to thee, giveth thee nothing better than Himself.[78]

The Spirit did not assume creature-form.[79] He is consubstantial and coeternal with the Father and the Son.[80] He is the communion of divine mutual love between the Father and the Son.

The Holy Spirit is a certain unutterable communion of the Father and the Son; and on that account, perhaps, He is so called, because the same name is suitable to both the Father and the Son. For He Himself is called specially that which they are called in common; because both the Father is a spirit and the Son a spirit, both the Father is holy and the Son holy. In order, therefore, that the communion of both may be signified from a name which is suitable to both, the Holy Spirit is called the gift of both. And this Trinity is one God, alone, good, great, eternal, omnipotent; itself its own unity, deity, greatness, goodness, eternity, omnipotence.[81]

The Spirit is both the Spirit of God who gave Him, and ours who have received Him. . . . The Father and the Son are a Beginning of the Holy Spirit, not two Beginnings; but as the Father and Son are one God, and one Creator, and one Lord relatively to the creature, so are they one Beginning relatively to the Holy Spirit. But the Father, the Son, and the Holy Spirit is one Beginning in respect to the creature, as also one Creator and one God.[82]

We must now treat of the Holy Spirit, so far as by God's gift is

permitted to see Him. And the Holy Spirit, according to the Holy
Scriptures, is neither of the Father alone, nor of the Son alone, but of
both; and so intimates to us a mutual love, wherewith the Father and
the Son reciprocally love one another.[83]

Wherefore also the Holy Spirit consists in the same unity of substance,
and in the same equality. For whether He is the unity of both, or the
holiness, or the love, or therefore the unity because the love, and
therefore the love because the holiness, it is manifest that He is not
one of the two, through whom the two are joined, through whom the
Begotten is loved by the Begetter and loves Him that begat Him.[84]

The Holy Spirit is the Spirit of the Father and of the Son. "He
who sees the Father and the Son sees also the Holy Spirit of the
Father and the Son."[85] In his commentary on John's Gospel,
Augustine writes:

For the Holy Spirit is not that of the Father only nor of the Son only,
but the Spirit of the Father and of the Son. For it is written, "If any
man love the world, the Spirit of the Father is not in him." And again,
"Whoso hath not the Spirit of Christ is none of His." The same, then,
is the Spirit of the Father and of the Son. Therefore, the Father and
the Son being named, the Holy Spirit also is understood because He is
the Spirit of the Father and of the Son.[86]

Again, in Sermon XXI on Matthew 12:32, he reiterates that the
Holy Spirit is the Spirit of both the Father and of the Son:

Ye know, Dearly beloved, that in that invisible and incorruptible
Trinity, which our faith and the Church Catholic maintains and
preaches, God the Father is not the Father of the Holy Spirit, but of
the Son; and that God the Son is not the Son of the Holy Spirit, but of
the Father; but that God the Holy Spirit is the Spirit not of the Father
only, or of the Son only, but of the Father and the Son.[87]

The Spirit is begun by the Father and the Son:

The Father and the Son are a Beginning of the Holy Spirit, not two
Beginnings; but as the Father and Son are one God, and one Creator,
and one Lord relatively to the creature, so are they one Beginning in
respect to the creature, as also one Creator and one God.[88]

Because the Holy Spirit is the Spirit of both the Father and the
Son, it follows that He proceeds from both. In this Augustine gives
definitive shape to the Western Church's position, in contrast to
that of the Eastern Church which teaches procession from the
Father through the Son.

Why, then, should we not believe that the Holy Spirit proceedeth also
from the Son, seeing that He is likewise the Spirit of the Son? For did
He not so proceed, He could not, when showing Himself to His
disciples after the resurrection, have breathed upon then, and said,
"Receive ye the Holy Spirit." For what else was signified by such a
breathing upon then, but that from Him also the Holy Spirit
proceedeth?[89]

And we are so taught that He proceeds from both, because the Son
Himself says, He proceeds from the Father. And when He had risen
from the dead, and had appeared to His disciples, "He breathed upon

them, and said, Receive the Holy Ghost," so as to show that He proceeded also from Himself.[90]

I had taught them by testimonies of the Holy Scriptures that the Holy Spirit proceeds from both, I continue: "If, then, the Holy Spirit proceeds both from the Father and from the Son, why did the Son say, 'He proceedeth from the Father?' " Why, think you, except as He is wont to refer to Him, that also is that which He saith, "My doctrine is not mine own, but His that sent me?" If, therefore, it is His doctrine that is here understood, which yet He said was not His own, but His that sent Him, how much more is it there to be understood that the Holy Spirit proceeds also from Himself, where He so says, He proceedeth from the Father, as not to say, He proceedeth not from me? From Him, certainly, from whom the Son had his Divine nature, for He is God of God, He has also, that from Him too proceeds the Holy Spirit; and hence the Holy Spirit has from the Father Himself, that He should proceed from the Son also, as He proceeds from the Father.[91]

While the Trinity is of one essence, and is inseparable and operates inseparably,[92] there are distinctions to be drawn between the three Persons. Augustine now is faced with the nearly impossible task of explaining what these distinctions are. His own moral preoccupations lead him to compare God's trinitarian being to the memory, intellect, and will in the human psyche.[93] The Holy Spirit is likened to the faculty of the human will. Therefore, the Spirit is the Person in the Trinity who renews the human moral faculty so that man can obey God's law.

We, however, on our side affirm that the human will is so divinely aided in the pursuit of righteousness, that . . . he receives the Holy Ghost, by whom there is formed in his mind a delight in, and a love of, that supreme and unchangeable good which is God, even now while he is still "walking by faith" and not yet "by sight;" in order that by this gift to him of the earnest, as it were, of the free gift, he may conceive an ardent desire to cleave to his Maker, and may burn to enter upon the participation in that true light, that it may go well with him from Him to whom he owes his existence. A man's free-will [sic], indeed, avails for nothing except to sin, if he knows not the way of truth; and even after his duty and his proper aim shall begin to become known to him, unless he also take delight in and feel a love for it, he neither does his duty, nor sets about it, nor lives rightly. Now, in order that such a course may engage our affections, God's "love is shed abroad in our hearts," not through the free-will which arises from ourselves, but "through the Holy Ghost, which is given to us."[94]

In a unique sense the Spirit is the Gift of God, the Gift of both the Father and the Son to the Church:

For truly the same Jesus Christ, the only-begotten, that is, the only Son of God our Lord, was born of the Holy Spirit and the Virgin Mary. And certainly the Holy Spirit is the Gift of God, which gift is in truth itself equal to the Giver.[95] For without the Gift of God, that is, without the Holy Spirit, through whom charity is diffused in our hearts, the law can command, but cannot help.[96]

Augustine indicates that the Holy Spirit actually has been given twice, once when after the Resurrection Jesus breathed on the face of His disciples, and said, "Receive ye the Holy Ghost;" and again when, ten days after the Ascension, the Holy Spirit descended on those waiting in the Upper Room.[97]

Augustine likens the Holy Spirit to fire, because when He came on the Day of Pentecost "there appeared unto them cloven tongues like as of fire, and it sat upon each of them" (Acts 2:3), and because Jesus said, "I am come to send fire on the earth" (Luke 12:49).[98] The Spirit also is called the stream of that river which makes glad the City of God.[99] As the Gift of God, He is the one and only Fountain. Augustine exclaims, "God's Spirit calls you to drink of it; God's Spirit calls you to drink of Himself."[100]

The Spirit also is described as the Sword of the Lord,[101] the Creator, the Bread, the Shepherd, and the Unchangeable Spirit.[102] He is the Energizer who renews the moral faculty of man, and the heavenly Teacher leading man into all truth as Christ had been the great Teacher while on earth.

> "And ye have no need that any man teach you, because His unction teacheth you concerning all things." Then to what purpose is it that "we," my brethren, teach you? If "His unction teacheth you concerning all things," it seems we labor without a cause. And what mean we, to cry out as we do. Let us leave you to His unction, and let His unction teach you. . . . [But] the sound of our words strikes the ears, the Master is within. Do not suppose that any man learns ought from man. We can admonish by the sound of our voice; if there be not One within that shall teach, vain is the noise we make. . . . I, for my part, have spoken to all; but they to whom that Unction within speaketh not, they whom the Holy Ghost within teacheth not, those go back untaught. The teachings of the master from without are a sort of aids and admonitions. He that teacheth the hearts, hath His chair in heaven. . . . Where His inspiration and His unction is not, in vain do words make a noise from without.[103]

Such heavenly teaching is life-giving, unlike the law, which, without the Spirit, is the letter that killeth.[104] The very presence of the Holy Spirit is God's law written in the hearts of men. By His presence the love of God is shed abroad, fulfilling the law, and marking the end of the commandments.[105] The gift of the Holy Spirit is true grace. It is He who reproves the world of sin.

> The Lord, when promising that He would send the Holy Spirit, said, "When He is come, He will reprove the world of sin, and of righteousness, and of judgment." What does it mean? . . . Why is it, then, He attributeth this to the Holy Spirit, as if it were His proper prerogative? Is it that, because Christ spake only among the nation of the Jews, He does not appear to have reproved the world, inasmuch as one may be understood to be reproved who actually hears the reprover; while the Holy Spirit, who was in His disciples when scattered throughout the whole world, is to be understood as having reproved not one nation, but the world? . . . But in my opinion,

because there was to be shed abroad in their hearts by the Holy Spirit
that love which casteth out the fear, that might have hindered then
from venturing to reprove the world which bristled with persecutions,
therefore it was that He said, "He shall reprove the world:" as if He
would have said, He shall shed abroad love in your hearts, and having
your fear thereby expelled, ye shall have freedom to reprove.[106]

He who reproves of sin also remits sin. This the Spirit does by
man, Augustine insists, although He also can remit even without
the aid of man.[107] Remission of sins is the gift of the Holy Spirit in
the Church. Outside of the Church there is no Holy Spirit and no
such forgiveness.

And thus sins, because they are not forgiven out of the Church, must
be forgiven by that Spirit, by whom the Church is gathered together
into one. In fact, if any one out of the Church repent him of his sins,
and for this so great sin whereby he is an alien from the Church of
God, has an heart impenitent, what doth that other repentance profit
him? seeing by this alone he speaketh a word against the Holy Ghost,
whereby he is alienated from the Church, which hath received this
gift, that in her remission of sins should be given in the Holy Ghost.[108]

For outside the Church there is no remission of sins. She received as
her very own the pledge of the Holy Spirit, without whom no sin
whatever is remitted, so that those to whom sins are remitted receive
life everlasting.[109]

The Spirit is received only in the Church, and that by the
imposition of hands.

But when it is said that "the Holy Spirit is given by the imposition of
hands in the Catholic Church only, I suppose that our ancestors meant
that we should understand thereby what the apostle says, "Because
the love of God is shed abroad in our hearts by the Holy Ghost which
is given unto us." For this is that very love which is wanting in all who
are cut off from the communion of the Catholic Church; and for lack
of this, "though they speak with the tongues of men and of angels,
though they understand all mysteries and all knowledge, and though
they have the gift of prophecy, and all faith, so that they could remove
mountains, and though they bestow all their goods to feed the poor,
and though they give their bodies to be burned, it profiteth them
nothing." But those are wanting in God's love who do not care for the
unity of the Church; and consequently we are right in understanding
that the Holy Spirit may be said not to be received except in the
Catholic Church.[110]

If baptism remains with the man who secedes from the Church, the
Holy Spirit withdraws.

He [Cyprian] says "that the Church, and the Spirit, and baptism, are
mutually incapable of separation from each other, and therefore" he
wishes that "those who are separated from the Church and the Holy
Spirit should be understood to be separated also from baptism." But
if this is the case, then when any one has received baptism in the
Catholic Church, it remains so long in him as he himself remains in
the Church, which is not so. For it is not restored to him when he
returns, just because he did not lose it when he seceded. But as the
disaffected sons have not the Holy Spirit in the same manner as the

beloved sons, and yet they have baptism; so heretics also have not the Church as Catholics have, and yet have baptism. "For the Holy Spirit of discipline will flee deceit," and yet baptism will not flee from it. And so, as baptism can continue in one from whom the Holy Spirit withdraws Himself, so can baptism continue where the Church is not.[111]

By the Holy Spirit man is given not only remission of sins, but a love for God which aids him in his pursuit of righteousness. The human will is divinely assisted by the Holy Spirit. Man becomes obedient to God's law as the Spirit pours out the love of God in the human heart. It is this Augustinian comprehension of God's immediate involvement in the life of man through the Holy Spirit—justification by grace through faith—that most significantly influences Protestant reformers eleven centuries later.

We, however, on our side affirm that the human will is so divinely aided in the pursuit of righteousness, that (in addition to man's being created with a free-will [*sic*], and in addition to the teaching by which he is instructed how he ought to live) he receives the Holy Ghost, by whom there is formed in his mind a delight in, and a love of, that supreme and unchangeable good which is God, even now while he is still "walking by faith" and not yet "by sight;" in order that by this gift to him of the earnest, as it were, of the free gift, he may conceive an ardent desire to cleave to his Maker, and may burn to enter upon the participation in that true light, that it may go well with Him to whom he owes his existence. . . . God's "love is shed abroad in our hearts," not through the free-will, which arises from ourselves, but "through the Holy Ghost, which is given to us."[112]

A holy life is the gift of God, not only because God has given a free-will, to man, without which there is no living ill or well; nor only because He has given him a commandment to teach him how he ought to live, but because through the Holy Ghost He sheds love abroad in the hearts of those whom he foreknew, in order to predestinate them; whom He predestinated, that He might call them; whom He called, that he might justify them; and whom he justified, that He might glorify them.[113]

We are assisted by divine aid towards the achievement of righteousness, not merely because God has given us a law full of good and holy precepts, but because our very will, without which we cannot do any good thing, is assisted and elevated by the importation of the Spirit of grace, without which help mere teaching is "the letter that killeth," forasmuch as it rather holds them guilty of transgression, than justifies the ungodly.[114]

Now this Spirit of God, by whose gift we are justified, whence it comes to pass that we delight not to sin, in which is liberty; even as, when we are without this Spirit, we delight to sin, in which is slavery, from the works of which we must abstain; this Holy Spirit, through whom love is shed abroad in our hearts, which is the fulfillment of the law, is designated in the gospel as "the finger of God." Is it not because those very tables of the law were written by the finger of God, that the Spirit of God by whom we are sanctified is also the finger of

God, in order that, living by faith, we may do good works through love?[115]

The expression "finger of God" is used frequently to designate the Spirit in His role of reaching out to touch man, in inspiring biblical writers, and in nourishing the believer:

> Now it is said of Moses himself, by the magicians of king Pharaoh, when they were conquered by him, "This is the finger of God." And what is written, "The heavens shall be rolled up as a book." Although it be said of this ethereal heaven, yet naturally, according to the same image, the heavens of books are named by allegory. "For I shall see," he says, "the heavens, the works of Thy fingers:" that is, I shall discern and understand the Scriptures, which Thou, by the operation of the Holy Ghost, hast written by Thy ministers.[116]

> The Law then written by the finger of God was given on the fiftieth day after the slaughter of the lamb, and the Holy Ghost descended on the fiftieth day after the Passion of our Lord Jesus Christ . . . now in the fulness of love, not in the punishment of fear.[117]

> For in the case of the people of Israel likewise, from the day on which they first celebrated the Passover in a figure by killing and eating a sheep, with the blood of which their doorposts were marked to preserve them unharmed—from that day, I say, the fiftieth day was completed when they received the law written by the finger of God, by which name we have already said that the Holy Spirit is typified; as after the Passion and Resurrection of our Lord, who is the true Passover, on the fiftieth day the Holy Spirit Himself was sent to the disciples, no longer, however, typifying the hardness of their hearts by tables of stone; but when they were gathered together in one place in Jerusalem itself, "suddenly there came a sound from heaven as of a rushing mighty wind, and there appeared to them parted tongues as it were of fire, and they began to speak with tongues."[118]

> It also received the law written by the finger of God, by which name the Holy Spirit is signified, as is most plainly declared in the Gospel. For God is not limited by bodily form, nor are we to think of members and fingers in His case, even as we see them in ourselves. But because it is through the Holy Spirit that the gifts of God are apportioned among the saints, so that while they vary in power, yet they do not depart from the harmony of love; and because again it is in the fingers that a certain division is especially apparent, yet without any separation from unity; either because of this or for some other reason the Holy Spirit has been called the finger of God.[119]

Augustine clearly distinguishes between the Spirit's work in the remission of sins and in the nourishment of the believer.

> But it is one thing to be born of the Spirit, another to be nourished by the Spirit; just as it is one thing to be born of the flesh, which happens when the mother is delivered of her child; another to be nourished by the flesh, which happens when she gives suck to her infant, who turns himself that he may drink with pleasure thither whence he was born, to have life; that he may receive the support of life from thence, whence he received the beginning of his birth. We must believe then that the first blessing of God's goodness in the Holy Ghost is the remission of sins.[120]

Not only is man dependent on the Holy Spirit for love, he also needs divine knowledge. By the Spirit man knows God in part. He leads into all truth, although this is not complete here. Yet it will be in the hereafter.

> On receiving the Spirit of God, we learn also what takes place in God: not the whole, for we have not received the whole. We know many things from the pledge; for we have received a pledge, and the fullness of this pledge shall be given hereafter. Meanwhile, let the pledge console us in our pilgrimage here; because he who has condescended to bind himself to us by a pledge, is prepared to give us much. If such is the token, what must that be of which it is the token?[121]

> Accordingly, when He says, "He will teach you all truth," or "will guide you into all truth," I do not think the fulfillment is possible in any one's mind in this present life (for who is there, while living in this corruptible and soul-oppressing body, that can know all truth, when even the apostle says, "We know in part"?), but because it is effected by the Holy Spirit, of whom we have now received the earnest, that we shall attain also to the actual fullness of knowledge: whereof it is said by the same apostle, "But then face to face;" and, "Now I know in part, but then shall I know even as also I am known;" not as a thing which he knows fully in this life, but which, as a thing that would still be future on to the attainment of that perfection, the Lord promised us through the love of the Spirit, when He said, "He will teach you all truth," or "Will guide you unto all truth."[122]

The Spirit assists the saints in praying when they know not how to pray (Romans 8:26):

> When the apostle said, "We know not what we should pray for as we ought," he immediately added, "But the Spirit Himself maketh intercession for us with groanings which cannot be uttered. He that searcheth the hearts knoweth what is in the mind of the Spirit, because He maketh intercession for the saints according to the will of God"—that is to say, He makes the saints offer intercessions.[123]

Having been reconciled with his Maker, man is introduced to the secret things of God by the Holy Spirit:

> And inasmuch as, being reconciled and called back into fellowship through love, we shall be able to become acquainted with all the secret things of God, for this reason it is said of the Holy Spirit that "He shall lead you into all truth."[124]

When the Gift of God, the Holy Spirit, was outpoured on the Day of Pentecost, the Decalogue was promulgated a second time. This time it was a law of love and not of fear. Man was instructed to love God and his neighbor. Herein the City of God was made glad.

> Jesus being glorified after His Resurrection, glorified after His Ascension, on the day of Pentecost came the Holy Spirit, and filled the believers, who spake with tongues, and began to preach the Gospel to the Gentiles. Hence was the City of God made glad, while the sea was troubled by the roaring of its waters, while the mountains were confounded, asking what they should do, how drive out the new doctrine, how root out the race of Christians from the earth. Against

whom? Against the streams of the river making glad the City of God. For thereby showed He of what river He spake; that He signified the Holy Spirit, by "the streams of the river make glad the City of God."[125]

The descent of the Spirit at Pentecost was marked by the tongues of many nations. Tongues were replaced thereafter as a test of the Spirit's presence by the bond of peace.

With a view to this fellowship they to whom He first came spake with the tongues of all nations. Because as by tongues the fellowship of mankind is more closely united; so it behoved that this fellowship of the sons of God and members of Christ which was to be among all nations should be signified by the tongues of all nations; that as at that time he was known to have received the Holy Ghost, who spake with the tongues of all nations; so now he should acknowledge that he has received the Holy Ghost, who is held by the bond of the peace of the Church, which is spread throughout all nations. Whence the Apostle says, "Endeavouring to keep the unity of the Spirit in the bond of peace."[126]

Time and again Augustine denies any continuity in the Church of the gift of tongues. The following are but examples:

In the earliest times, "the Holy Ghost fell upon them that believed: and they spake with tongues," which they had not learned, "as the Spirit gave them utterance." These were signs adapted to the time. For there behooved to be that betokening of the Holy Spirit in all tongues, to shew that the Gospel of God was to run through all tongues over the whole earth. That thing was done for a betokening, and it passed away. In the laying on of hands, now, that persons may receive the Holy Ghost, do we look, that they should speak with tongues?

Or when we laid the hand on these infants, did each one of you look to see whether they would speak with tongues, and, when he saw that they did not speak with tongues, was any of you so wrong-minded as to say, These have not received the Holy Ghost. . . . If then the witness of the presence of the Holy Ghost be not now given through these miracles, by what is it given, by what does one get to know that he has received the Holy Ghost? Let him question his own heart. If he love his brother, the Spirit of God dwelleth in him.[127]

Why then is the Holy Spirit given now in such wise, that no one to whom it is given speaks with divers tongues, except because that miracle then prefigured that all nations of the earth should believe, and that thus the gospel should be found to be in every tongue?[128]

How then, brethren, because he that is baptized in Christ, and believes on Him, does not speak now in the tongues of all nations, are we not to believe that he has received the Holy Ghost? God forbid that our heart should be tempted by this faithlessness. Certain we are that every man receives: but only as much as the vessel of faith that be shall bring to the fountain can contain, so much does He fill of it. Since, therefore, the Holy Ghost is even now received by men, some one may say, why is it that no man speaks in the tongues of all nations? Because the Church itself now speaks in the tongues of all nations.[129]

For the Holy Spirit is not only given by the laying on of hands amid

the testimony of temporal sensible miracles, as He was given in former
days to be the credentials of a rudimentary faith, and for the extension
of the first beginnings of the Church. For who expects in these days
that those on whom hands are laid that they may receive the Holy
Spirit should forthwith begin to speak with tongues? but it is
understood that invisibly and imperceptibly, on account of the bond
of peace, divine love is breathed into their hearts, so that they may be
able to say, "Because the love of God is shed abroad in our hearts by
the Holy Ghost which is given unto us."[130]

But, continues Augustine, there are many operations of the Spirit.
The Spirit's gifts are likened to stars, upon which the babe in Christ
must be content to gaze until he is able to look upon the Sun—to be
illuminated or to eat solid meat.[131] True gifts will bear examination.
Augustine suggests the following as a test to determine whether the
spirit is of God:

Therefore by this understand ye the spirit that is from God. Give the
earthen vessels a tap, put them to the proof, whether haply they be
cracked and give a dull sound: see whether they ring full and clear, see
whether charity be there.[132]

Augustine, while denying tongues in his own day, quite readily
admits to numerous contemporary miracles. He takes pains to
relate certain wonders occurring in his own church at Hippo, which
bear resemblance to "gifts of healing by the same Spirit,"
mentioned by Paul in 1 Corinthians 12:9. In the following account
Augustine describes his own reaction and that of his congregation
to two such miracles:

Even now, therefore, many miracles are wrought, the same God who
wrought those we read of still performing them, by whom He will and
as He will; but they are not as well known, nor are they beaten into the
memory, like gravel, by frequent reading, so that they cannot fall out
of mind. For even where, as is now done among ourselves, care is
taken that the pamphlets of those who receive benefit be read publicly,
yet those who are present hear the narrative but once, and many are
absent; and so it comes to pass that even those who are present forget
in a few days what they heard, and scarcely one of them can be found
who will tell what he heard to one who he knows was not present.

One miracle was wrought among ourselves, which, though no greater
than those I have mentioned, was yet so signal and conspicuous, that I
suppose there is no inhabitant of Hippo who did not either see or hear
of it, none who could possibly forget it. There were seven brothers and
three sisters of a noble family of the Cappadocian Caesarea, who were
cursed by their mother, a new-made widow, on account of some
wrong they had done her, and which she bitterly resented, and who
were visited with so severe a punishment from Heaven, that all of
them were seized with a hideous shaking in all their limbs. Unable,
while presenting this loathsome appearance, to endure the eyes of
their fellow-citizens, they wandered over almost the whole Roman
world, each following his own direction. Two of them came to Hippo,
a brother and a sister, Paulus and Palladia, already known in many
other places by the fame of their wretched lot. Now it was about

fifteen days before Easter when they came, and they came daily to church, and specially to the relics of the most glorious Stephen, praying that God might now be appeased, and restore their former health. There, and wherever they went, they attracted the attention of every one. Some who had seen them elsewhere, and knew the case of their trembling, told others as occasion offered. Easter arrived, and on the Lord's day, in the morning when there was now a large crowd present, and the young man was holding the bars of the holy place where the relics were, and praying suddenly he fell down, and lay precisely as if asleep, but not trembling as he was wont to do even in sleep. All present were astonished. Some were alarmed, some were moved with pity; and while some were for lifting him up, others prevented them, and said they should rather wait and see what would result. And behold! he rose up, and trembled no more, for he was healed, and stood quite well, scanning those who were scanning him. Who then refrained himself from praising God? The whole church was filled with the voices of those who were shouting and congratulating him. Then they came running to me, where I was sitting ready to come into the church. One after another they throng in, the last comer telling me as news what the first had told me already; and while I rejoiced and inwardly gave God thanks, the young man himself also enters, with a number of others, falls at my knees, is raised up to receive my kiss. We go in to the congregation: the church was full, and ringing with shouts of joy, "Thanks to God! Praised be God!" every one joining and shouting on all sides, "I have healed the people," and then with still louder voice shouting again. Silence being at last obtained, the customary lessons of the divine Scriptures were read. And when I came to my sermon, I made a few remarks suitable to the occasion and the happy and joyful feeling, not desiring them to listen to me, but rather to consider the eloquence of God in this divine work. The man dined with us, and gave us a careful account of his own, his mother's, and his family's calamity. Accordingly, on the following day, after delivering my sermon, I promised that next day I would read his narrative to the people. And when I did so, the third day after Easter Sunday, I made the brother and sister both stand on the steps of the raised place from which I used to speak; and while they stood there their pamphlet was read. The whole congregation, men and women alike, saw the one standing without any unnatural movement, the other trembling in all her limbs; so that those who had not before seen the man himself saw in his sister what the divine compassion had removed from him. In him they saw matter of congratulation, in her subject for prayer. Meanwhile, their pamphlet being finished, I instructed them to withdraw from the gaze of the people; and I had begun to discuss the whole matter somewhat more carefully, when lo! as I was proceeding, other voices are heard from the tomb of the martyr, shouting new congratulations. My audience turned round, and began to run to the tomb. The young woman, when she had come down from the steps where she had been standing, went to pray at the holy relics, and no sooner had she touched the bars and rose up cured. While, then, we were asking what had happened, and what occasioned this noise of joy, they came into the basilica where we were, leading her from the martyr's tomb in perfect health. Then, indeed, such a shout of wonder rose from men and women together, that the exclamations and the tears seemed like never to come to an end. She was led to the place where she had a little before stood trembling. They now rejoiced that she was like her brother, as before they had mourned that she remained unlike him; and as they had not yet uttered their prayers in her behalf, they perceived that their intention of doing so had been speedily heard. They shouted God's praises without words, but with such a noise that our ears could scarcely bear it.[133]

Although Augustine does not suggest in his narrative that any one person exercised a gift of healing, the miraculous recoveries reported here involve divine intervention in response to the prayers of the Hippo congregation and those healed. While Augustine holds that certain signs and wonders have ceased, he readily acknowledges that the involvement of God through the Holy Spirit in human affairs still includes miraculous intervention, bypassing natural processes and exceeding normal human expectations.

Augustine's impact on the medieval Catholic Church and on Evangelical Protestantism can hardly be overstated. His development of the Nicene dogma of the Trinity, his formulation of the double procession of the Holy Spirit, and his clear definition of the sacrament as a visible sign of invisible grace, mark him as one of the most formative pneumatological thinkers of Christian history.

Notes to Chapter 7

[1]Note Jerome's caustic remarks in which he calls Ambrose a plagiarist who spoiled the good which he stole from the Greeks, in Rufinus, *Apology* ii.23-25, NPF 2nd Series 3:470-471.

[2]See Paul Henry, "The Adversus Arium of Marius Victotinus, the First Systematic Exposition of the Doctrine of the Trinity," *Journal of Theological Studies* n.s. 1 (1950):42-55.

[3]On Hilary and the doctrine of the Holy Spirit see J.M. McDermott, "Hilary of Poitiers: The Infinite Nature of God," *Vigiliae Christianae* 27, no.3 (1973):172-202.

[4]Hilary of Poitiers, *On the Trinity* vii.26, NPF 2nd Series 9:144-145.

[5]Ibid., ii.1, NPF 2nd Series 9:52. Cf. iv. 33, NPF 2nd Series 9:81.

[6]Ibid., ii.5, NPF 2nd Series 9:53.

[7]Hilary of Poitiers, *On the Councils* liii, NPF 2nd Series 9:20.

[8]*On the Trinity* ii.6-7, NPF 2nd Series 9:53-54. Here Hilary anticipates the negative theology of Pseudo-Dionysus and many of the medieval mystics.

[9]Ibid., xii.56, NPF 2nd Series 9:233.

[10]Ibid.

[11]Ibid., i.13, viii.53, ix.1, 8, xii.20, NPF 2nd Series 9:43, 153, 155, 157, 222-223.

[12]Ibid., xi.44, NPF 2nd Series 9:216.

[13] Ibid., ii.7, NPF 2nd Series 9:54.

[14] Swete, 304, insists that Hilary is in line with the Eastern doctrine of procession.

[15] *On the Trinity* viii.20, NPF 2nd Series 9:143.

[16] Ibid., iv.16, 21, NPF 2nd Series 9:73-78.

[17] Ibid., x. 15-16, NPF 2nd Series 9:186.

[18] Ibid., ii.33-34, NPF 2nd Series 9:61.

[19] Ibid., ii.35, NPF 2nd Series op. cit.

[20] Ibid., viii.30, NPF 2nd Series 9:146.

[21] Ibid., viii.28, NPF 2nd Series 9:145.

[22] Hilary of Poitiers, *Life of St. Honoratus*, in *Early Christian Biographies* (Washington, D.C.: The Catholic University of America Press, 1952), 378.

[23] Rufinus, *Apology* ii.23-25, NPF 2nd Series 3:470-471.

[24] Swete, 318.

[25] Joseph P. Christopher, trans., *St. Augustine: the First Catechetical Instruction*, ACW 2:132 n. 220, observes, "The allegorical method of exegesis was, therefore, a powerful weapon against the Manichaeans, for it struck at the literalism upon which most of the Manichaean objections, particularly to the Old Testament, were based."

[26] Ambrose, *Of the Holy Spirit* i.16. 177-179, NPF 2nd Series 10:113-114.

[27] Ibid., i.7.85, NPF 2nd Series 10:104.

[28] Ibid., i.4.61, NPF 2nd Series 10:101

[29] Ibid., i.16,181, NPF 2nd Series 10:114.

[30] Ibid., i.16,182, NPF 2nd Series, op. cit.

[31] Ibid., i.4.56-61, NPF 2nd Series 10:101.

[32] Ibid., i.2.31, NPF 2nd Series 10:97

[33] Ibid., i.7.84, NPF 2nd Series 10:104.

[34] Ibid., i.7.89, NPF 2nd Series 10:105.

[35] Ibid., i.14.160-170, i.15.171, ii.1.19, ii.4.31, ii.5.35, NPF 2nd Series 10:111-112, 113, 117, 118, 119.

[36] Ibid., i.9.102, ii.7.64, NPF 2nd Series 10:107, 122.

[37] Ibid., iii.18.135-137, NPF 2nd Series 10:154.

[38] Ibid., iii.18.141-143, NPF 2nd Series 10:155.

[39] Ibid., i.3.40, NPF 2nd Series 10:98.

[40] Ibid., ii.1-2,19-20, NPF 2nd Series 10:117.

[41] Ibid., ii.12.142, NPF 2nd Series 10:133.

[42] Ibid., i.11.121, NPF 2nd Series 10:109.

[43] Ambrose, *On the Christian Faith* ii.8.92, NPF 2nd Series 10:274.

[44] *Of the Holy Spirit* iii.8.48, NPF 2nd Series 10:141-142.

[45] Ibid., ii.12.130, NPF 2nd Series 10:131. For other examples see

ii.11.118, ii.12.134, NPF 2nd Series 10:130, 132.

[46]Ibid., i.11.119, NPF 2nd Series 10:109.

[47]Ibid., i.15.172, NPF 2nd Series 10:113.

[48]Ibid., ii.5.34, NPF 2nd Series 10:119.

[49]Ibid., ii.5.38, 41, iii.1.1-2, NPF 2nd Series 10:119, 135.

[50]Ibid., iii.14.98-99, NPF 2nd Series 10:149.

[51]Ibid., ii.10.110, NPF 2nd Series 10:129.

[52]Ibid., i.7.89, NPF 2nd Series 10:105.

[53]Ibid., ii.13.143, NPF 2nd Series 10:133.

[54]Ibid., i.11.121, NPF 2nd Series 10:109.

[55]Ibid., ii.9.93, NPF 2nd Series 10:126.

[56]Ibid., i.prologue.18, NPF 2nd Series 10:96.

[57]Ambrose, On the Mysteries iv.20, NPF 2nd Series 10:319.

[58]Of the Holy Spirit iii.10.68, NPF 2nd Series 10:144.

[59]On the Mysteries ix.59, NPF 2nd Series 10:325.

[60]Ambrose, On the Sacraments v.17, Corpus scriptorum ecclesiasticorum latinorum 73:65 (Henceforth CSEL).

[61]Norman Joseph Belval, The Holy Spirit in Saint Ambrose (Romae: Officium Libri Catholici, 1971), 68.

[62]On the Mysteries vii.42, NPF 2nd Series 10:322.

[63]Ambrose, Concerning Repentance i.2.8, NPF 2nd Series 10:330.

[64]Of the Holy Spirit i.5.62, NPF 2nd Series 10:101.

[65]Ibid., i.15.172, NPF 2nd Series 10:113.

[66]Ibid., i.16.177-179, NPF 2nd Series 10:113-114.

[67]Ibid., i.9.102, NPF 2nd Series 10:107.

[68]Ibid., i.14.165, NPF 2nd Series 10:112.

[69]Ibid., i.16.178, NPF 2nd Series 10:113-114.

[70]Ibid., i.8.93, NPF 2nd Series 10:106.

[71]Ibid., ii.10,109, NPF 2nd Series 10:128.

[72]Ibid., i.5.74, NPF 2nd Series 10:103.

[73]Ibid., i.5.80, NPF 2nd Series, op.cit.

[74]Among the many studies of Augustine's doctrine of the Holy Spirit, the following are of special value: Jacques Verhees, "Die Bedeutung des Geistes Gottes in Leben des Menchen nach Augustin's Frühester Pneumatologie (Bis 391)," Zeitschrift für Kirchengeschichte 88, no.3-4 (1977):161-189, and Gabriel Pont, Les dons de l'Esprit Saint dans la pensée de saint Augustin (Sierre: Martigny:Editions Château Ravére, 1974).

[75]Augustine, Sermon xxi.5, NPF 2nd Series 6:320.

[76]Ibid., xxi.18, NPF 1st Series 6:324.

[77]Ibid. Also see Augustine, First Catechetical Instruction xxvii.55, ACW 2:87.

[78]Sermon lv.4, NPF 1st Series 6:431. Cf. Augustine, On the

Gospel of St. John, tractate xcv.1, NPF 1st Series 7:369.
[79]*On the Gospel of St. John*, tractate xcix.1, NPF 1st Series 7:381.
[80]Ibid., tractate lxxiv.1, NPF 1st Series 7:333.
[81]Augustine, *On the Trinity* xi.12, NPF 1st Series 3:93.
[82]Ibid., xiv.15, NPF 1st Series 3:95.
[83]Ibid., xvii.27, NPF 1st Series 3:215.
[84]Ibid., vi.5.7, NPF 1st Series 3:100.
[85]Augustine, *On the Spirit and the Letter* lix, NPF 1st Series 5:110. Also Augustine, *Enchiridion (Faith, Hope, and Charity)* iii.9, ACW 3:18, and *On the Trinity* vi.5.7, NPF 1st Series 3:100.
[86]*On the Gospel of St. John*, tractate ix.7, NPF 1st Series 7:65.
[87]*Sermon* xx.18, NPF 1st Series 6:323-324.
[88]*On the Trinity* v.14, NPF 1st Series 3:95.
[89]*On the Gospel of St. John*, tractate xcix.7, NPF 1st Series 7:383-384.
[90]*On the Trinity* xv.45, NPF 1st Series 3:224.
[91]Ibid., xv.27.48, NPF 1st Series 3:225-226. Cf xxi.20.29, NPF 1st Series 3:84-85, in which Augustine discusses the relationship of mission to procession.
[92]Augustine asks how the Incarnation can be limited to the Person of the Son alone. It must be the act of the entire Trinity, although One Person only becomes incarnate. *Letter* xi, NPF 1st Series 1:229.
[93]*On the Trinity* x.11. 17-18, NPF 1st Series 3:142-143.
[94]*On the Spirit and the Letter* v, NPF 1st Series 5:84-85. On other occasions Augustine likens Persons within the Trinity to Eternity, Truth, Goodness (*Sermon* xxi.18, NPF 1st Series 6:324), and to mind, its self-knowledge, and its self-love. (*On the Trinity* ix.5.8, NPF 1st Series 3:129.)
[95]*Enchiridion (Faith, Hope and Charity)* xi.37, ACW 3:45. Also see *Enchiridion* xii.40, ACW 3:48; *Sermon* xxi.18, NPF 1st Series 6:324.
[96]*Enchiridion*, xxi.117, ACW 3:109.
[97]Augustine, *Against the Epistle of Manichaeus* x.11, NPF 1st Series 4:134.
[98]*Sermon* xxi.19, NPF 1st Series 6:324.
[99]Augustine, *On the Psalms* xlvi.7, NPF 1st Series 7:157.
[100]Augustine, *Homilies on I John*, LCC 8:315.
[101]*On the Psalms* xciii.3, NPF 1st Series 8:457.
[102]*Sermon* lv.4, NPF 1st Series 6:431.
[103]Augustine, *The Epistle of St. John*, homily iii.13, NPF 1st Series 7:481.
[104]*On the Spirit and the Letter* v-vi, NPF 1st Series 5:84-85.
[105]Ibid., xxxvi, NPF 1st Series 5:98.

[106]*On the Gospel of St. John*, tractate xcv.1, NPF 1st Series 7:368-369.

[107]*Sermon* xlix.10, NPF 1st Series 6:419.

[108]Ibid., xxi.28, NPF 1st Series 6:328.

[109]*Enchiridion (Faith, Hope, and Charity)* xvii.65, ACW 3:66.

[110]Augustine, *On Baptism, Against the Donatists* iii.16.21, NPF 1st Series 4:442-443.

[111]Ibid., v.23.33, NPF 1st Series 4:475.

[112]*On the Spirit and the Letter* v, NPF 1st Series 5:84-85.

[113]Ibid., vii, NPF 1st Series 5:85.

[114]Ibid., xx, NPF 1st Series 5:91.

[115]Ibid., xxviii, NPF 1st Series 5:95.

[116]*On the Psalms* viii.7, NPF 1st Series 8:29.

[117]*On the Psalms* xci.16, NPF 1st Series 8:451.

[118]*First Catechetical Instruction* xxiii.41, ACW 2:73.

[119]Ibid., xx.35, ACW 2:65.

[120]*Sermon* xxi.19, NPF 1st Series 6:324.

[121]*On the Gospel of St. John*, tractate xxxii.5, NPF 1st Series 7:194.

[122]Ibid., tractate xcvi.4, NPF 1st Series 7:373.

[123]Augustine, *On the Soul and Its Origin* iv.13, NPF 1st Series 5:359. Also see Augustine, *On the Gift of Perseverance* lxiv, NPF 1st Series 5:551

[124]Augustine, *On Faith and the Creed* ix.19, NPF 1st Series 3:330.

[125]*On the Psalms* xlvi.7, NPF 1st Series 8:157. Also *First Catechetical Instruction* xxiii.41, ACW 2:72-73.

[126]*Sermon* xxi.28, NPF 1st Series 6:328.

[127]*The Epistle of St. John*, homily vi.10, NPF 1st Series 7:497-498.

[128]Augustine, *The Answer to the Letters of Petilian, the Donatist* ii.32.74, NPF 1st Series 4:548.

[129]*On the Gospel of St. John*, tractate xxxii.7, NPF 1st Series 7:195.

[130]*On Baptism, Against the Donatists* iii.16.21, NPF 1st Series 4:443.

[131]Augustine, *The Confessions* xii.18.23, NPF 1st Series 1:197-198.

[132]*The Epistle of St. John*, homily vi.13, NPF 1st Series 7:500.

[133]Augustine, *The City of God* viii, NPF 1st Series 2:490-491.

EPILOGUE

On the very day that Augustine died (August 28, 430), the city which he had served as bishop for so many years was under siege by the barbarian Vandals. Soon afterward Hippo was taken and destroyed by the invaders. A few decades later the entire Western Empire fell in ruins. As Augustine had foreseen, the City of Man had collapsed. But the City of God continued to flourish wherever the ideas of Augustine and his predecessors fell like seeds into fertile soil, producing abundant fruit in nations and countries of which they had never heard. Their voices continued to resound through Christian centuries to come, enriching the spiritual understanding and encouraging the piety of future generations which sought after "the deep things of God."

The person and the work of the Holy Spirit filled a large place in ancient Christian teaching. As the experience of the Church grew and her outlook expanded, she began to grasp the mysteries of the nature of the Spirit and His relationship within the Godhead, as well as the great range of His activity in the total panorama of divine involvement in human affairs. Although ancient Christians walked in different paths than their spiritual descendents, they were led by the same Spirit of God. The substance of their teachings, therefore, should serve as steppingstones for those who continue to look to the Holy Spirit to lead into all truth.

PRIMARY SOURCES: COLLECTIONS

ACW   *Ancient Christian Writers,* New York: Newman Press, 1946—.

ANF   *Ante-Nicene Fathers,* New York: Christian Literature Company, 1890-97. Reprint, Grand Rapids, Michigan: Eerdmans, 1980-82.

CSEL   *Corpus scriptorum ecclesiasticorum latinorum.* Vindobonae, apud C. Geroldi filium, etc., 1866-1913.

FC   *The Fathers of the Church,* Washington: Catholic University of America Press, 1947—.

LCC   *The Library of Christian Classics,* Philadelphia: Westminster Press, 1953—.

NHL   *The Nag Hammadi Library,* James M. Robinson, ed., New York: Harper and Row, 1981.

NPF   *Nicene and Post-Nicene Fathers,* 1st Series. New York: Christian Literature Company, 1887-94. Reprint, Grand Rapids, Michigan: Eerdmans, 1971-80.
Nicene and Post-Nicene Fathers, 2nd Series. New York: Christian Literature Company, 1890-1900. Reprint, Grand Rapids, Michigan: Eerdmans, 1978-80.

PG   *Patrologia cursus completus. Series Graeca,* Jacques Paul Migne, ed., Pariis, J. P. Migne, 1859-87.

PL   *Patrologia cursus completus. Series Latina,* Jacques Paul Migne, ed., Pariis, J. P. Migne, 1844-1904.

SELECTED EDITIONS AND SECONDARY SOURCES

Anderson, Floyd, ed. *Council Daybook: Vatican II, Sessions 1 and 2.* Washington, D.C.: National Catholic Welfare Conference, 1965.

Aranda, Antonio. "El Espiritu Santo en la 'Exposicion de fe' de S. Gregorio Taumaturgo." *Scripta Theologica* 10, no. 2 (1978): 373-407.

Armstrong, Deborah Pease. "And in the Holy Ghost." *The Life of the Spirit* 7 (May 1953): 497-508.

Ash, James L., Jr. "The Decline of Ecstatic Prophecy in the Early Church." *Theological Studies* 35 (June 1976): 227-252.

Athanassakis, Apostolos N., trans. *The Life of Pachomius.* Missoula, Montana: Scholars Press, 1975.

Barnett, Maurice. *The Living Flame: Being a Study of the Gift of the Spirit in the New Testament, with Special Reference to Prophecy, Glossolalia, and Perfection.* London: The Epworth Press, 1953.

Belval, Norman Joseph. *The Holy Spirit in St. Ambrose.* Romae: Officium Libri Catholici, 1971.

Berry, Colman J., ed. *Readings in Church History.* New York: Newman Press, 1960.

Bilaniuk, Petro B. T. "The Monk as Pneumatophor in the Writings of St. Basil the Great." *Diakonia* (Fordham) 15, no. 1 (1980): 49-63.

Blackman, E. C. *Marcion and His Influence.* London: Society for the Promotion of Christian Knowledge, 1948.

Bresson, Bernard L. *Studies in Ecstasy.* New York: Vantage Press, 1966.

Brewer, E. Cobham. *A Dictionary of Miracles: Imitative, Realistic, and Dogmatic.* Philadelphia: Lippincott, 1966.

Brumback, Carl. *Suddenly . . . From Heaven.* Springfield, Missouri: Gospel Publishing House, 1961.

Burgess, Stanley M. "Medieval Examples of Charismatic Piety in the Roman Catholic Church." In *Perspectives on the New Pentecostalism,* Edited by Russell P. Spittler. Grand Rapids, Michigan: Baker, 1976.

Burkhard, Neunheuser. "Taufe im Geist: Der Heilige Geist in den Riten der Taufliturgie." *Archiv für Liturgiewissenschaft* 12 (1970): 268-284.

Campbell, Ted A. "Charismata in the Christian Communities of the Second Century." *Wesleyan Theological Journal* 17, no. 2 (Fall 1982): 7-25.

Campbell, Theodore C. "The Doctrine of the Holy Spirit in the Theology of Athanasius." *Scottish Journal of Theology* 27 (1974): 408-443.

Campenhausen, Hans von. *Ecclesiastical Authority and Spiritual Power in the Church of the First Three Centuries.* Translated by J. A. Baker. Stanford, California: Stanford University Press, 1969.

Clarke, W. K. L. *The Ascetic Works of St. Basil.* London: Society for Promoting Christian Knowledge, 1925.

Collins, James J. "The Holy Spirit's Transforming Activity in Gregory of Nyssa's Sacramental Theology." *Diakonia* (Fordham) 12, no. 3 (1977): 234-243.

Cutten, George B. *Speaking in Tongues.* New Haven, Connecticut: Yale University Press, 1927.

Dalton, Robert Chandler. *Tongues like as of Fire.* Springfield, Missouri: Gospel Publishing House, 1945.

Damaskinos, M. "La disponbilité au Saint Esprit et la fidélité aux origines d'après les Pères grecs." *Istina* 19 (1974): 49-64.

_____. *Platonisme et Theologie mystique.* Paris: Aubier, 1944.

Daniélon, Jean. *From Glory to Glory.* New York: Scribner's, 1961.

Deferrari, Roy Joseph, ed. *Early Christian Biographies.* Washington, D.C.: The Catholic University of America Press, 1952.

Dewar, Lindsay. *The Holy Spirit and Modern Thought.* London: Mowbray, 1959.

Dix, Gregory. *Le Ministère dans l'Église Ancienne (des annes 90 à 410).* Neuchatel: Delachaux et Niestle, 1955.

_____. *The Treatise on the Apostolic Tradition of St. Hippolytus of Rome.* London: Society for Promoting Christian Knowledge, 1968.

Doresse, Jean. *The Secret Books of the Egyptian Gnostics.* New York: Viking Press, 1970.

du Plessis, David. "Golden Jubilees." *International Review of Missions* 48 (April 1958): 193-194.

Easton, Burton Scott, trans. *The Apostolic Tradition of Hippolytus.* Cambridge: Cambridge University Press, 1935.

Egert, Eugene. *The Holy Spirit in German Literature until the End of the Twelfth Century.* The Hague and Paris: Mouton, 1973.

Ephiphanius. *Opera Omnia in duos tomos distributa.* Parisiis: Sumptibus Michaelis Sonnii, Claudii Morélli, et Sebastiani Cramoisy, 1622.

Eusebius. *Preparation for the Gospel.* Translated by Edwin H. Gifford. Oxford: Clarendon Press, 1903.

Evans, H. M. "Tertullian: Pentecostal of Carthage." *Paraclete* 9, no. 4 (Fall 1975): 17-21.

Fedwick, Paul Jonathan. *The Church and the Charisma of Leadership in Basil of Caesarea*. Toronto: Pontifical Institute of Mediaeval Studies, 1979.

Foerster, Werner, ed. *Gnosis: A Selection of Gnostic Texts*. Oxford: Clarendon Press, 1972.

_____. "Two Fourth-Century Witnesses on the Charismata." *Paraclete* 4, no. 4 (Fall 1970): 17-22.

Floris, Andrew T. "Chrysostom and the Charismata." *Paraclete* 5, no. 1 (Winter 1971): 17-22.

Fonlipps, Hans. "Ordination in den Pastoralen." Ph.D. diss., Heidelberg, 1974.

Grant, Robert. *The Letter and the Spirit*. New York: Macmillan, 1957.

Gribomont, Jean. "Saint Basile et le monachisme enthousiaste." *Irenikon* 53, no. 2 (1980): 123-144.

Hanson, R. P. C. "Basil's doctrine of tradition in relation to the Holy Spirit." *Vigilae Christianae* 23 (December 1968): 241-255.

_____. "The Divinity of the Holy Spirit." *Church Quarterly* 1 (April 1969): 298-306.

Harnack, Adolph von. *History of Dogma*. 7 vols. Translated from the 3rd German Edition by Neil Buchanan. New York: Russell and Russell, 1958.

Haroutunian, Joseph. "The Church, the Spirit, and the Hands of God." *Journal of Religion* 54, no. 2 (1974): 154-165.

Hedrick, Charles W. "Christian Motifs in the Gospel of the Egyptians." *Novum Testamentum* 23 (1981): 242-260.

_____. "Kingdom Sayings and Parables of Jesus in the Apocryphon of James: Tradition and Redaction." *New Testament Studies* 29 (January 1983): 1-24.

Hendry, George S. *The Holy Spirit in Christian Theology*. Philadelphia: Westminister, 1956.

Henry, Paul. "The Adversus Arium of Marius Victorinus, the First Systematic Exposition of the Doctrine of the Trinity." *Journal of Theological Studies* n.s. 1 (1950): 42-55.

Heston, Edward L. "The Spiritual Life and the Role of the Holy Ghost in the Sanctification of the Soul, as Described in the Works of Didymus of Alexandria." Dissertatio ad laurem in facultate theologica Pontificiae Universitatis Gregorianae, 1938.

Hippolytus. *Philosophumena*. Translated by F. Legge. London: Society for Promoting Christian Knowledge, 1921.

Holl, Karl. *Enthusiasmus und Bussgewalt beim griechischen*

Mönchtum: eine Studie zu Simeon dem Neuen Theologen.
Leipzig: J. C. Hinrichs, 1898.

————. *Gessammelte Aufsätze zur Kirchengeschichte II, der Osten.* Tübingen: verlag von J. C. B. Mohr (P. Siebeck), 1928.

Horton, Wade H., ed. *The Glossolalia Phenomenon.* Cleveland, Tennessee: Pathway Press, 1966.

Hunter, Harold. "Tongues-speech: A Patristic Analysis." *Journal of the Evangelical Theological Society* 23, no. 2 (June 1980): 125-137.

Hussey, M. Edmund. "The Theology of the Holy Spirit in the Writings of St. Gregory of Nazianzus." *Diakonia* (Fordham) 14, no. 3 (1979): 224-233.

Jaeger, Werner. *Early Christianity and Greek Paideia.* Cambridge, MA: Belknap Press of Harvard University Press, 1961.

————. *Gregor von Nyssa Lehre von Heiligen Geist.* Aus dem nachlase Hsg. von H. Dorries. Leiden: Brill, 1966.

————. *Gregorii Nysenni Opera.* Leiden: Brill, 1952.

Jaschke, Hans-Jochen. *Der Heilige Geist im Bekenntnis der Kirche. Eine Studie zur Pneumatologie des Irenäus von Lyon im Aufgang von altchristliche Glaubensbekenntnis.* Munster, Verlag Aschendorff, 1976.

Kalin, E. R. "Inspired Community: A Glance at Canon History." *Concordia Theological Monthly* 43 (September 1971): 541-549.

Kannengeiser, Charles. "Athanasius of Alexandria and the Holy Spirit between Nicea I and Constantinople I." *Irish Theological Quarterly* 48 (1981): 166-180.

Kelly, J. N. D. *Early Christian Creeds.* New York: Longmans, 1972.

Kendrick, Klaude. *The Promise Fulfilled.* Springfield, Missouri: Gospel Publishing House, 1959.

Kydd, Ronald. "Novatian's *De Trinitate*, 29: Evidence of the Charismatic?" *Scottish Journal of Theology* 30 (1977): 313-318.

Kingdon, F. "The Holy Comrade." *Methodist Review* 113 (March 1930): 200-208.

Klauser, Theodor. *Der Ursprung der bischöflichen Insignien und Ehrenrecht; Rede gehalten beim Antritt der Rektorats der Rheinischen Friedrich-Wilhelms-Universität zu Bonn am 11. Dez. 1948.* Frefeld: Scherpe, 1949.

Knox, R. A. *Enthusiasm: A Chapter in the History of Religion.* Oxford: Clarendon Press, 1962.

Labroille, Pierre de, ed. *Les sources de l'histoire du montanisme.*

Fribourg: Librairie de l'Universite (O. Gschwend), 1913.
Ladaria, Luis F. *El Espiritu en Clemente Alejandrino. Estudio teologico-antropologico.* Madrid: UPCM, 1950.
_____. *El Espiritu Santo en San Hilario de Poitiers.* Madrid: EAPSA, 1977.
Lewis, Warren. *Witnesses to the Holy Spirit: An Anthology.* Valley Forge, Pennsylvania: Judson Press, 1978.
Lightfoot, J. B. *The Apostolic Fathers.* Grand Rapids: Baker Book House, 1980.
McDermott, J. M. "Hilary of Poitiers: The Infinite Nature of God." *Vigiliae Christianae* 27, no. 3 (1973): 172-202.
McDonagh, Hilary. "The Divine Mission of the Holy Ghost." *The Life of the Spirit* 7 (May 1953): 495-497.
MacIntyre, J. "The Holy Spirit in Greek Patristic Thought." *Scottish Journal of Theology* 7 (1954): 353-375.
Malherbe, Abraham J. "The Holy Spirit in Athenagoras." *Journal of Theological Studies* n.s. 20, no. 2 (October 1969): 538-542.
Meredith, Anthony. "The Pneumatology of the Cappadocian Fathers and the Creed of Constantinople." *Irish Theological Quarterly* 48 (1981): 196-211.
Newbigin, Leslie. *The Household of God: Lectures on the Nature of the Church.* New York: Friendship Press, 1954.
Nuttall, Geoffrey F. *The Holy Spirit in Puritan Faith and Experience.* Oxford: Basil Blackwell, 1946.
O'Connor, Edward D. *Pope Paul and the Spirit.* Notre Dame, Indiana: Ave Maria Press, 1978.
Opitz, Helmut. *Ursprünge frühkatholischen Pneumatologie.* Berlin, Evangelische Verlagsanstalt, 1960.
Opsahl, Paul D., ed. *The Holy Spirit in the Life of the Church from Biblical Times to the Present.* Minneapolis: Augsburg, 1978.
Pagels, Elaine. "Gnosticism." In *Interpreter's Dictionary of the Bible: Supplementary Volume.* New York: Abingdon, 1976.
Parmentier, M. F. G. " 'Montanisme' als etiket voor religieus enthousiasme." *Nederlands Theologisch Tijdschrift* 32, no. 4 (1948): 310-317.
Paulsen, H. "Die bedeutung des montanismus für die herausbildung des kanons." *Vigiliae Christianae* 32, no. 1 (1978): 19-52.
Phipps, Lee Ralph. "The Holy Spirit and Christian Mysticism." *Methodist Review* 113 (May 1930): 408-413.
Piepkorn, Arthur Carl. "Charisma in the New Testament and the Apostolic Fathers." *Concordia Theological Monthly* 42 (1971): 369-389.

Pont, Gabriel. *Les dons de l'Esprit Saint dans la pensée de saint Augustin.* Sierre: Martigny: Éditions Chateau Ravire, 1974.

Procopius. *Secret History.* Translated by Richard Atwater. Ann Arbor, Michigan: Ann Arbor Paperbacks, 1963.

Ramsey, Michael. *Holy Spirit.* Grand Rapids, Michigan: Eerdmans, 1977.

Reid, H. M. B. *The Holy Spirit and the Mystics.* London: Hodder and Stoughton, 1925.

Ritter, Adolph Martin. *Charisma im Verständnis des Joannes Chrysostomes und seiner zeit.* Göttingen: Vandenhoeck and Ruprecht, 1972.

Robeck, Cecil M., Jr. "Montanism: A Problematic Spirit Movement." *Paraclete* 15, no. 3 (Summer 1981): 24-29.

_____. "Visions and Prophecy in the Writings of Cyprian." *Paraclete* 16, no. 3 (Summer 1982): 21-25.

Russell, Jeffrey Burton. *A History of Medieval Christianity: Prophecy and Order.* New York: Thomas Y. Crowell, 1968.

Saake, Helmut. *Pneumatologica: Untersuchungen zum Geistverstandnis im Johannes-evangelium bei Origenes and Athanathius von Alexandreia.* Frankfurt A. M.; Diagonal-Verlag, 1973.

Schmidt, Carl, ed. *Pistis Sophia.* Leiden: Brill, 1978.

Shapland, C. R. B., trans. *The Letters of St. Athanasius Concerning the Holy Spirit.* London: The Epworth Press, 1951.

Sohm, Rudolph. *Kirchenrecht.* 2 vols. Leipzig: Verlag von Duncker und Humblot, 1892.

_____. *Outlines of Church History.* Translated by May Sinclair. London: Macmillan, 1904.

Staats, Reinhart. "Die Basilianische Verherrlichung des Heiligen Geistes auf dem Konzil zu Konstantinopel 381." *Kerygma und Dogma* 25 (Oct.-Dec. 1979): 232-253.

Stagg, Frank, E. Glenn Hinson, and Wayne E. Oates. *Glossolalia: Tongue Speaking in Biblical, Historical, and Psychological Perspective.* Nashville and New York: Abingdon Press, 1967.

Stam, John E. "Charismatic Theology in the Apostolic Tradition of Hippolytus." In *Current Issues in Biblical and Patristic Interpretation,* Edited by Gerald F. Hawthorne. Grand Rapids, Michigan: Eerdmans, 1975.

Stephanou, Eusebius A. "The Charismata in the Early Church Fathers." *The Greek Orthodox Theological Review* 21 (Summer 1976): 125-146.

Swete, Henry Barclay. *The Holy Spirit in the Ancient Church.* London: Macmillan, 1912.

Tillich, Paul. *A History of Christian Thought.* New York: Harper and Row, 1968.

Trigg, Joseph W. "The Charismatic Intellectual: Origen's Understanding of Religious Leadership." *Church History* 50 (1981): 5-19.

Van Dusen, Henry Pitt. "Caribbean Holiday." *Christian Century* 72 (August 17, 1955): 946-947.

_____. "The Third Force in Christendom." *Life* 44 (June 9, 1958): 13.

Verhees, Jacques. "Die Bedeutung des Geistes Gottes in Leben des Menchen nach Augustin's Frühester Pneumatologie (Bis 391)." *Zeitschrift für Kirchengeschichte* 88, no. 2-3 (1977): 161-189.

Watkin-Jones, Howard. *The Holy Spirit from Arminius to Wesley.* London: Epworth, 1929.

_____. *The Holy Spirit in the Mediaeval Church.* London: Epworth, 1922.

Weinal, Heinrich. *Die wirkungen des geistes und der geister in nachapostolischen zeitalter bis auf Irenäus.* Tübingen, Druck von H. Lampp, 1898.

Welch, Herbert. "The Neglected Doctrine of the Spirit." *Methodist Review* 113 (May 1930): 323-335.

Williams, Charles. *The Descent of the Dove: A Short History of the Holy Spirit in the Church.* Grand Rapids, Michigan: Eerdmans, 1939.

Williams, George, and Edith Waldvogel. "A History of Speaking in Tongues and Related Gifts." In *The Charismatic Movement,* Edited by Michael P. Hamilton. Grand Rapids, Michigan: Eerdmans, 1975.

Wynne, John J. *The Great Encyclical Letters of Pope Leo XIII.* New York and Cincinnati: Benziger Brothers, 1903.

Yamamura, K. "Development of the Doctrine of the Holy Spirit in Patristic Philosophy: St. Basil and St. Gregory of Nyssa." *St. Vladimers Theological Quarterly* 18, no. 1 (1974): 3-21.

Yanguas, Jose Maria. "La divinidad del Espíritu Santo en S. Basilio." *Scripta Theologica* 9, no. 2 (1977): 485-539.

INDEX

God, 60; life and lifegiver, 160; light and lightgiver, 160; living water, 178; magnet drawing men to God, 71; mind of the world/eternal mind, 152; minister of the incarnate Word, 30; *nesamah*, 2; oil of gladness, 178; ointment of Christ, 174; one of the two hands of God, 58-59, 87; plentitude of all divine gifts, 114-115; *pneuma*, 2; power, 175; power of God, 29; power that gives life, 135; princely Spirit, 160; regal gold, 71; the right, 160; river, 173-174; rope lifting man to God, 20; *ruah*, 2; the sender, 160; the separator, 160; Spirit of adoption, 109; Spirit of God, 109; Spirit of God and Christ, 109; Spirit of grace, 109; Spirit of holiness, 109; Spirit of Jesus Christ, 109; Spirit of promise, 109; Spirit of revelation, 109; Spirit of the Father, 109; Spirit of the Lord, 109; Spirit of truth, 109; Spirit of wisdom and understanding, of counsel and might, of knowledge, of godliness, and of the fear of God, 109-110; spring of Goodness, 160; stream, 173; treasure more brilliant than royal treasures, 125; wings of the soul, 30; wisdom, 32, 58-59, 100

—nature and work of the Holy Spirit: anointing by the Spirit, 44; continuous involvement in human affairs, 4; creation, 32, 58, 75, 118; creativity of the Holy Spirit, 156; creator of the Church, 137; divinity, 18, 95, 114, 167, 169; giving immortality to man, 25; grieving the Spirit, 23; heavenly teaching, 184; helping with human infirmities, 125, 188; illumination of human mind, 142, 178; Incarnation, 28, 59; indwelling of Spirit, 22, 23; inspiration, 17, 19, 31, 71, 114; inspiration of the New Testament, 17, 114; inspiration of the Old Testament, 17, 114; late development of pneumatology, 133; ministry of Holy Spirit, 21; not created, 74, 124, 135, 144; nourishing believers, 187-188; ordination, 81-83; outpouring of Spirit, 22; perfection through the Spirit, 61, 79-80, 142, 150-151; procession of the Holy Spirit, 31, 75, 95, 96, 114, 118, 120, 133, 138-139, 164, 169, 175-176, 182-183; prophetic role of Spirit, 119; protection for man against evil spirits, 30, 109; redemptive role, 60; revealing kingdom of heaven to martyrs, 109; revealing things of God, 176; sanctifying believer, 23, 111, 117-118, 146, 148, 170, 178-179; sealing by the Spirit, 118; the Spirit and the priest, 157-158, 178; searching hearts, 125; spiritual freedom and discipline, 142; subordination of Spirit to Father and Son, 71, 74; through Whom man is adopted, 135; unction of the Spirit, 44, 60, 64, 111, 115, 118, 129; unique work of Spirit, 63; uniting/blending Christ with the Church, 176

—fruits of the Holy Spirit: 3, 75, 79-80, 110-111, 122, 125, 149, 151

—gifts of the Holy Spirit: 3, 9, 13, 20, 22, 29, 33, 40, 60-62, 65-67, 70, 72, 76-77, 79, 81, 85-86, 103-104, 108, 115-116, 120-122, 125-126, 139-143, 158-159, 171, 188-192

Philosophumena, 37
Photius, Photinians, 180
Phrygia, 50
Pistis Sophia, 54
Plato, Platonism, 29, 30, 71
Pneumatomachi, 95, 117, 134. *See also* Macedonians, Tropici
Pneumatophor, 144
Polemics, and polemicists, 12
Polycarp, d. ca. 155, bishop of Smyrna, 13, *20-21*, 58
Praxeas, ca. 200, theologian at Rome, 48, 51, 67
Presbyters, 81, 89-90
Priesthood, 157-158, 178
Priscilla, second-century Montanist prophetess, 49, 64, 67
Procopius, 56
Prophets and prophecy, 3, 4, 12, 13, 20, 21, 29, 45, 49-53, 61-62
—false prophets, 22-23
—true prophets, 23
Pseudo-Clement. *See Clement, Second Epistle of*

Quadratus, 103

Radical Reformation, 53
Ramsey, Michael, 5
Redemption, 29, 38, 48, 60, 177
Resurrection, 4
Roman Empire, 12, 100, 197

Sabellius, and Sabellianism, 48, 92, 101, 102, 166, 182. *See also* Monarchianism
Sacraments, 43-44, 57, 64, 106-112, 146-148, 157, 177-178
Sadducees, 152, 182
Satan. *See* Devils
Scripture, 16, 17, 18, 19, 25, 26, 29, 31, 71, 73, 95, 107, 114, 160, 168, 172-174
Second Treatise of the Great Seth, 36
Serapion, d. ca. 362, bishop of Thmuis in Lower Egypt, 95, 104, 117
Simon Magus, 37, 107
Smyrna, 20, 21
Soteriology, 3
Spirit. *See* Holy Spirit
Swete, Henry Barclay, 5, 73, 172

Tatian, d. after 172, apologist, *29-30*
Teachers, 21